D'Sozo

Reversing the worst evil

Dave Fiedler

To Larry Cook,
A normal guy whose unusual courage led to great things.

Also by Dave Fiedler
Hindsight: Seventh-day Adventist
History in Essays and Extracts

Adventist City Missions, Inc.
www.AdventistCityMissions.org

Printed by Remnant Publications
www.remnantpublications.com
800-423-1319

Table of Contents

As religious teachers,
we are under obligation to teach our students
how to engage in medical missionary work.

—Ellen G. White
The Christian Educator,
October 1, 1898

Foreword

WE live in times that call for new thinking, or should I say renewed thinking. This book is just that, "renewed thinking." If the concepts found here were rightly applied, it would solve the health care problems many nations face. But there is more. If applied in Christian churches, especially Seventh-day Adventist churches, we would see physical, emotional and spiritual life spring forth, and thousands of lives saved (the word *sozo* in Greek can be translated either "salvation" or "health") eternally.

I believe, along with the author of this book, that this will happen! I saw glimpses of it as the author and myself, along with a number of dedicated medical missionaries, worked together in Wichita, Kansas. Doors opened within the medical, business, legal and religious community that we served. People recognized that our local Adventist church was, through humble service, making a difference! They saw that our church could provide things that large companies and government agencies could not—health information that was not only evidence based, but sacrificially laced, and care that really was care. The results were simply undeniable both experientially and clinically. The real need of our day is not simply health education—we have excellent information. What is needed is health information coupled with power to put it into practice, that is power to change.

A physician friend, Dr Tim Howe, put it this way at a recent AMEN (Adventist Medical Evangelism Network) Conference:

> "Health education alone is not medical missionary work. Health education does not provide healing any more than the law of God provides salvation. To re-

alize health or salvation the transforming power of God must be experienced. The Apostle Paul said, "I am not ashamed of the gospel for it is the power of God unto salvation." The Greek word "sozo," translated as salvation in this text, is also translated in scripture as healing. In the truest sense health and salvation are one. Both are gained, not through a knowledge of law, be it health law or moral law, but rather through God's redeeming, restoring power. Imparting health information without the gospel may lead some to better temporal health for a time, but all those who embrace health information suffused with the gospel will be led to life and life eternal. This is true medical missionary work."

I believe that God longs to pour out His power on and through His church. And I believe that ultimately He will. Notice how Ellen White, a truly inspired early Adventist pioneer put it:

> The Lord has presented before me that many, many will be rescued from physical, mental, and moral degeneracy through the practical influence of health reform. Health talks will be given, publications will be multiplied. The principles of health reform will be received with favor, and many will be enlightened. The influences that are associated with health reform will commend it to the judgment of all who want light, and they will advance step by step to receive the special truths for this time. Thus truth and righteousness will meet together. *Testimonies*, vol. 6, 378–379

This is going to happen, and it will happen as soon as individuals, as churches, as educators, as conference leaders submit themselves to God's plans and priorities.

Before I let you get started with this fascinating and timely book, I leave you with a quote that God used to underline the urgency and relevance of the concepts found in this book. Here it is:

> "As religious aggression subverts the liberties of our nation, those who would stand for freedom of conscience will be placed in unfavorable positions. For their own sake, they should, while they have opportunity, become intelligent in regard to disease, its causes, prevention and cure. And those who do this will find a field of labor anywhere. There will be suffering ones, plenty of them, who will need help, not only among those of our own faith, but largely among those who know not the truth.
>
> "The shortness of time demands an energy that has not been aroused among those who claim to believe the present truth." *Counsels on Health, 506*

This passage not only paints a precise picture of the times we live in, it also underlines the necessity for renewed thinking, for d'Sozo thinking, and the vital necessity for a last-day d'Sozo demonstration.

May God's spirit inspire you as you read, and then may that same Spirit lead you to be used to reverse "the greatest evil."

Don Mackintosh
Director, NEWSTART Global

Foreword

MEDICAL Missionary work has been my interest since childhood. It was the reason I went to Medical school, and it remains my reason for continuing to practice medicine today.

I well remember seeing its power as I worked alongside my father and mother (O.J. and Millie Mills), as well as those they were mentoring. I was able to watch firsthand the power of physicians working in concert with ministers to save people from sickness *and* sin.

I highly recommend this book to anyone who is serious about medical missionary work. While I could give many reasons for this recommendation, I'll put forward just two: First, I've worked with Dave Fiedler first hand, and know that this is not just a book of solid research (though it is that, complete with references), it is also a book informed by life experience. Second, I've seen with joy the real, gospel-powered change that has come in the lives of the many who came into the fold as the fruit of a solid physician/minister team in Wichita, Kansas. For over a decade, Pastor Don Mackintosh and my parents, as well as committed clinicians such as Kevin Bryant, MD, and a host of others, blended our efforts with the faithful members of a local church and saw God's power displayed as a result of these convictions and activities.

Phil Mills, MD
Past President of AMEN,
the Adventist Medical Evangelism Network

Introduction

PETER and John stood arraigned before the highest court of the land, charged with the unlikely crime of healing a lame man. Opportunity at last being given to answer the charge, Peter spoke up clearly:

> If we this day are judged for a good deed done to a helpless man, by what means he has been made well, let it be known to you all, and to all the people of Israel, that by the name of Jesus Christ of Nazareth, whom you crucified, whom God raised from the dead, by Him this man stands here before you whole. This is the "stone which was rejected by you builders, which has become the chief cornerstone." Nor is there salvation in any other, for there is no other name under heaven given among men by which we must be saved. —Acts 4:9–12

To those listening, nothing would have stood out in what he said. A miracle? Yes, that was unusual, but his words? Nothing special there.

But in Simon Peter's words lay a profound truth that he had learned from none other than the Messiah, the Son of God, the Savior of men. When he had stopped at the Beautiful Gate and healed the lame man, he had done only the same as his Master had done. This was fitting, for the Master's work had not ended with His return to heaven, it had merely been left in His disciples' hands to carry on in His stead.

And so it was that when Peter said that the man had been made well, and when he spoke of the only name by which men may be saved, he used the same words His master had used. To heal. To save. In Greek the root is *sozo*. So closely related are ministry to body and soul that a single word describes both. This is as God would have them, united.

And when that which God has united is split asunder, we are told, "there is placed on our churches the worst evil that can be placed there."[1] How did this happen? How can it be corrected?

The answers come through understanding the purpose and process of the Great Controversy, and learning the lessons of "our past history."[2] Those answers put this sacred, dual ministry into the hands of every Christian believer at an appropriate level for the experience, strength and training of each.

This larger picture, and fuller context, highlight the freedom and the joy of walking as Jesus walked, of learning "the true interpretation of the gospel,"[3] and taking up a "work identical with the work that Christ did."[4]

Though still imperfectly understood, and even more poorly practiced, this is the meaning of d'Sozo. God has a plan for it in every life, including yours. I trust it will bless you as it has me.

Dave Fiedler
December 2012

---

1. *Medical Ministry*, 241
2. *Life Sketches*, 196
3. *Review and Herald*, March 4, 1902
4. *Medical Ministry*, 24

Chapter One

A Drama in Four Acts

THE best place to start is always at the beginning. That's what the Bible does in Genesis.[1] And in John[2]... but these are two different "beginnings." We'll be starting at the beginning, too, but we're going to yet another "beginning."

> You are of your father the devil, and the desires of your father you want to do. He was a murderer from the beginning, and does not stand in the truth, because there is no truth in him. When he speaks a lie, he speaks from his own resources, for he is a liar and the father of it.[3]

This, of course, is the beginning of sin. At the moment of its inception, sin held in its very being the twin evils of murder and untruthfulness. It has never changed. But the verse also speaks of "the truth." This is not a reference to honesty as a general principle. "The truth" is what Lucifer walked away from when sin entered his mind and heart.

We all know that the Bible says, "sin is the transgression of the law,"[4] or, as in some modern versions, "sin is lawlessness." And since "Your law is truth,"[5] it all seems simple, and consistent, though perhaps a bit nebulous.

Since sin differed from God's will, we may assume that Lucifer—at some tragic point in time—came to believe that *he* had a better grasp of the situation than God did. That *he*, Lucifer, the highest of the angels, would be better served following his own plan rather than following God's plan. Did he convince himself that it was in others' best interest as

---

1. In the beginning God created the heaven and the earth. Genesis 1:1
2. In the beginning was the Word, and the Word was with God, and the Word was God. John 1:1
3. John 8:44
4. 1 John 3:4
5. Psalms 119:142

well? Did he see himself as the benefactor of the universe? If so, it was only the first of many such cases of self-deception. What actually mattered was that he didn't think God's plan was in his best interest.

In other words, God wasn't taking care of Lucifer as well as Lucifer could take care of Lucifer. That, right there, is the basic Lie.[6] From it come all manner of sins:

1. If I don't believe God will take care of me, that's a loss of faith.
2. If I think I can do a better job of taking care of myself than God can, that's pride (and stupidity, by the way).
3. If I try taking care of myself in some way other than what God asks me to, that's plain old disobedience.
4. If my influence convinces someone else that "self-serving" is a better law of life than "service," that's lying.
5. And if I put myself first, instead of loving my neighbor as myself, that's stealing, and—under enough pressure—it will become murder.

This is all wrong, and it has been a problem for us ever since Lucifer deceived Eve and persuaded Adam that he had a better plan for them than God did. And so we ask, "Why did God let Satan sin? Why didn't He just *vaporize* him and get it over with?"

Those may be fair questions, but they are only one small step away from saying, "God *should* have vaporized him." Which is to say, "God didn't take care of my best interest. I could do a better job...."

And thus we usually manage to convince ourselves that we are at least looking for answers to the big question. Seldom, though, do we realize the starkness of the issues the rest of the universe is focused on. They look at the origin of sin and recognize the central question: "Can God be trusted? Even when He says to do something that makes no sense to me? Even now, when He says *some* angels, and *some* people must die? Even when He says He wants to bring human sinners back to heaven, but completely closes the door on my angelic friends?"

A Sense of Scale

Before we look at God's response to all this, we need to understand that self-serving actually is a big deal. It might seem to be making a mountain out of a molehill to get so wrought up over a difference of opinion. Why not just "live and let live"? And, for that matter, why pay any attention to it all?

---

6. Consider 2 Thessalonians 2:11—And for this reason God will send them strong delusion, that they should believe the lie.

To answer those questions in a way that makes sense is the purpose of the next twenty-two chapters. For now, we'll illustrate the value of "faith" by saying, "If you believe the Spirit of Prophecy, you can see from these quotations about 'the Law of Life' that self-serving is a big issue."

Self-renouncing love is the law of life.[7]

The circuit of beneficence is... the law of life.[8]

The great law of life is a law of service.[9]

To give is to live.[10]

Self-sacrifice is the law of self-preservation.[11]

Self-renunciation is the great law of self-preservation, and self-preservation is the law of self-destruction.[12]

And so the contrast between "the Truth" and "the Lie" was stark. God said, "Trust Me, I will freely provide all that is truly for your good, I only ask that you make the good of others your first interest," and Lucifer said "God has placed other considerations above my best interest; for that, He cannot be trusted, and I must care for myself at others' expense if need be."

How high were the stakes? Perhaps an illustration will help:

Pretend that one hundred people were stranded on a conveniently un-inhabited tropical island. How would the society structure itself? On one end of the spectrum is something like this: "Listen up, everyone! We've got to stick together for safety. Never leave camp without telling someone, and never leave camp alone. As long as we take care of each other, we'll all be OK."

On the other end of the spectrum is this: "This is bad. Who knows what sort of situation we're up against? And what do I know about all these people? I better get a club, maybe make a knife from some scrap metal. Need to be looking out for Number One."

Both scenarios are easy to imagine, and both approaches might actually work to keep people alive....

Unless there is only enough food on the island to support twenty people. Then what? Simple human reason tells us that generosity becomes suicide.

---

7. *Desire of Ages,* 19
8. *Desire of Ages,* 21
9. *Education,* 103
10. *Desire of Ages,* 623
11. *Education,* 110
12. *Signs of the Times,* July 1, 1897

And so the question comes down to this: "Can I follow the Golden Rule in dealing with others and trust God to supply for my best good, or am I better off reserving the right to take care of myself first?"

How Do You Fight a Lie?

Lucifer's influence spread. Questions were raised much faster than answers were coming. Could God be trusted? Or is self-serving the next big thing? Should I believe God, or Lucifer?

It may be helpful to think of this whole situation as an exercise in divine Damage Control, not that foreign to something in Public Relations 101. But when it comes to combating negative propaganda, the simple answer is that there is no way to "pronounce" oneself honest and trustworthy. Once the doubt is implanted, the only remedy is through demonstration. For anything less, the response will be, "You can *say* you're honest, but why should I believe *you,* You might be lying to me like Lucifer said."

Stage One

And so began what we know today as the Great Controversy. Let's look at that, but let's start when Jesus was talking to the seventy disciples who had just come back from their missionary tour. They said "Lord, even the demons are subject to us in Your name."

And Jesus said something a little strange. According to Luke, His first response was:

> And He said to them, "I saw Satan fall like lightning from heaven."[13]

When did this happen? When did Satan fall like lightning from heaven? When he sinned and got kicked out, obviously. And any good Seventh-day Adventist would likely think of this passage:

> And war broke out in heaven: Michael and his angels fought with the dragon; and the dragon and his angels fought, but they did not prevail, nor was a place found for them in heaven any longer. So the great dragon was cast out, that serpent of old, called the Devil and Satan, who deceives the whole world; he was cast to the earth, and his angels were cast out with him.[14]

In passing, we should note that linking these two passages in our minds like this amounts to equating Jesus' word "fall," with John's phrase "cast out." Also, before we go on, let's put a label on this occasion of Satan's "fall." We'll call it "Stage One," for reasons that will be apparent shortly.

---

13. Luke 10:18
14. Revelation 12:7–9

Stage Two

But now we move on to "Stage Two," and the plot thickens slightly. Notice this verse:

> Now is the judgment of this world; now the ruler of this world will be cast out.[15]

Again, these are Jesus' words, but on a different occasion. This was said just shortly before the crucifixion, and Jesus set it clearly in the future tense. We generally see the near-future "now" that He spoke of as the crucifixion. But that prompts us to ask if "cast out" in this verse is the same as the "cast out" in Revelation 12. If so, would that mean that Revelation 12 is in some way speaking of the cross?

Maybe this will help:

> Christ bowed His head and died, but He held fast His faith and His submission to God. "And I heard a loud voice saying in heaven, Now is come salvation, and strength, and the kingdom of our God, and the power of His Christ: for the accuser of our brethren is cast down, which accused them before our God day and night." Rev. 12:10.[16]

Why is Ellen White quoting *that* verse when she's talking about the crucifixion? We just looked at verses 7–9 and saw the fall of Satan from heaven back before the creation of our world. How could the very next verse be talking about the crucifixion? And, for what it's worth, is there any difference between the "cast down" in this verse, and the "cast out" in verse nine?

Don't worry, this next quotation will start to make sense of it:

> After the crucifixion, [Satan] saw that he had over reached himself....
>
> Satan saw that his disguise was torn away, that the character he had tried to fasten on Christ was fastened on himself. It was as if he had the second time fallen from heaven.[17]

At the cross? The second time? It's like there is something about these two events—the fall of Satan in heaven and the death of Christ on the cross—that is so similar that inspired writers get them all mixed up together. Fascinating!

Actually, Ellen White sometimes made the linkage even stronger:

> God... looked upon the victim expiring on the cross, and said, "It is finished. The human race shall have another trial." The redemption price was paid, and Satan fell like lightning from heaven.[18]

---

15. John 12:31
16. *Desire of Ages*, 761
17. *Manuscript Releases*, vol. 12, 411
18. *Youth's Instructor*, June 21, 1900

But he wasn't even *in* heaven then! How could he fall *from* heaven? And on that happy note, we will move on.

Stage Three

These verses are familiar, indeed we just read the first one a moment ago. Nevertheless, read them again and think of the big picture:

> Then I heard a loud voice saying in heaven, "Now salvation, and strength, and the kingdom of our God, and the power of His Christ have come, for the accuser of our brethren, who accused them before our God day and night, has been cast down. And they overcame him by the blood of the Lamb and by the word of their testimony, and they did not love their lives to the death. Therefore rejoice, O heavens, and you who dwell in them! Woe to the inhabitants of the earth and the sea! For the devil has come down to you, having great wrath, because he knows that he has a short time."[19]

Notice the details:

1. The "accuser of our brethren" has been cast down.
2. A group of people have beaten the devil, placing their lives at risk in the process.
3. Because they overcame, everyone in "the heavens" rejoices.
4. But everyone on "earth" or in the "sea" is in trouble because the devil is running out of time, and he's really mad about it.

Now just step back mentally, look at that sequence, and ask yourself, "What does this sound like? When is all this supposed to happen?"

Yes. You're right. It does sound like the time of the end. That's the way Ellen White used it here:

> The apostle John in vision heard a loud voice in heaven exclaiming: "Woe to the inhabiters of the earth and of the sea! for the devil is come down unto you, having great wrath, because he knoweth that he hath but a short time." Revelation 12:12. Fearful are the scenes which call forth this exclamation from the heavenly voice. The wrath of Satan increases as his time grows short, and his work of deceit and destruction will reach its culmination in the time of trouble.[20]

So now we've got three separate historical episodes portrayed in Revelation chapter twelve. It may seem confusing, but hold on; it gets better!

Notice that group of people who beat the devil in the last days. For general purposes at least, we might call them the 144,000. Here's a statement that fits in with them right at this point. We don't have all the

---

19. Revelation 12:10–12
20. *Great Controversy*, 623

pieces in place yet to get this one locked into the puzzle properly, but it's worth a moment's thought anyway:

> Satan... is an accuser of the brethren, and his accusing power is employed against those who work righteousness. The Lord desires through His people to answer Satan's charges by showing the results of obedience to right principles.[21]

This role of God's people will come up again. And the "right principles" spoken of here are important, too. But let's just note that this process is accomplished through "showing" more than through "telling." And now we're circling back on our trail, to right where we started. But this time it's—

Stage Four

> Like the apostles, the seventy had received supernatural endowments as a seal of their mission. When their work was completed, they returned with joy, saying, "Lord, even the devils are subject unto us through Thy name." Jesus answered, "I beheld Satan as lightning fall from heaven."

This is familiar, but notice what Ellen White sees in this occasion that we might not have:

> The scenes of the past and the future were presented to the mind of Jesus. He beheld Lucifer as he was first cast out from the heavenly places. He looked forward to the scenes of His own agony, when before all the worlds the character of the deceiver should be unveiled. He heard the cry, "It is finished" (John 19:30), announcing that the redemption of the lost race was forever made certain, that heaven was made eternally secure against the accusations, the deceptions, the pretensions, that Satan would instigate.
>
> Beyond the cross of Calvary, with its agony and shame, Jesus looked forward to the great final day, when the prince of the power of the air will meet his destruction in the earth so long marred by his rebellion. Jesus beheld the work of evil forever ended, and the peace of God filling heaven and earth.
>
> Henceforward Christ's followers were to look upon Satan as a conquered foe. Upon the cross, Jesus was to gain the victory for them; that victory He desired them to accept as their own. "Behold," He said, "I give unto you power to tread on serpents and scorpions, and over all the power of the enemy: and nothing shall by any means hurt you."[22]

Do you see all four stages of the process? The scenes of past and future? The order is jumbled a bit so they show up as 1, 2, 4, 3, but they're all there in a single place. Here's an itemized list:

---

21. *Christ's Object Lessons*, 296
22. *Desire of Ages*, 490

1. 6,000 years ago—The members of the Godhead understood Satan's plans and arguments, and rejected them because Omniscience knew from all eternity the evil of sin.
2. 2,000 years ago—Angels and the inhabitants of the unfallen worlds understood Satan's plans and arguments, and rejected them because they saw the murderous character of Satan revealed at the cross.
3. Near future (hopefully)—The 144,000 will understand Satan's plans and arguments, and will reject them because "obedience to right principles" has prepared them to understand—and successfully resist—the fiercest temptations ever brought to mortal man.
4. 1,000 years later—The wicked will understand Satan's plans and arguments after seeing the course of Satan throughout the conflict with heaven, and they, too, will reject them.

Because the need for this whole process is not understood, people often misunderstand the crucifixion and thus cause themselves a lot of confusion. This is where the whole "it's all done at the Cross" problem gets its start. We have plenty of reasons to be thankful for the Great Controversy concept that has been entrusted to Adventism.

The Power of Demonstration

Far from being the end of God's work, the cross is, well, somewhere in the middle, chronologically. There were issues that just hadn't been addressed yet. We looked at a statement from *Desire of Ages* back on page 21 that spoke of Christ's death, and quoted Revelation 12:10 in that connection. That was interesting enough, but look at the next two paragraphs!

> Satan saw that his disguise was torn away. His administration was laid open before the unfallen angels and before the heavenly universe. He had revealed himself as a murderer. By shedding the blood of the Son of God, he had uprooted himself from the sympathies of the heavenly beings. Henceforth his work was restricted. Whatever attitude he might assume, he could no longer await the angels as they came from the heavenly courts, and before them accuse Christ's brethren of being clothed with the garments of blackness and the defilement of sin. The last link of sympathy between Satan and the heavenly world was broken.
>
> Yet Satan was not then destroyed. The angels did not even then understand all that was involved in the great controversy. The principles at stake were to be more fully revealed. And for the sake of man, Satan's existence must be continued. Man as well as angels must see the contrast between the Prince of light and the prince of darkness. He must choose whom he will serve.[23]

---

23. *Desire of Ages*, 761

So the first thing we see is that the crucifixion revealed Satan's princi-ples in a way that nothing else had ever done. Ellen White specifically says he had "revealed himself as a murderer." But hadn't that been done back when Abel was killed? Or by however many million murders there were in the first four thousand years of earth's history. Don't they count for something? Well, evidently not as murder victims, in the eyes of an-gels, anyway. How could that be?

It seems to be a categorical distinction... and the most significant diff-ference between Jesus and all the rest was that Jesus hadn't sinned. He (alone) was innocent. Satan had the perfect cover for all the rest: "Don't blame *me*! It's *God's* law that says sinners have to die!" But that line didn't work with Jesus... and all the universe learned something that they had never really *known* before. That's the power of demonstration.

But the statement goes on: The last "link of sympathy" was gone now, at least with the unfallen worlds. Bear in mind that the word "sympathy" doesn't always mean the "Oh! you poor thing, you" kind of sympathy. This was more the "I sympathize with your position" kind of philosophi-cal or intellectual sympathy. And after the cross, that was gone.

And yet the process of discrediting Satan's false positions must go on. There were things for both men and angels still to learn.

Stop a moment and think about that "for the sake of man, Satan's ex-istence must be continued" idea. If you've ever wanted to say, "Oh, you shouldn't have!" this might be the time. But you would be wrong, of course. God *should* have, and He did, because the long-term gain more than justifies the process of demonstration. It's the only way to learn these lessons well.

Things to Learn

Speaking of learning lessons, think about Stage Three for a moment. Basically, this is the 144,000 who will learn that they have no cause for sympathy with the devil, either. Think of it this way: Adam and Eve chose the knowledge of good and evil. How much evil do you think God's people are going to have to learn about?

Or think of it this way: Jesus promises that He won't allow us to be "tempted above that ye are able," and we rightly take comfort in the promise. But what do you suppose Satan's doing with that? Can you imagine the "interfering with the investigation" and "tampering with the witness" claims he is making? And he's got a point; how can God say that His people have rejected Satan's plan of government if he's never even been able to give them his best sales pitch?

No, this process is not over yet, but the plan is in place and the process is well under way. One day it will be finished, and all will see that methodically, step-by-step, the Lord has provided the demonstration that alone could vindicate His government. One group after another, sometimes willingly, sometimes only through force of circumstances, has seen that God's ways are, and always have been, perfect.

Just four steps. It almost seems simple. But it isn't. It's so complicated, so difficult, so costly, that sometimes even Satan has been left wondering what God would do next. But when it's done, it will be seen by all that there was no other possible means to do what God has done.

In the next two chapters we'll see some of that complexity, some of the elegance with which this crisis is being handled. We'll also see what God will do about the one class of people not covered in the steps above.

Chapter Two

Harder Than It Looks!

IN the first chapter we looked at an overview of the Lord's Damage Control plan. His government stands accused, not only of not having the best system of governance, but of callously refusing to improve when a better system was developed by Lucifer. Such are the claims in sweeping terms. There are details, of course, the most basic of which is that the law is "arbitrary," based on a "because I said so," rather than on any real connection to cause and effect. This is a fascinating study, but we will merely touch it lightly in this volume.

For the moment, our concern is the process of completely discrediting Lucifer's deadly claims and deceptions. We've seen his four "falls from heaven," in which his positions are systematically shown to be based entirely on lies. The claim that the law couldn't be kept was disproved by the simple expediency of having Someone keep it perfectly. That, by the way, is the power of demonstration.

Another claim of Lucifer's was that God required self-sacrifice of His subjects, but that He selfishly claimed their entire allegiance and continuous service for Himself. This, too, was proven false, by means of the greatest possible sacrifice, freely given for the undeserving. That's the power of demonstration.

That much (and more, of course) was done at the cross. It's in the past, and can not be changed. Thus we turn our attention to the future.

The Work Yet to Be Done

Perhaps the first contrast that comes to mind when we look forward is that, this time, human beings are more involved. A lot of them. One hundred and forty-four thousand of them. And whether you take that as a literal or a figurative number, it's still people, and even the best of them are a far cry from the Son of God. That could be worrisome, but let's back up to familiar ground. Let's start with a text:

> And this gospel of the kingdom will be preached in all the world as a witness to all the nations, and then the end will come.[1]

A familiar verse, and a familiar sequence of events, but ask yourself why it should be like this. Why should the gospel need to go to all the world before the end comes?

One standard answer is something along the lines of, "So everyone will have a chance to be saved."

Really? Do you believe that? Do you believe that the billions upon billions of people (give or take) who have lived and died without ever hearing the gospel are just *automatically* consigned to hell fire?

Sure, some people believe that. Are you one of them? What about the people who will need to have the wounds in the hands of Christ explained to them in heaven?[2] What about the Gentiles who "do by nature the things contained in the law,... [and] are a law unto themselves."[3] And then there are the Spirit of Prophecy comments:

> How surprised and gladdened will be the lowly among the nations, and among the heathen, to hear from the lips of the Saviour, "Inasmuch as ye have done it unto one of the least of these My brethren, ye have done it unto Me"! How glad will be the heart of Infinite Love as His followers look up with surprise and joy at His words of approval![4]

Heathen, yes. Surprised, yes. Banished to hell? Not without some very creative obfuscatory exegesis! The point is, people don't absolutely have to hear the gospel in order to be saved. So... why *does* the gospel need to go to all the world before the end comes?

That's a good question, so we're going to hang on to it while we consider a related question: Which gospel is "this gospel"?

"This Gospel"

Imagine for a moment that two or three extremely wealthy oil sheiks became Christian and pooled all their resources to provide a communication system that could reach everyone on earth (or at least their cellphones). Then imagine that they could somehow ensure that everyone

1. Matthew 24:14
2. Zechariah 13:6
3. Romans 2:14
4. *Desire of Ages,* 638

would listen for three solid hours every Sunday evening. If they gave that time slot to the pope and had him preach an evangelistic series to every person on earth, how many weeks would it take for the end to come?

Not sure? How about Benny Hin, or Jerry Falwell, or James Dobson, or Joel Osteen? How long for one of them?

And this little game can come uncomfortably close to home as well. What if we made it Ted Wilson, or Dwight Nelson, or Doug Batchelor, or Mark Finley, or David Asscherick?[5]

The point is this: the "gospel to all the world" is not a matter of quantity alone. Everyone on earth could hear "a gospel" and it wouldn't accomplish what we might have expected. But "this gospel" is different. "This gospel" is complete, mature, and powerful enough to bring on "the end." Makes you wonder, "How?" doesn't it? Keep reading.

The logic of the case makes it clear that our inability to present "this gospel" is closely tied to the sealing of God's people. And that's a serious problem. Maybe not so much of a problem for those of us living in what passes for comfort here on earth, but what about the millions who suffer from malaria, or starvation, or political unrest, or any of the dozens of things we have here to make life only marginally better than death? For them—and the generations of "them" yet to come—delay is terrible.

And, of course, if we are talking of the toll from delay, we have to consider this as well:

> Those who think of the result of hastening or hindering the gospel think of it in relation to themselves and to the world. Few think of its relation to God. Few give thought to the suffering that sin has caused our Creator. All heaven suffered in Christ's agony; but that suffering did not begin or end with His manifestation in humanity. The cross is a revelation to our dull senses of the pain that, from its very inception, sin has brought to the heart of God.[6]

Simply put, time is the tax master that extracts payment in suffering. Delay is at best a tragedy. And yet, this very delay is Scriptural:

> After these things I saw four angels standing at the four corners of the earth, holding the four winds of the earth, that the wind should not blow on the earth, on the sea, or on any tree. Then I saw another angel ascending from the east, having the seal of the living God. And he cried with a loud voice to the four angels to whom it was granted to harm the earth and the sea, saying, "Do not harm the earth, the sea, or the trees till we have sealed the servants of our God on their foreheads."[7]

---

5. The author means no disrespect to either these brethren or to those who are not on the list!
6. *Education*, 263
7. Revelation 7:1–3

Sealed In Their Foreheads... Someday

Notice what is holding up progress. It's the sealing, or the lack of it, that forces the delay. Apparently the sealing is actually an *essential* component of God's last day plan of action. It's more like a heart or a liver, than an appendix or a tonsil. All of which raises an interesting question: What's so important about the sealing of God's people? What difference would it make if it never happened? And if it does happen... well, what does that *do*?

A heart is necessary because things won't work without blood making the rounds. And a liver is necessary to keep the body's chemical balance within livable tolerances. In other words, they're functional, they have a purpose, they accomplish something important.

What does the sealing do?

One thing it *doesn't* do is indicate that the sealed ones have "graduated." The seal can't be a sign of achievement, per se, because the great achievement, the final exam, of the 144,000 comes *after* the sealing.

Remember the "power of demonstration"? That's what the sealing is all about. Consider this verse:

> To the intent that now the manifold wisdom of God might be made known by the church to the principalities and powers in the heavenly places.[8]

God's church is intended to serve as a demonstration of God's wisdom. Until we're ready to do that, He has to wait. That's a tall order, and it leads to one obvious question: What "manifold wisdom of God" are we talking about? If we're supposed to demonstrate something, it seems like a good idea to know what it is!

So... who is going to claim to know the "manifold wisdom of God"? It almost sounds blasphemous to make such a claim. That's a line we don't want to cross, but consider what we can deduce by asking four fairly straight-forward questions:

1. What plans are being held up?

Well, since everything is waiting on the sealing, it's safe to say that all the "normal" last day events would be included. The big, obvious ones would be the close of probation, the time of Jacob's trouble, the second coming, the righteous in heaven, and the destruction of the wicked.

2. What "wisdom of God" could possibly require demonstration?

8. Ephesians 3:10

Take a look at the list in question one. Which of them need demonstration? Remember, demonstration is especially called for as a measure to allay concern. Which of the above might raise concerns?

Since this demonstration is *by* the church, it's not *for* the church. It's for the *rest* of the universe. So what might their concerns be?

Of the list of major events, there are two which stand out as obvious, legitimate concerns from their perspective: the idea of taking sinners into heaven, and the plan to execute the wicked. Remember, they were there when sin began; they've seen the whole gruesome experiment down here; and they have good reason to see that it never happens again.

On the second count, remember that—for all their hatred and perhaps fear of sin—they still have good memories. How long did Lucifer and Gabriel work together as best friends? How much fun did the angels have back in the old days, singing in the choir that Lucifer directed?

They will have questions... first and foremost, "Isn't there some way to save our friends?" Really, isn't there *something* God could do?

3. What specifics need to be demonstrated?

How do you go about demonstrating that genuine, participatory sinners with a rap sheet longer than we can imagine, are now safe to admit into the society of heaven?

This is no place for some sort of executive pardon from the Governor or President; this is the place for solid evidence of reformation. This is no laughing matter. How can you know that John Doe is safe to take to heaven? The stark simplicity of this obviously vital question tells us a great deal about the plan of salvation.

Let's approach it through an illustration.

Suppose a teacher gave a math test—and everyone flunked! But suppose the teacher announced later that seven students would get passing grades anyway. You'd want to know what made those seven different, wouldn't you?

And if the teacher said, "It's because they have blue eyes," you wouldn't think it was fair—especially if your eyes were brown! But why not? What's wrong with using eye color as a criterion. After all, the teacher is the authority; can't he do want he wants in his classroom?

We would all reject such arguments, and probably the teacher, too. The problem is that blue eyes have nothing to do with math tests. That's just not a good reason because there isn't any cause and effect relationship, no basis in "reality."

What *would* be a good reason for giving A's to students who flunked the test? Maybe if the class studied the lesson again, and then took another test. If the seven students showed they had learned how to do the math—that would make more sense. But does that second test guarantee that they'll never again make a mistake on another math problem? In other words, tests like that are better at judging past behavior than they are at predicting future behavior.

So, does it sound like a good idea to take people to heaven? Even people who have passed a second test? What a risk!

And what about those who failed twice? What if the teacher gave them another chance? Wouldn't they learn sometime? How many chances should someone get before the teacher says, "I give up! This student is hopeless"?

How can you say that—when the consequence isn't just a failing grade... it's eternal death? Especially when the curve seems so ridiculously high! One sin—*just one!*—and it's a mandatory death penalty. It hardly seems fair. Think of the friendly little retired lady that grows roses in her flower bed, and shares cookies and milk with the neighborhood school kids... but never accepted Christ as her Savior.

For that, she has to *die*? And why can't God just *do something* about this? He's God! Can't He do anything He wants?

So... back to our question: What specifics need to be demonstrated? To justify His government's rulings on the reward of the righteous and the destruction of the wicked, God needs to do at least three things:

A. Show that there is a good, "reality-based" reason some are lost and some are saved. This can't be "blue eyes" or even "dunked in the baptistry." There must be some genuine cause-and-effect relationship to the individual's status of lost or saved.

This is necessary to counter Satan's claim that because God's people have sinned, they are no more entitled to salvation than he is. Or, better yet, from Satan's point of view, that he deserves salvation just as much as they do!

B. Show that the people He wants to take to heaven (all clearly guilty in the past) are now safe to have there. And consider the stakes—these people are not just "going to heaven," they are to be exalted above the angels, to sit with God on His throne!

This allays the concern of the unfallen inhabitants of the universe about taking human beings to heaven. In order to be "completely saved," the righteous need to be "completely safe."

C. Show that there is nothing more that even God Himself can do to help the wicked (who—despite their present wickedness—have been loved deeply by both angels and human beings in the past).

This establishes God's love and justice as being entirely compatible. For the wicked to be "completely condemned," they need to be "completely hopeless."

This is getting complex.... Four questions.... Three requirements. But cheer up; the hard part is over, because our fourth question is simple—

4. Can the sealing really demonstrate all that?

And fortunately the answer is, Praise God! Yes it can! Well... two out of three, anyway.

Chapter Three

Unrolling the Scroll

B ACK on page 30, we asked "what does the sealing *do?*" The next few
pages were spent looking at issues that are just crying out to be
proved by demonstration. And now we'll be looking at how the sealing
plays into that whole process. So let's get started by listing off some basic
information about the seal of God:

1. The seal of God (Revelation seven and nine) is contrasted with the
   mark of the beast (Revelation thirteen).
2. A seal—an official sign of authority—gives the essential information
   (usually the name, title, and jurisdiction) of the individual, organization, or government it represents.
3. This information is found in the Sabbath commandment: Name—
   LORD; Title—Creator; Jurisdiction—Heaven and earth.
4. The mark of the beast is readily identified as the claim to have
   changed the Sabbath to Sunday.

So far, so good. The Sabbath is the seal of God's government. Knowl-
edgeable and determined opposition to God's authority, in the form of
Sunday exaltation, will be the mark of the beast. This is all normal Seventh-day Adventist eschatology, and on the next page we have these
things mapped out on a simplified chart of last day events.

It's not the most complete chart of its kind, and it certainly isn't to
scale, so don't make more of it than it's worth. But all we need right now

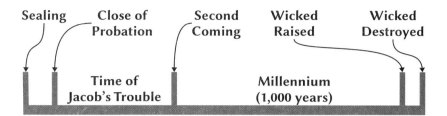

is a basic outline, and that's what this provides. There are just three key things that are important to us at the moment:

1. The seal of God is placed in the foreheads of the 144,000 before the close of probation.
2. The close of probation marks the end of Christ's work as High Priest in the most holy place of the heavenly sanctuary.
3. The conflict between the observance of Sabbath and the mark of the beast reaches its peak during the "time of Jacob's trouble," when those resisting the combined religious/political authority of the world are condemned to death.

Remember, diplomas don't get handed out before finals, so the seal isn't an honor for passing the test of the time of Jacob's trouble. But what *is* the seal for? What does it *contribute* to the plan of salvation? And why do the angels have to hold the four winds of trouble until the sealing is finished? There's a connection here, but what is it? The clue is in the name.

How Did Jacob Get Into This?

Biblical names are important, and this isn't the time of Abraham's trouble. Not Jonah, Jeremiah, or anyone else. So what makes Jacob special?

It was Jeremiah who first used the Jacob imagery:

> For thus says the LORD: "We have heard a voice of trembling, of fear, and not of peace. Ask now, and see, whether a man is ever in labor with child? So why do I see every man with his hands on his loins like a woman in labor, and all faces turned pale? Alas! For that day is great, so that none is like it; and it is the time of Jacob's trouble, but he shall be saved out of it."[1]

Remember the setting? Jacob is returning home after his twenty-year absence when he gets word that his brother Esau is coming with four hundred armed men. This is not a good sign!

---

1. Jeremiah 30:5–7

Realizing his only hope is God, Jacob spends the night praying. At midnight, someone "attacks" him.... For the story, we go to Genesis:

> Then Jacob was left alone; and a Man wrestled with him until the breaking of day. Now when He saw that He did not prevail against him, He touched the socket of his hip; and the socket of Jacob's hip was out of joint as He wrestled with him. And He said, "Let Me go, for the day breaks." But he said, "I will not let You go unless You bless me!"... And He said, "Your name shall no longer be called Jacob, but Israel; for you have struggled with God and with men, and have prevailed."[2]

For expanded coverage, we have the Spirit of Prophecy. The whole of chapter 18 in *Patriarchs and Prophets* would be good to read in this connection, but for the sake of space we will simply focus on brief excerpts:

> While he was thus battling for his life, the sense of his guilt pressed upon his soul; his sins rose up before him, to shut him out from God.[3]

The picture we get is that, while in the middle of a five-hour-long fight to the death, the sense of guilt actually became the central issue. Guilt which brought discouragement and despair, and could only be resisted through faith in the promises of God. Notice the basic nature of Jacob's sin:

> The error that had led to Jacob's sin in obtaining the birthright by fraud was now clearly set before him. He had not trusted God's promises, but had sought by his own efforts to bring about that which God would have accomplished in His own time and way.[4]

In other words, Jacob lost faith in God and thought he had found a better way to take care of himself. Sound familiar?

> During the patriarch's long night of wrestling, Satan endeavored to force upon him a sense of his guilt, in order to discourage him, and break his hold upon God. When in his distress Jacob laid hold of the Angel, and made supplication with tears, the heavenly Messenger, in order to try his faith, also reminded him of his sin, and endeavored to escape from him.[5]

This is peculiar. Satan and the Angel were both reminding Jacob of his sin, but one was seeking to drive him to despair and the other was carefully watching the beneficial "trial of his faith."

---

2. Genesis 32:24–28
3. *Patriarchs and Prophets*, 197
4. *Patriarchs and Prophets*, 197–198
5. *Patriarchs and Prophets*, 201

The stranger placed his finger upon Jacob's thigh, and he was crippled instantly. The patriarch now discerned the character of his antagonist.... It was Christ, "the Angel of the covenant," who had revealed Himself to Jacob.[6]

And here is the crisis point. We may think it had to be a good thing for Jacob to realize he had been wrestling with "the Angel," but consider: After five hours of wrestling for his life (and no one around to impose International Olympic Committee regulations), what do you suppose Jacob had done to his opponent? If you had just flattened God's nose with your forehead, tried to take a chunk out of His upper arm with your teeth, and tried to destroy His kidney with your elbow... are *you* going to think He's happy with you?

Jacob could either say, "Look what I did to Him, He's got to hate me," or "He could have killed me anytime He wanted, He must love me." Under that kind of pressure and fatigue, what might you have said? This is no idle question, because—

> Jacob's experience during that night of wrestling and anguish represents the trial through which the people of God must pass just before Christ's second coming....
>
> Such will be the experience of God's people in their final struggle with the powers of evil. God will test their faith, their perseverance, their confidence in His power to deliver them. Satan will endeavor to terrify them with the thought that their cases are hopeless; that their sins have been too great to receive pardon. They will have a deep sense of their shortcomings, and as they review their lives their hopes will sink.[7]

And that's not all. The worst is yet to come. Only once in all her writing did Ellen White spell it out so clearly.

It Appears to Them...

> Those who live in the last days must pass through an experience similar to that of Jacob. Foes will be all around them, ready to condemn and destroy. Alarm and despair will seize them, for it appears to them as to Jacob in his distress, that God himself has become an avenging enemy.[8]

This is why it is the time of *Jacob's* trouble. This is not the same test the martyrs faced. Despite their suffering, they had the sense of God's acceptance and approval. Not so at the end of time, and for a shockingly simple reason. This test, in order to guarantee that the righteous are safe to save, must be the hardest of all possible tests of faith.

---

6. *Patriarchs and Prophets*, 197
7. *Patriarchs and Prophets*, 201–202
8. *Signs of the Times*, November 27, 1879

Since the basic issue of sin has always been "will God take care of me?" there can be no harder test than for God to "*obviously*" be seeking my harm. Do I trust Him *now?*

There have been foreshadowings of this test. Job is the standout example from the Old Testament. "Though he slay me, yet will I trust Him,"[9] he said. And, of course, in the New Testament we have Christ Himself crying out, "My God, My God, why have You forsaken Me?"[10]

It is in this path that the 144,000 are called to walk. When every sensory input is screaming "God has abandoned you!" faith in His promise of love will alone prevail. Ellen White's account of the end continues:

> Dangers thicken on every side, and it is difficult to fix the eye of faith upon the promises amidst the certain evidences of immediate destruction. But in the midst of revelry and violence, there falls upon the ear peal upon peal of the loudest thunder. The heavens have gathered blackness and are only illuminated with the blazing light and terrible glory from Heaven. God utters his voice from his holy habitation. The captivity of his people is turned. With sweet and subdued voices they say to one another, "God is our friend."[11]

That realization, growing out of those circumstances, and demonstrated by victory in that test, is what the angels are looking for. That level of faith will mark the 144,000 as secure for eternity.

But what about everyone else?

The Function of the Seal

Now, at last, we can put the pieces together to tie off some loose ends that we've left flapping in the breeze. The function, purpose, or contribution of the whole sealing process is one of these, and farther back was the question of why "this gospel" has to go to all the world. And the answer is "demonstration." But what does the seal demonstrate?

We'll approach it as a matter of science. Among the most highly regarded of scientific experiments are those which are carefully constructed to eliminate all variables other than the point in question. When there is only one "independent variable" on the input side, and only one "dependent variable" on the output side, the results of the experiment are very hard to refute.

How about an example for the non-scientific types? Think about balloons. On the input side we have one variable—the gas that fills the bal-

---

9. Job 13:15
10. Mark 15:34
11. *Signs of the Times*, November 27, 1879

loon, and for our purposes we limit that selection to either standard atmospheric air or helium. On the output side we have only one variable—the location of the balloon when released, and after extensive testing we find only two outcomes, on the floor and at the ceiling.

It seems like a simple experiment. What could go wrong? Well, uncontrolled variables could go wrong. What if there were a big fan blowing through the room? Or what if the air mixture were heated above the ambient temperature of the room? Or what if some of the balloons were made of some industrial weight material? All of a sudden it looks like we might get some confusing results.

The problem, of course, is uncontrolled variables. God has a problem like that. Remember the heathen who've never heard the gospel? That's an uncontrolled variable. Think of the sincere believers who have never heard of the Sabbath? That's an uncontrolled variable.

You can't make a crucial demonstration with uncontrolled variables in the experiment. So what to do? Simple—take "this gospel" to every man, woman, and child on planet earth. Suddenly knowledge is no longer a variable. And though it might be hard for human eyes to see it, that leaves only one significant variable: faith in God.

Some people have it, and some people don't. And those who have it, receive the seal of God. Then, in a stunningly nerve-wracking display of divine confidence, Christ announces to the universe, "These 144,000 are Mine. They trust Me. They've shown that in their respect for My Sabbath, and they understand 'this gospel.' They don't know it, but they are now prepared to withstand the most hellish temptations that Satan can muster up. What's more, they will withstand the hardest of all possible tests, which I alone can administer. I've marked them with My seal... now *watch this!*"

Then the four angels let go of the four winds, chaos ensues, and in due time God Himself appears to be the avenging enemy of the only ones on earth faithful to His law. To some degree they understand that great issues are at stake in their experience. In the midst of their distress, they realize that, "should they prove unworthy, and lose their lives because of their own defects of character, then God's holy name would be reproached."[12]

What? One with the seal of God on his forehead who fails the test? The hypothesis of human redemption discredited? The omniscience of God proven false? The government and justice of heaven disgraced? Lucifer justified? Rebellion immortalized?

---

12. *Great Controversy*, 619

To bear the seal of God is no light matter, not the place for the spiritually weak. Every deception, every threat and fear and bribe and appeal to human weakness and appetite will be brought to bear:

[Some,] overwhelmed with consternation, will be ready to exclaim: 'Had we foreseen the consequences of our words, we would have held our peace.' They are hedged in with difficulties. Satan assails them with fierce temptations. The work which they have undertaken seems far beyond their ability to accomplish. They are threatened with destruction. The enthusiasm which animated them is gone; yet they cannot turn back. Then, feeling their utter helplessness, they flee to the Mighty One for strength.[13]

And when it all looks hopeless, then, in some unspecified manner, God Himself appears ready to stab them in the back. But faith falls at His feet and cries out, "I will not let You go unless You bless me!" At last, they hear the voice of God announcing their deliverance. Only then do they realize, fully, that "God is our friend."

When the results are in, it will be seen that every person on earth with faith passed the test, every person without faith failed the test, and God accurately marked every individual with, or without, His seal.

What does this prove? It proves that the 144,000 are safe to save. It proves that faith, plus knowledge of "this gospel," invariably produces victory over sin. And it proves that God is an infallible judge of faith.

Those last two items are crucial, because they provide the rationale for dealing with that one previously mentioned group who don't have a special "Satan falls from heaven" event just for them.

Who is this? The righteous dead. We'll use a hero of the Lord's cause as an illustration. His name was Martin Luther, and he understood a thing or two about justification by faith. But some of the details of "this gospel" were unavoidably fuzzy in his mind.

As a result, Luther held to a few positions that would make us squirm today. Infant baptism, for instance, and predestination. As to his personal life, well he was a German, which meant that his humor was a bit coarse, and his diet was worse—along the lines of roast beast, sauerkraut, and beer. And there were some troubling lapses in judgment, like the time he realized that the Jews weren't going to accept the Reformation—he thought the best thing would be to simply kill them all.

Does Martin Luther sound like a good candidate for heaven? Really?

Of course he's a good candidate! Jesus simply shows that the Investigative Judgment found Luther had faith in God. The other issues?

13. *Great Controversy*, 610

There's no problem there, he'll learn "this gospel" in heaven. And the combination of true faith and that knowledge *always* produces victory.

And with the evidence in place, Gabriel and all the host of heaven offer no objection, but rejoice that a sinner has been reclaimed.

So, in the end, Luther had it right. Righteousness is *sola fide*. And lest anyone be tempted to think this opens the door to a cheap grace kind of faith, remember who is the Judge of true faith, and what is the test that confirms it.

But What of the Others?

We've seen how the sealing and the time of Jacob's trouble answer the concerns of the unfallen universe about the safety of redeeming sinners. But there is a flip side to that coin, and nothing yet has addressed the concern over the harshness of the law that says sinners—*all* sinners—must die in the fires of hell.

It's easy now, perhaps, to say, "That's God's law. It's good." But what if the sinner in question is your mother, son, father, daughter, husband, wife, or friend? What then? Until the justice of that law is demonstrated, God has a problem....

Fast forward a thousand years. The millennium is over; the wicked have been raised; the Holy City has descended. Time has been given them, and Satan has deceived them (*again!*). Now the decisive moment has come:

> At last the order to advance is given, and the countless host moves on—an army such as was never summoned by earthly conquerors, such as the combined forces of all ages since war began on earth could never equal. Satan, the mightiest of warriors, leads the van, and his angels unite their forces for this final struggle. Kings and warriors are in his train, and the multitudes follow in vast companies, each under its appointed leader.
>
> With military precision the serried ranks advance over the earth's broken and uneven surface to the City of God. By command of Jesus, the gates of the New Jerusalem are closed, and the armies of Satan surround the city and make ready for the onset.[14]

Did you catch it?

Something absolutely incredible just happened. No, not the army surrounding the city. That's what armies do. The whole purpose of Satan's last ditch effort is to tear God from the throne and take it himself. Nothing unexpected there.

---

14. *Great Controversy*, 664

The amazing thing is what Jesus did. He closed the gates. That means they had been *open*. With the wicked of all ages outside the city, the gates were left open! And, as if to remove all doubt about what the gates were for, Jesus first resurrects the wicked, then summons the New Jerusalem, and in sight of all the wicked, He leads the righteous through the gates and into the city.[15]

We are not told what this means. And, certainly, it would be foolish to give anyone the idea that he could find acceptance with the Lord at that late date. And yet... the gates were open....

And that raises a question. Would Jesus, the One who is "the same yesterday, today, and forever,"[16] the One who said "whoever comes to Me I will by no means cast out,"[17] the One who has "no pleasure in the death of the wicked"[18]—would "this same Jesus"[19] let a repentant and trusting sinner into the city?

It's hypothetical, of course, since in all the multitudes of the lost there is not one with faith in God's good will to venture anywhere near those open doors. Does Jesus invite them? We are not told, but it would not change the outcome. Just as the 144,000 passed the hardest possible test of faith to answer one question of the unfallen universe, so the wicked have answered another by failing the easiest of all tests.

There is nothing more that even God can do for them. They just don't trust Him. Destruction is the most merciful option. But first there is the necessity for Satan's final fall from heaven.

Alone... So Very Alone

Next comes the final judgment, with its panoramic presentation of the entire conflict. With this evidence before them, every knee shall bow and every tongue confess the justice and righteousness of God. But—

> Notwithstanding that Satan has been constrained to acknowledge God's justice and to bow to the supremacy of Christ, his character remains unchanged. The spirit of rebellion, like a mighty torrent, again bursts forth.... He rushes into the midst of his subjects and endeavors to inspire them with his own fury and arouse them to instant battle. But of all the countless millions whom he has allured into rebellion, there are none now to acknowledge his supremacy. His power is at an end.[20]

15. *Great Controversy*, 662–663
16. Hebrews 13:8
17. John 6:37
18. Ezekiel 33:11
19. Acts 1:11
20. *Great Controversy*, 671

The conflict is over. All that must be demonstrated, has been... almost. One revelation remains. The scroll, front and back, must now be revealed to all. None but Christ can do so, and up to this point He has chosen to do so gradually, over time. We have lessons to learn before all is revealed:

> The light we have received upon the third angel's message is the true light. The mark of the beast is exactly what it has been proclaimed to be. Not all in regard to this matter is yet understood, nor will it be understood until the unrolling of the scroll; but a most solemn work is to be accomplished in our world. The Lord's command to His servants is: "Cry aloud, spare not, lift up thy voice like a trumpet, and show My people their transgression, and the house of Jacob their sins."[21]

> God had a knowledge of the events of the future, even before the creation of the world. He did not make his purposes to fit circumstances, but he allowed matters to develop and work out. He did not work to bring about a certain condition of things, but he knew that such a condition would exist. The plan that should be carried out upon the defection of any of the high intelligences of heaven—this is the secret, the mystery which has been hid from ages.[22]

But when all is done, the "ages" are past and eternity is to begin. The scroll is to be revealed, that, to some degree, we might understand the omniscient foreknowledge of God. This, too, is a part of His plan to strengthen the confidence of all His creatures, to further ensure that "afflfliction will not rise up a second time."[23]

> There in His open hand lay the book, the roll of the history of God's providences, the prophetic history of nations and the church. Herein was contained the divine utterances, His authority, His commandments, His laws, the whole symbolic counsel of the Eternal, and the history of all ruling powers in the nations. In symbolic language was contained in that roll the influence of every nation, tongue, and people from the beginning of earth's history to its close.

> This roll was written within and without. John says: "I wept much, because no man was found worthy to open and to read the book, neither to look thereon." The vision as presented to John made its impression upon his mind. The destiny of every nation was contained in that book. John was distressed at the utter inability of any human being or angelic intelligence to read the words, or even to look thereon. His soul was wrought up to such a point of agony and suspense that one of the strong angels had compassion on him, and laying his hand on him assuringly said, "Weep not: behold, the Lion of the tribe of Judah, the Root of David, hath prevailed to open the book, and to loose the seven seals thereof."

---

21. *Testimonies*, vol. 6, 17
22. *Signs of the Times* , March 25, 1897
23. Nahum 1:9

John continues: "I beheld, and, lo, in the midst of the throne and of the four beasts, and in the midst of the elders, stood a Lamb as it had been slain, having seven horns and seven eyes, which are the seven Spirits of God sent forth into all the earth. And He came and took the book out of the right hand of Him that sat upon the throne."

As the book was unrolled, all who looked upon it were filled with awe. There were no blanks in the book. There was space for no more writing.[24]

Where Do You Go After the End?

In three chapters we have traced in broad outline the work of God in response to the accusations of Lucifer. We call this the Great Controversy, and justly so. But, now what?

Now we return to the "real world," the distorted, artificial, superficial place we live on a daily basis. Gone are the sweeping vistas of great principles and vast ages. Instead we find the routine of jobs, school, bills, and whatever else.

What does the great vision have to do with daily reality? How can we as individuals, as local churches, as a world-wide church, move forward with the Lord's work? How do *we* make a demonstration of His principles? These are the questions that remain, the issues addressed by the following chapters.

Knowing that the scroll is not yet fully revealed, everyone should realize that neither this book, nor any other by human authors, will contain all we will need to know. But that there is a work to be done, a message to be proclaimed, is obvious. Perhaps, after these three chapters, it is also obvious that proclamation must be combined with demonstration; that God's wisdom exceeds our own; that His methods alone will succeed.

It is to the easily overlooked simplicity of the very methods that Jesus used that we now turn our attention. Our focus now is d'Sozo.

---

24. *Manuscript Releases*, vol. 20, 197

Chapter Four

The Right Arm Rises

IT is famously dangerous to establish doctrine on a single text, and one might surmise that to do so on two texts is only marginally better. But no idea or theory or even narrative arrives fully developed. There is always an introductory phase where the range of discussion is undefined, explanations only partial, and documentation incomplete. The table must be set before dinner can be served.

And so we begin with two data points, displayed here with almost no context whatsoever. They were both written by Ellen White in the early years of the twentieth century, and at present will merely serve as points of departure:

> I want to tell you that when the gospel ministers and the medical missionary workers are not united, there is placed on our churches the worst evil that can be placed there.[1]

> The truth for this time, the third angel's message, is to be proclaimed with a loud voice, meaning with increasing power, as we approach the great final test. This test must come to the churches in connection with the true medical missionary work, a work that has the great Physician to dictate and preside in all it comprehends.[2]

And So the Story Begins...

There was a time when Adventists didn't speak of medical missionaries at all. Not that the idea was entirely absent, but the term hadn't yet come into vogue. In fact, the phrase "medical missionary" didn't appear

---

1. *Sermons and Talks*, 347
2. *Ellen G. White 1888 Materials*, 1710

in the *Review and Herald* until November 21, 1893, and never made it into the *Testimonies,* until vol. 6, 203, published in 1901.

Before then, anything done in that direction was known as "Christian help work," or sometimes "benevolent work." Another way to indicate the same idea of service to others was a quotation from, or even just an allusion to, the fifty-eighth chapter of Isaiah. But, even though the idea wasn't entirely foreign to the church, it's probably fair to say that none too much was done along those lines.

The Seventh-day Adventist Benevolent Association was formed in 1868 to foster this sort of work. Unfortunately, this was largely in reaction to the failure of the church to provide for Hannah More, an experienced foreign missionary, teacher, author, and preacher. Miss More had worked at a mission amongst the Cherokee Indians of Oklahoma, a mission in Sierra Leone started by survivors of the *Amistad,* and another mission in Liberia.[3] Back in the States on furlough in 1863, she met Stephen Haskell, who gave her some books on the Sabbath.

Not until she had returned to Liberia did she fully weigh out this strange new teaching, but when she did, she concluded it was the truth—something that she felt her fellow missionaries would naturally love to hear about. But it turned out they did not want to hear her new beliefs, and they eventually fired her for keeping Sabbath.

Left in a far-off foreign country without financial support, she was forced to pay her own way back to the States, and finally on to Battle Creek. This was the home of the truths she had come to love, but Battle Creek proved not to be a home to Hannah More.

It was her misfortune to arrive at Adventist headquarters when James and Ellen White were out of town on an extended camp meeting tour. Sadly, the Whites never met Miss More in person. After thoroughly "making the rounds" of the institutions and members of the church in Battle Creek in an effort to find work and housing, the middle-aged, single woman with unfashionably old clothes was running out of money. Was it the clothes? Or Hannah herself? Having suffered from eye trouble for many years, she now wore large glasses which magnified her eyes, and one of them was essentially blind and unfocused.[4] Physically unimpressive, somewhat worse the wear from crossing the Atlantic Ocean six times and spending years in the jungles of Africa, the graying, mid-

---

3. Isabel B. Weigold, *Hannah Moore,* (ISBN 978-0-595-43135-9)
4. Isabel B. Weigold, *Hannah Moore,* 86

dle-aged missionary seemed not to fit in well with the relatively refined society of Battle Creek's West End.

As a stop-gap measure, she sought employment and housing with some former co-workers, a Baptist family who now lived in northern Michigan. While there, she contracted tuberculosis from the poor conditions of her unheated but often smoky attic quarters. Miss Hannah More died in March of 1868.

From Ellen White's comments, we can gain a sense of God's perspective of this matter:

> In this testimony I speak freely of the case of Sister Hannah More, not from a willingness to grieve the Battle Creek church, but from a sense of duty. I love that church notwithstanding their faults. I know of no church that in acts of benevolence and general duty do so well. I present the frightful facts in this case to arouse our people everywhere to a sense of their duty. Not one in twenty of those who have a good standing with Seventh-day Adventists is living out the self-sacrificing principles of the word of God.[5]

Perhaps the most startling note of alarm was simply that our neglect of this woman—whom no one in Battle Creek had ever met before she showed up on their doorstep, so to speak—was more significant than we would like to think:

> In the case of Sister Hannah More, I was shown that the neglect of her was the neglect of Jesus in her person. Had the Son of God come in the humble, unpretending manner in which He journeyed from place to place when He was upon earth, He would have met with no better reception.[6]

The First Efforts

And so, with this circumstance as a backdrop, the Seventh-day Adventist Benevolent Association was formed in 1868. By 1887, there were thirty-seven Adventist "city missions" in operation; but in 1888 only twenty-two were reported.[7] What a disaster—forty percent of the "benevolent work" lost in a single year!

Actually, it was more of a tempest in a teapot. The "city missions" reported in 1887 were mostly small endeavors, and their loss doesn't seem to have concerned anyone very much. The numerical discrepancy may have simply been the result of negligent (or, perhaps, *realistic*) reporting.

---

5. *Testimonies*, vol. 1, 632
6. *Testimonies*, vol. 2, 140
7. *1888 General Conference Daily Bulletin*, 26

Six years later, the status of the Benevolent Association was summed up like this: "This Association, through lack of support, and, perhaps, in consequence of being overshadowed by other enterprises, was allowed to lapse, and very little has been heard of it for quite a number of years."[8]

But for the benevolent work itself, 1888 turned out to be a banner year! It happened, of all places, at Minneapolis... at the General Conference session held there... through the teaching of two young ministers from the West Coast, and the heart response of thirty-six-year-old John Harvey Kellogg.

To understand the next fifty years of denominational history, it is necessary to take the influence of J.H. Kellogg into account. By any measure, he was one of the movers and shakers of the denomination, and to this day he remains the most colorful character Adventism has ever produced.

What was Kellogg like? Intelligent, insecure, independent, proud, generous, decisive, and controlling. His medical training had made him the most highly educated man in the church. His unsuccessful courtship of Miss Mary Kelsey had strained relations somewhat with the young man she chose to marry instead: Willie White. And—as we'll see—Kellogg's vigorous advocacy of health reform, combined with the failure of some of the church's ministers to practice it (especially a vegetarian diet) had caused him to lose confidence in them.

Kellogg was all this in 1888, to one degree or another, but none of these traits is as important to our story as one other thing which Kellogg was just then: He was converted. Nearly a decade-and-a-half later, Ellen White remembered it clearly:

> After the meeting at Minneapolis, Dr. Kellogg was a converted man, and we all knew it. We could see the converting power of God working in his heart and life.[9]

Now to understand this statement, it must be borne in mind that Dr. Kellogg was by this time an established figure in the church. He had been Medical Director of the Sanitarium for a dozen years already. It's not like he was the town drunk. But here he was now, in late 1888, early 1889—a converted man, and so obviously so that everyone knew it. It was clearly visible to all. And that raises an interesting question: What had changed? It's not that Dr. Kellogg suddenly began attending Sabbath services at the Dime Tabernacle, or that he stopped going to the local bar, or that he paid up on tithe that he had withheld in the past.

So what had changed? Perhaps this statement will help:

---

8. *The Medical Missionary*, February 1894, 33
9. *1903 General Conference Bulletin*, 86

While [the believer] is justified because of the merit of Christ, he is not free to work unrighteousness. Faith works by love and purifies the soul. Faith buds and blossoms and bears a harvest of precious fruit. Where faith is, good works appear. The sick are visited, the poor are cared for, the fatherless and the widows are not neglected, the naked are clothed, the destitute are fed.[10]

It seems that this is the kind of conversion that Dr. Kellogg experienced. As might be expected, a change of heart like this could simmer along in one's own personal experience for a while, but in Kellogg's case it wasn't long before it came out into plain sight. He was, after all, a promoter, a go-getter, not one to sit on the sidelines of life.

A year-and-a-half after the Minneapolis meetings, Kellogg was in northern Michigan—about fifty miles from Hannah More's grave—talking to Ellen White about starting an orphanage. She later wrote to the medical workers in Battle Creek:

While in Petoskey I had some conversation with your physician-in-chief in regard to establishing a home for orphan children at Battle Creek. I said that this was just what was needed among us as a people, and that in enterprises of this kind we were far behind other denominations.[11]

Now Kellogg had something to work toward, and he set about to see that it got done. The opportunity would come at the next General Conference Session, March 5–25, 1891.

General Conference, 1891

On Monday morning, the 16th of March, Kellogg spoke to the delegates. His topic was "Our Orphans." In a straight forward manner the doctor told of his research on Seventh-day Adventist orphans. A letter of inquiry sent to five hundred thirty-six leaders within the denomination had resulted in a list of two hundred twenty-two orphans. This was complicated, however, by the doctor's figures coming from the Obituaries section of the *Review*. During the last five years, that publication had listed seven hundred seventy-four children who had been orphaned.

Since church leaders could only list two hundred twenty-two orphans, that might mean that the other five hundred fifty-two orphans had been cared for... but since no one could actually say *where* or *by whom* these orphans were being cared for, it seemed more probable that the five hundred thirty-six church leaders were simply out of touch with the subject.

10. *Selected Messages*, Book One, 398
11. *Testimonies*, vol. 8, 133

When the dust finally settled on the issue, a committee of seven was formed to work with the General Conference committee to establish "a home for orphans and destitute aged persons to be called the 'James White Memorial Home.'"[12]

The developmental path of the orphanage seemed straight-forward: raise funding, erect building, select staff, secure operating budget. It wasn't necessarily going to be easy, but it wasn't exactly brain surgery, either. But there was another plot line playing out during those meetings of the General Conference that was inextricably intertwined with the story of the orphanage. This had to do with Kellogg's relationship with the ministers of the church. Simply put, that relationship was already challenged, and some of Kellogg's comments at the session probably did nothing to help.

Eight days before his speech on "Our Orphans," Kellogg had addressed the International Health and Temperance Association and given his perspective on Adventist health reform. There is no way to know who all was listening that afternoon, but in any case, the full speech was printed in the *General Conference Daily Bulletin* for all to read. The preamble to Kellogg's account of the Association's activities provides a good introduction to the tensions between him and the ministers:

> The American Health and Temperance Association, or, as it is now called, the International Health and Temperance Association, was organized a little more than twelve years ago, and I am glad to be able to announce today that it is still alive, and threatens to continue to live for some time to come in spite of the many dangers which have threatened it and the many obstacles which it has encountered.
>
> The time when this association was organized, was an opportune one. Something more than a dozen years before, there had been a very active and earnest agitation of health and temperance principles among our people, which had resulted in the adoption, by the majority of those who at that time constituted the denomination, of many very important reforms. Intoxicating drinks and tobacco had been practically excluded from the denomination. Elder White wrote, in 1870:
>
> "As a people, we have discarded the use of tobacco in all its forms. Thank God for so glorious a victory over perverted appetite! In the annual assemblies of the leading men of our denomination, not the least taint of the filthy weed can be discovered by sight or smell. Our people have also discontinued the use of tea and coffee, as unnecessary, expensive, and injurious to health. Here another victory has been gained.

---

12. *1891 General Conference Daily Bulletin*, 177–178, 206

"But the reform among us does not stop here. Our people have put away the use of swine's flesh, and, to a great extent, of flesh meats generally. This they have done from a conviction that flesh is not the most nutritious or the most healthful food for man. While flesh-meats stimulate, they do not build up the system, as other foods do. This was once an experiment with our people; now it is demonstrated.

"Seventh-day Adventists have adopted two meals a day, instead of three. But this is not a denominational law with them, as their church organization and discipline have nothing to do with regulating such matters. Yet in most cases they discard flesh-meats, and partake of food but twice each day. These facts we have learned from personal observation in holding camp-meetings with them from Maine to Kansas, during the past summer. Our ministers preach hygiene reform, and live it wherever they go. And our many publications carry it to the doors of all our people. Thousands have testified to the benefits of the changes they have made. They report better health, and an increase of physical strength. Ask them if they can perform as much labor without meat and without the third meal as they could before they made the changes, and they will tell you that since their present habits have become fully established, they can endure more labor, and that they enjoy life much better. This is the experience of all, whether professional or laboring men."

Unfortunately, the good work of reform had, by the end of another decade, not only ceased its onward progress, but there had been a very marked retrograde; other issues, coming before the people, had attracted their attention, and the promulgation of health principles had ceased to receive the influence necessary to keep them before the people.

No regular means had been provided for systematic consideration of these principles, and as a consequence new converts to the faith received little or no instruction in them. Large numbers of young ministers and licentiates had entered the field as preachers who had never received adequate instruction in health principles, and who consequently were not prepared either to appreciate their importance or to instruct the people in their precepts.

In consequence a great backsliding had begun and had progressed to an extent which was not fully comprehended until the circulation of the teetotal pledge, at the camp-meetings held during 1879, developed the fact that hundreds among us were addicted to the habitual use of tea and coffee, and that it could no longer be said, "Not the least taint of the filthy weed would be discovered," for in some instances leading members of churches, in a few cases even officers of churches, were found to be habitual users of the filthy weed. There were found among the ministers even, not a few who complained that the pledge was too strong, a criticism which from their standpoint was eminently proper, since the pledge evidently prohibited the strong tea to which such critics were almost universally found to be addicted.

Unquestionably the organization of the American Health and Temperance Association exerted a great influence in checking, to some degree at least, the course of emigration in the direction of the Egypt from which the grand principles of health and temperance reform, given to our people by the Lord through the Testimonies of Sister White, had but a few years ago so gloriously emancipated a whole denomination.

The backward movement continued, however, until it seemed almost like a stampede. Men and women who had for years testified to the great benefits received from the adoption of health principles, suddenly discovered that health reform did not agree with them; that two meals a day were insufficient to support a working man, especially brain workers, who need more nourishment than those who use their muscles only; that good beef steak was necessary for good health; that good cheese was essential to good digestion, and a cup of strong tea, now and then, to relieve sick headache, not particularly objectionable, and possibly of service as a preventive.

The provision stands and boarding-tents at camp-meetings ceased to be object lessons for our people and those not of our faith, in healthful dietetics. The camp-meeting provision stand in the last decade has rarely failed to include in its stock a good supply of lard crackers, ginger snaps, baker's pies and cakes of various sorts, dried beef, smoked halibut, sale codfish, smoked herring, painted candies and unwholesome knick-knacks of various sorts, a good supply of cheese, ripe enough to be buried and lively enough to move on if not kept in a cage, and in the background might usually be seen, arranged in a picturesque manner, sundry coils of sausage, warranted, however, to be bologna, as I have frequently been told, which is a guarantee that the article is not Simon pure swine's flesh, but a miscellaneous assortment of all manner of beasts.

Two or three years ago I spent a few unhappy hours upon a camp-ground, the main entrance of which was flanked upon one side by a huge sign, "Ice-cream," and upon the other side, "Hot Peanuts." The book tent bore no sign at all, which was perhaps just as well under the circumstances. The ground was well carpeted with peanut shells, the constant snapping of which furnished punctuation marks for the discourses of the ministers from the speaker's stand.

With such examples to the flock at camp-meetings, the annual gatherings which our people are earnestly exhorted by the ministers to attend for the purpose of "drawing near to the Lord and seeking a more complete consecration of soul and body to the service of God," it cannot be considered a matter of wonderment that in their home life our people have for some years back not been making progress in the reforms which God so graciously placed in our hands more than a quarter of a century ago, for us to cherish and practice for our own good, and to develop and promulgate for the benefit of our fellow-men; and it is not a matter of astonishment that even beneath the shadow of the Sanitarium, which in the providence of

God was established to be a means by which these reforms should be fostered and encouraged, there should be found tea bibbers and coffee topers, while among the families of the denomination there are probably to be found few indeed who do not daily gather about the flesh pots, and, to use the graphic words of a vegetarian heathen, "Chaw with bloody teeth the bleeding bread."

With this state of things, the description of which I assure you is not overdrawn, it should [not] be a matter of surprise to us that the American Health and Temperance Association has not been in a very flourishing state as an organization, or that it has been difficult to maintain a lively interest in its State and local organizations. Nevertheless something has been accomplished. The officers of the society having recognized the impossibility of doing much more than maintain an existence, have sought to at least keep the association alive, and have earnestly endeavored to accomplish what they could in the promotion of its principles, particularly in the education of our people.[13]

Start-up Costs

When the 1891 General Conference formally authorized the orphanage project, they considered as well the need for funding. The trustees of the institution were told they could make general appeals to the church membership through the church's publications, and the Sabbath School offerings from the second quarter of 1892 were slated for the orphanage.

One of the more noteworthy appeals came from Ellen White:

A good move was made at the late General Conference in the representation of the subject to our brethren assembled, and in the decision that an orphans' home should be established. Now that the impetus has been given to the work by those who realize the great need, let every one stand ready to act a part in helping it forward.[14]

The Sabbath School offerings amounted to a little more than $7,000; beyond that, individual pledges for several thousand dollars were made, but many remained unfulfilled. In general though, the response was... well, perhaps "tepid" is the word.

What could they do? Why was there so little interest?

Actually, there was a great deal of interest in the orphanage, it's just that it was all on the part of orphans and those who had been caring for them:

As soon as it was known that provision was to be made for needy little ones, applications began to pour in from all parts of the United States; and in a short time, even before any definite arrangements were made by the committee, quite a number of children had gathered from various quarters. These were placed in

---

13. *1891 General Conference Daily Bulletin*, 41–42
14. *The Medical Missionary*, June 1, 1891

the care of a suitable person, and located in a building set aside for the purpose, by the Battle Creek Sanitarium.

Several urgent appeals were sent out for funds for the erection of the necessary building, but the receipts were exceedingly slow and the donations meager, being largely from the poor, whose sympathies are usually the most easily reached.

The fact that there was even in prospect a home for destitute children brought out very forcibly another fact; viz., that there were hundreds of needy children whose cases had not been brought to public notice, who were candidates for a place in the Home.

The outlook seemed anything but encouraging; but the committee at last determined to make a beginning with the few thousand dollars which had been received, although the amount was only sufficient to erect a cottage of moderate size, after making a small payment on the land purchased for a site. Those chiefly interested in the promotion of the enterprise were greatly distressed on account of the situation, especially in view of the numerous applications and the pitiful and urgent character of many of the cases.[15]

In this funding drought, Kellogg began to pray that the Lord would send a generous donor—and in April 1892, He did just that. One day a woman walked into Kellogg's office and introduced herself as Mrs. Caroline Haskell. She was a total stranger to Kellogg (and no relation to Elder Stephen Haskell, by the way).

After making some general inquiries about the work of the Sanitarium, she asked if there was any project of the institution that she might be able to help along with a gift of several thousand dollars. Kellogg mentioned the "endowed bed" program which provided free hospital services for people unable to pay themselves. But Mrs. Haskell was thinking on a larger scale than that, and told Kellogg so. Making a quick adjustment, the Doctor shared the dream of constructing an orphanage:

"That," said the lady, "is just such an enterprise as I should like to assist, and I should like to talk with you further in reference to your plans."

A few days later Mrs. Haskell examined the plans which had been prepared for the building of an orphans' home. She at once recognized the fact that they were insufficient for the purpose, and in several ways might be greatly improved. After some thought, she made a proposition which was almost startling to us, coming as it did from one who was so lately a stranger to us and our work. It was to erect the entire building herself, at a cost of $30,000, provided it might stand as a memorial of her deceased husband. Mr. Haskell, she added, had been greatly interested in boys; he had reared more than one orphan lad to manhood, and had contributed many thousands of dollars to institutions for boys.

15. 1897 Year Book of the International Medical Missionary and Benevolent Association, 82–83

Mrs. Haskell's plan once formed, she did not linger about carrying it out. New designs were prepared and submitted to her, with which she expressed her satisfaction, and by midsummer the funds were in the hands of the committee and the ground broken for the new building.[16]

Despite a slight delay caused by revising the plans, by August of 1892 the construction was begun in earnest. In February 1893 Kellogg said the home was nearly complete, but the formal dedication came nearly a year later, in January 1894. It was a big occasion, with speeches by the president of the State Board of Charities and Corrections, as well as Uriah Smith, John Loughborough, Dr. Kellogg, and the matron of the home, Mrs. E.H. Whitney. The Haskell Home seemed to be off and running.

The Need In Chicago

In the meantime, there had been other developments in related areas. The background for all this was Dr. Kellogg's visit to New York back in 1889. He would later comment:

> I never had much faith in God until I went down to the Jerry McAuley Mission in New York City, and saw how the Lord could save drunkards.[17]

The impressions made then, and reinforced later through his familiarity with the well-known city mission work of Dr. Dowkonnt, developed into an interest in outreach to the poor and "degraded" population of the large cities. Kellogg wanted to begin working in Chicago, but finances were a hurdle. The first open door in that direction came as the culmination of an unusual train of circumstances:

> In the summer of 1891 there was under treatment at the Sanitarium at Battle Creek a young lady, the daughter of a wealthy banker residing in Chicago. After a few weeks' treatment the young lady returned to her home in Chicago, accompanied by a Sanitarium nurse. Some weeks later, a critical surgical operation was performed by a Chicago surgeon, from which she did not recover. On her deathbed she expressed her high appreciation of the efficiency of the methods of nursing and treatment employed at the Sanitarium, and of the kindness and Christian courtesy exhibited by the nurses there, and exacted from her father a pledge that he would employ a Sanitarium nurse to work among the poor of Chicago.
>
> A few months later, a letter was received from him, asking that a nurse be sent to engage in work among the poor, at his expense. After careful consideration of the matter, the request was granted, and in 1892, a trained nurse from the Sanitarium was sent to Chicago to work in connection with the Visiting Nurses Association.

16. *1897 Year Book of the International Medical Missionary and Benevolent Association*, 94–95
17. *1897 General Conference Bulletin*, 292

Soon there were nurses from the Sanitarium who volunteered to give several weeks' time to visiting among the poor of Chicago, their fellow nurses aiding them to meet the expenses.[18]

Christian Help Bands

Even before the first Sanitarium nurse went to Chicago, Dr. Kellogg was thinking of ways to carry on a simpler work in Battle Creek—and everywhere else, for that matter. The first time the Christian Help Band idea was published seems to have been in February 1892.[19] In this article, Dr. Kellogg outlines the idea, and mentions a single "pioneer band" of workers drawn from the nursing staff of the Sanitarium. Like many good ideas, it seems this one had some success and then died away. It needed a good "shot in the arm" to get it going.

The stories Kellogg brought back from Chicago were the perfect catalyst for reviving the Christian Help Bands. If a single Adventist nurse—funded by a non-Adventist, and working under the direction of the non-Adventist "Visiting Nurses Association"—could take on the toughest sections of Chicago, surely a sanitarium full of Adventist doctors and nurses could do *something* for the poor of Battle Creek! Once again it was Dr. Kellogg who kicked the ball to keep it rolling:

> A little meeting of Sanitarium helpers, presided over by Dr. Kellogg, met at eight o'clock on the evening of November 15, 1892, to consider the question of Christian Help work. Dr. Kellogg spoke of the good such a band of workers could do, in looking up those in the city who were not able to take care of themselves, in providing, as far as possible, food, clothing, and such other things as they were in need of, and helping them in every way to a higher appreciation of life, and to know how to care for themselves and their children. This was the beginning of the organized effort of the Christian Help Bands.[20]

This turn of events was something new for the Adventists of Battle Creek. Like most new ideas or programs, this one needed some explaining. Wisely, it wasn't until the dust had settled and the work had taken

---

18. *1897 Year Book of the International Medical Missionary and Benevolent Association*, 61
19. Some question remains on this date, which is based on an article, presumably written by Dr. Kellogg, for which the author has been unable to locate a reliable original copy. The re-typed article from the private papers of Leah Schmitke (now deceased) is entitled "Christian Help Work," and is credited to the February 1892 edition of the *Medical Missionary* magazine. Unfortunately, the best source for such materials—the General Conference Archives' web site—doesn't have the *Medical Missionary* magazine. The best source in this particular case is Google Books, but they do not have the 1892 volume year.
20. *The Medical Missionary*, March/April 1893, 74

on a bit of routine that both an announcement and explanation of the program was provided for all to read. The account above continues:

Nine were chosen to make up the first band, a leader appointed, a gospel worker, a missionary nurse, three young men chosen as burden bearers, and three young women as mothers' helpers. This original band worked on for some weeks, devoting from one to six or more hours each week to the work, and calling on others to help them, when they found more than they could do. Others became anxious to aid, and names enough were soon handed to the committee to make four new bands, which were also set to work. The call-boys of the Sanitarium, not to be outdone in good works by their elders, also formed themselves into an auxiliary band, and though they could not work in just the same lines, have proved themselves very efficient in various directions, such as looking up old clothing, and gathering it up, distributing it, finding cases in need of help, running of errands, etc.

The whole number of visits made by these bands, as collected from the weekly reports is 293; but this falls somewhat short of the actual number. The instances where relief has been afforded to individuals are 263.

Some of the weekly reports of the bands are very suggestive. Of course they are too brief to be more than hints of the work done, but they speak for themselves, and show the nature of the work better than could be done in any other way. Let us look them over and gather some items:

"Two old ladies who needed wood split, and had no one to do it for them, were reported to the burden bearers, and a later report shows that the wood was split to the great gratitude of the lonely old ladies."

"A widow woman was found who was dependent on the renting of her rooms for support. Roomers were looked up and sent to her, so she was put in the way of self-support."

"A young woman was found in sore need of medical treatment, and was reported to the Hospital and treatment secured."

"Two cases on _____ street in need of clothing." The clothing was afterward supplied.

"A mother trying to take care of herself and child by washing, was helped to find work."

"Called on Mr. _____, whose wife was at the Hospital, found the house in sad condition, and helped clean it up."

"Patient previously visited and treated is improving and more cheerful, delights to read the Bible I sent him. Tears of gratitude filled his eyes when he received it. May the Lord convert him."

"Some good reading matter left with a family."

"Found a baby sick, little girl with tonsillitis," and at a later visit "the mother was down with rheumatism."

"Sent _____ to the dispensary for medicine."

"Invalid food furnished two cases."

"A family supplied with wood."

"Gave away five pairs of mittens, some food and tracts."

It's impossible to know exactly when this article was written, but it couldn't have been more than five months after the original band was formed. A lot had happened in those months, but the genius of the plan was that, except for serious medical cases, the services rendered were such that just about anyone could have a part. In fact, the article tells us that the idea was catching on:

Quite recently more names have been offered for Christian Help work, and have just been organized into bands, and territory laid out for them. There are now sixteen bands at the Sanitarium, besides the band of call-boys.[21]

If the nine-member band was the standard, that would mean one hundred forty-four people were now involved in Christian Help work—plus the call-boys, of course. And the next article in the paper, entitled "Christian Help Work in Ann Arbor," tells how the same work was begun there under the leadership of Dr. Daniel Kress "about the first of December, 1892."

It doesn't take a lot of imagination to believe that this sort of activity would have an impact on the communities targeted. But "communities" aren't won to Christ; people are. Was this kind of work having any success in soul-winning? The Ann Arbor article includes this note:

As the result of these efforts two men who had never made any profession of religion have been converted. Brother Kress, the leader of one of the bands, has been holding Bible studies with some who are much interested. "The people," he says, "are hungering for Bible truth. I do not remember of ever seeing such an interest. We have also formed classes for Bible study among the students. These are yet in their infancy, but a good interest is manifested. We can plainly see the fulfillment of the promise, 'And I, if I be lifted up, will draw all men unto me' and that he is the 'Desire of all nations.'"[22]

The two men who had "been converted" were the exception rather than the rule. Though many of the Help Band reports spoke of spiritual interactions with the people (praying, reading the Bible, formal Bible studies, or answering doctrinal inquiries), at the five-month mark it could not be said that there had been a large number of "conversions," let alone "baptisms." Help Band ministry had not produced a quick return on in-

21. *The Medical Missionary*, March/April 1893, 74–75

22. *The Medical Missionary*, March/April 1893, 76

vestment in that way; what remained to be seen was whether or not the number and quality measures would eventually validate the practice.

Meanwhile...

As a historical side note before moving on with the story, an introduction is in order. Though his name hasn't appeared in any of the selections included here, we should note that the leader of "Christian Help Band No. 1" and the author of the article describing the work in Battle Creek, was a young Australian by the name of A.W. Semmens. He plays a secondary role in our story—indeed, he is one of the great legion of "minor characters" who make up the mass of church history—but we will see him a time or two, and eventually back in his native land, a few years down the road, where he carried on the good work.

A second item, one that will take on greater significance as we continue this history, is a statement made by Ellen White at about this same time. Unlike Brother Semmens, the statement is well known, perhaps even "famous," but it has seldom been considered within the context presented here. The *Review and Herald* of November 22, 1893, contained these words:

> The time of test is just upon us, for the loud cry of the third angel has already begun in the revelation of the righteousness of Christ, the sin-pardoning Redeemer. This is the beginning of the light of the angel whose glory shall fill the whole earth.

The relationship between this "beginning" of the loud cry and the rise of medical missionary work is one of the central themes of all our further considerations.

The "Second Blessing"

This section's heading has nothing to do with Wesleyan theology; rather it is a reference to another significant financial event which may seem to be an outgrowth of everything we've covered so far, but one which actually comes from more complicated circumstances. Kellogg first hinted at this in the January 1893 edition of the *Medical Missionary*:

> Medical missionary work has been begun in Chicago, and through a recent "special providence," of which we will speak more fully next month, it will be possible to lay the foundation for a splendid work in that great city, which may be the means of accomplishing even more than our most sanguine hopes dared to expect when this work was mentioned in these columns two years ago.[23]

---

23. *The Medical Missionary*, January 1893, 12

What was this "special providence" which was to "lay the foundation for a splendid work" in Chicago?

A month later Kellogg introduced his topic by mentioning Mrs. Haskell's donation for the orphanage, and the businessman's donation that provided for the first missionary nurse to Chicago. He spoke of "the evident need for the enlargement of" medical missionary work in "the Western metropolis" and said that "it was determined, months ago, to undertake, if possible, a sanitarium hospital before the opening of the World's Fair." This is a reference to what had been planned as the 1892 "Columbian Exposition" originally intended to mark the 400th anniversary of the discovery of the New World. A variety of problems had delayed the fair, however, and as Kellogg was writing in early 1893, the opening day was still several months away.

The problem with this "sanitarium hospital" plan, of course, was the lack of funds. Hence Kellogg wrote:

> Under these circumstances the reader can well imagine the surprise and gratification afforded by a recent visit to the writer, of two gentlemen of wealth, who placed at the disposal of the committee the sum of $40,000 to be devoted to the purpose named. One of these gentlemen stated that for three months he had been impressed that he ought to make a liberal contribution to medical missionary work, and it was this impression that brought him to seek an interview for the purpose of ascertaining the needs of the work....
>
> Is there a single one of our readers who is not desirous of participating in a work which is blessed in so evident and remarkable a manner? We know of no similar experience anywhere in which so young an enterprise has received, within less than one short year, two such special providences as Heaven has bestowed upon our work. One of these provides a home for needy children; the other makes even more ample provision for the relief of the suffering sick. Let us all thank God and take courage.[24]

Five months later, it was plainly stated that the funds were provided by "Brethren Francis H. and Henry S.P. Wessels."[25] The Wessels family were from South Africa, and had come into wealth through the sale of property containing diamonds. They gave significant contributions to a variety of church projects during the 1890s and 1900s, but all was not as well as might appear from Kellogg's account of the situation. The Wessels family were relatively recent converts, and though probably as sincere as the "average" new believer, they had their weaknesses, too. Ellen

---

24. *The Medical Missionary*, February 1893, 37
25. *The Medical Missionary*, July 1893, 157

White commented some years later, revealing the surprising influence of mistakes made:

> The Wessels family have made large donations of money to Dr. Kellogg, as though he was the one who was to be steward of their means. The means that the Wessels family gave so abundantly in America should not have been handled by one man as he pleased, but by faithful stewards, who would have appropriated the money for the opening of the work in Africa. A great work might have been done in that field. Books should have been translated for use in fields needing strong missionary effort. Had the work been done that should have been done, the religious experience of the Dutch people would have been materially changed.
>
> This is where the young men of the Wessels family made a mistake. Mission fields in Africa were in their destitution crying to God for help and relief. They were starving for the light that should have shone in the dark places in regions beyond. This cruel, treacherous war would not have come at this time had the missionary work been done that the people of Africa were in suffering need of. The things which ought to have been done, but which have not been done testify to a neglect of duty.

The "cruel, treacherous war" she speaks of was the horrific Second Boer War, in which British forces employed "scorched earth" tactics, rounded up the civilian population—almost all women and children—and held them amid deadly conditions in a whole system of concentration camps. Approximately 27,000 died from starvation and disease. It is a sobering thought to consider what responsibility may rest on the heads of Seventh-day Adventists in this case. There are many lessons which might be drawn from this history, but our focus is the impact the Wessels' generosity had on Dr. Kellogg. Ellen White's letter continues:

> Let it never be forgotten that true Christianity comes through the engraving of Bible principles upon the heart and character. This must be an individual work, visibly expressed. Then true missionary work will be done. The Lord's means will be carefully invested.
>
> A class of workers should have been sent to Africa who would have tried by every means in their power to educate the people they came over to help. But some of those sent to Africa as missionaries needed the converting power of God upon their hearts....
>
> From the light God has given me, I know that He has not inaugurated such a work for our people to do as Dr. Kellogg has started in Chicago. In every city there should be missionaries, evangelists, appointed to work for the lower classes, who through abuse are ruining themselves. But all the resources are not to be used in this work, or the work of bringing the truth to other cities and missionary fields afar off from America will not be accomplished. God's money has been used lav-

ishly in some places, so that there is not means to invest in sustaining the gospel ministry in all parts of the world by voice and by the press.[26]

Buoyed by the "special providence" of an unfortunately misguided gift, Kellogg moved forward with his goal of establishing a full-scale "city mission" in the heart of Chicago. But as the notices which appeared monthly in the *Medical Missionary* made plain:

> The foundation for the Chicago Medical Mission was laid by the donation of $40,000 by Brethren Francis H. and Henry S.P. Wessels. It is understood, however, that this sum is not to be expended, but to be invested in permanent buildings and appliances. From $50 to $100 a week will be required to keep this mission in operation. Donations are solicited.[27]

The point is this—starting a project or an institution is a big step, but that's not all there is to it. Somehow, the operation has to be kept alive, and that takes money. How that played out in relation to other needs of the denomination in the coming years, turned into a major issue. And behind it all—behind the use of all talents, financial or otherwise—is the question of motive. In Dr. Kellogg's case, that was becoming a problem.

The Stage is Set

So here's the timeline we've covered so far:

- **November 1888**—Kellogg converted.
- **July 1890**—Kellogg seeks Ellen White's counsel regarding an orphanage.
- **March 1891**—General Conference votes to establish a home for orphans and the worthy aged.
- **February 1892**—Plan for Christian Help Bands first publicized.
- **Early 1892**—Non-Adventist businessman funds first nurse to Chicago.
- **April 1892**—Mrs. Haskell gives $30,000 for orphanage.
- **August 1892**—Construction begins on orphanage.
- **November 15, 1892**—Start of Christian Help Bands at the Sanitarium.
- **November 22, 1892**—Ellen White writes that "the loud cry of the third angel has already begun."
- **Late 1892 or early 1893**—Wessels brothers give $40,000 for city mission work in Chicago.

Everything is ready for the curtain to rise on the 1893 General Conference session.

---

26. *The Kress Collection*, 121–122
27. *The Medical Missionary*, July 1893, 157

Chapter Five

Into the Arena

FOR the last sixty-six days before Elder Olson's gavel called the delegates to order, there was no doubt as to the underlying tone of the 1893 General Conference session. Really, what could anyone expect once Ellen White's statement about the beginning of the loud cry came out in the *Review?* How could it be a business-as-usual session?

To Adventists living today, of course, 1893 is a distant era. If they know anything about that particular General Conference session at all, it's probably A.T. Jones and his "Third Angel's Message" series of sermons. And, to be honest, even those sermons wouldn't get the attention they do if it weren't for Ellen White's comment. More than anything else, it is the fact that the loud cry had "already begun" that has kept 1888, Minneapolis, Jones, Waggoner, et al., from being completely forgotten.

And so it was that barely two months after the landmark statement had appeared in print, the General Conference was to meet and conduct its regular business in the light of the loud cry. It should be no great surprise, then, that Jones spoke of the loud cry forty-eight times in his twenty-four meetings. Other speakers mentioned the issue as well, but none so often as A.T. Jones.

What is surprising, however, is that another speaker at that conference—one who addressed the loud cry even more directly than A.T. Jones (twenty-seven times in two meetings)—has been ignored as a commentator on the subject. Perhaps this speaker's thoughts did not "resonate" with his listeners. Perhaps they just couldn't see anything of value in his comments. Perhaps the fact that he was a physician rather than a theologian worked against him....

Dr. Kellogg was originally scheduled to give "six lessons on Medical Missionary Work" in the course of the 1893 General Conference session.[1] For reasons not known today, he ended up speaking eight times. It would seem from this turn of events that the doctor had some friends and supporters in church administrative positions. He was, after all, given the privilege of extra time to address the delegates.

But the issue was complex, and his relationships with church workers were not uniformly positive. Normally, his talks should be available in the pages of the *General Conference Daily Bulletin*. But that would be normal, and neither Dr. Kellogg nor the circumstances were normal.

As it turns out, those curious to see what the doctor had to say will not find their questions answered in the pages of the *Bulletin*. Despite a front page notice that Kellogg was to give six talks, they simply aren't there. All is not lost, however, for the talks were stenographically recorded and printed in an Extra edition of *The Medical Missionary* magazine. Like the *Bulletin*, this publication was printed at Battle Creek, but not by the Review and Herald. *The Medical Missionary* was a product of the Good Health Publishing Company. In other words, it was Kellogg's paper.

When the Extra came out, it bore on its front cover an explanation:

> This extra number of the *Medical Missionary*, and another extra number which will succeed it, comprise an abstract of the addresses pertaining to Medical Missionary Work delivered at the late SDA General Conference and the "Institute" preceding it, together with the business transacted by the Sanitarium Association and the International Health and Temperance Association, and the organization of the S.D.A. Medical Missionary and Benevolent Association. This number of the Extra is made up, except when otherwise stated, of addresses delivered before the Institute and the General Conference by Dr. J.H. Kellogg. It should be further stated that these extra numbers of the Medical Missionary will be sent to all subscribers to the *General Conference [Daily] Bulletin*, which should have contained the same matter; but the funds raised for the publication of the *Bulletin* having been exhausted, the publication of the report of meetings and other matters pertaining to Medical Missionary and Benevolent work was undertaken by the *Medical Missionary*.[2]

This financial explanation, of course, is nonsense.

Something Doesn't Add Up

Over the five-and-a-half weeks of meetings, the *Daily Bulletin* was published in twenty-six installments, ranging from as few as eight pages up to

1. *1893 General Conference Daily Bulletin*, January 27, 1893, 1
2. *The Medical Missionary*, Extra No. 1, March 1893, 1

forty-two pages in length. Dr. Kellogg's first presentation should have appeared in the sixth of these, dated February 6, 1893. To say that the "funds raised for the publication of the *Bulletin* [had] been exhausted" ten days into the meetings, or to imply that some bright accountant could tell so early on that the only way to stay on budget was to leave out the material that came from Dr. Kellogg, is simply not believable.

To expect the *Bulletin* to contain a record of every word spoken in the meetings is unrealistic, of course, but the team from the Review and Herald appears to have worked very hard to capture the action. In one exceptional case when they couldn't, this explanation was inserted:

> At the meeting of the [State Canvassing Agent's] convention held on Monday, an interesting paper was read by F.W. Morse, on the subject of re-canvassing territory, which cannot be inserted in the *Bulletin* for lack of space.[3]

It seems odd that Elder Morse's letter would be noticed like this, while Dr. Kellogg's eight talks received only one mention, and that simply in passing, when Elder A.T. Jones asked his audience:

> Don't you remember the other day in the talk that Dr. Kellogg gave us on the medical missionary work....[4]

This seems to be the only time Kellogg's presentations were mentioned in the *Daily Bulletin*.

Kellogg was always an active participant in organizational meetings, though, so it's not as as if he was simply forgotten. Of one General Conference business session held a week after Kellogg's last talk it was said, "Dr. Kellogg gave a report in regard to the Haskell Home and the James White Memorial Home. The particulars and statistics presented will probably appear in a later *Bulletin*."[5] But, no, those "particulars and statistics" made no appearance in the *Bulletin*. Was this because the allotted funds were "exhausted"? Really?

A far more plausible assessment is simply that someone remembered Kellogg's presentation at the last General Conference session, and saw no value in a repeat of the "lard crackers," "lively cheese," and "coiled sausage" comments. It's hard to imagine that anything other than an editorial decision decreed that Kellogg would almost entirely disappear from the official record.

---

3. *General Conference Daily Bulletin*, February 5, 1893, 143
4. *General Conference Daily Bulletin*, February 22, 1893; 343
5. *General Conference Daily Bulletin*, March 1, 1893; 437

The result is that Kellogg's perspective on the loud cry—imperfect though it was—has remained unconsidered by the church for more than a century. In the hope of changing this sad state of affairs, the following pages present a painfully abbreviated overview of Kellogg's talks.

The Preamble

Doctor Kellogg's first presentation was given on the fifth of February. He did not begin to analyze or comment upon the loud cry at the outset of his talks, and there is really no clear indication that he had any intent to do so. He began instead by addressing the "Needs and Opportunities for Medical Missionary Work," and he did so by calling the delegates' attention to "a few paragraphs from the writings of Sister White. In January, 1891, she wrote as follows":

> "How shall the Lord's work be done? How can we gain access to souls buried in midnight darkness? Prejudice must be met; corrupt religion is hard to deal with. The very best ways and means of work must be prayerfully considered. There is a way in which many doors will be opened to the missionary. Let him become intelligent in the care of the sick, as a nurse, or how to treat disease, as a physician, and if he is imbued with the spirit of Christ, what a field of usefulness is opened before him!"[6]

Kellogg continued to build his case for the need of medical missionary work and workers:

> We want men and women who will become medical missionaries. There are other things that we need, but we need men and women most of all. Medical missionaries are needed in every large city. Sister White says upon this subject, in a letter written last December:
> "In every large city there should be, not two or three, but scores [she is speaking of medical missionaries] of well-organized, well-disciplined workers."[7]

But a need for workers obviously entailed a need for the training of workers, and Ellen White had already said so:

> In a communication received from Sister White a few months ago, dated Preston, Australia, Sept. 16, 1892, she writes as follows:
> "I am much perplexed in regard to many matters concerning the education of men and women to become medical missionaries. I could wish that there were one hundred nurses in training where there is one."

---

6. *The Medical Missionary*, Extra No. 1, March 1893, 1; [*Counsels on Health*, 33].
   Many of the Ellen White quotations Kellogg used in these presentations were from personal letters written to him. References in such cases will be placed in brackets, and point to the most readily available current source of that material.
7. *The Medical Missionary*, Extra No. 1, March 1893, 3; [similar to *Medical Ministry*, 300]

That would make a considerable number. She further says:

"It ought to be thus. Both men and women can be more useful as medical missionaries than as missionaries without a medical education."[8]

One consistent feature of Kellogg's public presentations is a kind of informality in organization. Perhaps this was because all his talks were more or less extemporaneous. After all, for a man who dictates high-quality copy for book manuscripts while getting his exercise by riding around in circles on a bicycle, standing up in front of a live audience without speaking notes was no terror. He would come with a clear idea of what he wanted to say, mind you, and with the materials he might want to quote (usually from Ellen White), but the order of the delivery often seems to have been left for the spur of the moment to decide.

Think of that teacher you had who was easily distracted by anything interesting at the moment. Kellogg was a bit like that, and this next selection provides a hint of that flavor:

A gentleman who had just been married, came to the Sanitarium with his wife a year or two ago. The gentleman said to me, "Doctor, my wife and I were married yesterday. We have come here to learn how to cook hygienically. My business is urgent, I must go directly home, but I am going to leave my wife here a few weeks, to learn to cook. My brother was here some time ago, and gave me such an account of the Sanitarium that I made up my mind that I would have my wife come here and be instructed in cookery." So we gave her what instruction we could in a few weeks, and she went home to carry out what she had learned. There are many in this country who are hungry for this kind of knowledge.[9]

Sure, the story is amusing, but it was also a pretty good argument for training medical missionaries.

Another Day, Another Topic

The Doctor's second presentation, given February 9, was entitled "The Medical Missionary Himself," and dealt with the need for those in the Lord's work to maintain their own health. Despite the title of the talk, one gets the impression that much of what John Harvey had to say was primarily intended for—or directed at—the ministry. Given his concerns with the sometimes doubtful faithfulness of many of the ministers to the principles of health reform, it's little wonder he included this next topic:

Three or four hours after eating, a dyspeptic often feels giddy, stupid, and sleepy, with a dull headache, and a pressure in the back part of the head. He

---

8. *The Medical Missionary*, Extra No. 1, March 1893, 2; [similar to *Counsels on Health*, 503]
9. *The Medical Missionary*, Extra No. 1, March 1893, 4

thinks he has worked or studied too hard. That is all nonsense. A man may work every day as hard as he can, and not have the headache, or injure his brain. Few people have brains enough to be hurt by work. I am sure I have not. The trouble is not in the head; it is down below, in the stomach and in the alimentary canal, which become infected with poisons which are the product of bad diet, and thus the whole body is poisoned....

Sometimes it may be noticed that the white of the eye is dingy. Now it is not only the white of the man's eye that is dingy; but his muscles, his glands, nerves, even his brain, are dingy. Every portion of his body is saturated with these poisonous matters.

Calvinism originated in that kind of a body. ["Amen."] I have no doubt that the doctrine of everlasting torment originated in the same way, among the monks shut up in cloisters without exercise, until their bodies became saturated with those dingy poisons, and they wrote out their dingy theology under these influences. It appears from Calvin's diary, that within two weeks of the time when he signed the death warrant sentencing poor Servetus to be burned at the stake, he was suffering dreadful torments with a bad stomach. A man whose body is in this condition cannot have a clear head or clear ideas; he cannot be sharp-witted and keen-sighted; he cannot readily decide important questions. A man cannot have full command of his physical and mental powers when his brain is full of poison....

Exercise and temperance are the two most important means by which we may keep our bodies pure....

This is what science says, and now I will read something that the Lord says to us on this subject. God speaks to us through the Bible, through nature, and through special revelation. What nature shows us, is God's voice, as much as is inspiration. But the Lord gives us special revelations, because we are so dull in learning from the other sources of information which he has given us. It does not seem necessary for the Lord to tell us by special revelation that we ought to breathe and to exercise freely. Every animal knows this. Horses and colts, when turned into a pasture, do not go off into a corner and lie down and go to sleep. They immediately begin kicking up their heels and running races, although they have no driver to compel them to work. Every animal on the face of the earth, except man, knows enough to exercise. But man will shut himself up in his study, and try to get good service out of his dingy brain. No wonder his thoughts are often perverse and stupid. Because of our obtuseness, the Lord has given us special instructions upon this point. You will perhaps be astonished to hear what the Testimonies say upon the subject of the relation of mind and body:

"If you would exercise your muscles, your mind would be better balanced, your thoughts would be of a purer and more elevated character, and your sleep would be more natural and healthy."

She says here, "Your mind would be better balanced." Now if there is a man who needs to have his mind better balanced than a minister or a laborer in these institutions, I do not know who he is. Do not we, more than any other class of people on earth, need well balanced minds?[10]

The bulk of Kellogg's second talk serves mostly to tie together a number of choice quotations from Ellen White. Many were such that ministers might have felt like their toes had been stepped upon, and the modern-day reader is left trying to decide how much sympathy should go in which direction. Kellogg may have been too pointed in his delivery, but he certainly said nothing that wasn't supported by the numerous Spirit of Prophecy comments he quoted.

Readers with a natural inclination toward tactfulness and a desire to avoid confrontation will probably feel that the ministers were a little hard done by; readers who value "truth" above all else (and are comfortable with health reform in general and vegetarianism in particular) will likely find themselves cheering on the doctor. But isn't tactfulness a part of "truth," and isn't temperance a part of ministry?

In closing, Kellogg sought to show this inter-relatedness of health reform and the gospel. He introduced his point with one last quotation from Ellen White:

> "Our preachers should all be genuine, sincere health reformers, not merely adopting this reform because others do, but in obedience to the word of God." ["Amen."]
>
> What does that mean? It means that our preachers should all understand that the word of God says they must be genuine, sincere health reformers, and that they are not obeying God unless they are such. Now when you preach righteousness by faith, don't forget to put health reform in, and then I believe the third angel's message will go with greater power. Temperance is a part of the third angel's message. You can't preach the third angel's message without preaching hygiene and temperance in it. The Lord has put it there to make us better men and women, to save us from fanaticism, to give us health and strength and vigor with which to carry on this important work.[11]

It's Not Just the Ministers...

Talk number three came the next day, February 10. The title is straight forward and to the point: "The Duty of Doing Works of Charity and Benevolence." This sermon is about as simple as a sermon can be—"This is what the Bible says to do, and we haven't been doing it, so we need to

---

10. *The Medical Missionary*, Extra No. 1, March 1893, 7; [*Testimonies*, vol. 3, 235]
11. *The Medical Missionary*, Extra No. 1, March 1893, 10; [*Testimonies*, vol. 3, 311]

change." In contrast to the first two presentations, Kellogg didn't use a single word from Ellen White. But he used a *lot* of Bible.

> Charge them that are rich... that they do good, that they be rich in good works, ready to distribute,... laying up in store for themselves a good foundation against the time to come, that they may lay hold on eternal life. —1 Timothy 6:17–19[12]

> That the man of God may be perfect, thoroughly furnished unto all good works. —2 Timothy 3:17[13]

> Christians are exhorted to "be careful to maintain good works" [Titus 3:8, 14], not only to do good works occasionally, but to be constantly engaged in good works. In the same epistle, chap. 2:14, we read that Christ gave himself for us, that he might "purify unto himself a peculiar people zealous of good works." One of the characteristics of this peculiar people, according to the apostle Paul, is that they will be "zealous of good works."[14]

> If we have the idea that righteousness consists in good talk, it is only necessary to read a few Bible texts to be convinced of our error. In 1 John 3:7 the apostle tells us, "Let no man deceive you. He that doeth righteousness is righteous." It is possible that we may be deceived. The apostle warns us that a man is not righteous unless he works. It seems that righteousness is not so much a quality as an action. Righteousness is right doing, for we read in Isaiah 1:16–17, "Cease to do evil, learn to do well: seek judgment, relieve the oppressed." It is not simply to cease to do evil, but to "learn to do well." Righteousness is not a negative condition, a simple passive withholding from wrong doing, but a positive and zealous activity in doing good.[15]

> In Acts 10:38, Peter tells us that Christ "went about doing good." It is evident, then, that if we are Christ's servants, if we follow Christ, we must also go about doing good. We are not to wait for the opportunities for doing good to come to us, but we must *go about* doing good, seeking opportunities to do good, to help the needy, to bless and comfort the sorrowing, to uplift the fallen. We must search them out, not wait for them to hunt us up and move us to action by their appeals.

> How much have we done in this direction? How many of us have been *going about* "doing good," as Christ did? Is it not to be feared that too many of us are in a condition to be rebuked by the words of the apostle John (1 John 3:17), "But whoso hath this world's goods, and seeth his brother have need, and shutteth up his bowels of compassion from him, how dwelleth the love of God in him?"

> The apostle says, in substance, that if one sees another who is suffering and needy and afflicted, and turns away without ministering to his wants, he has not

---

12. *The Medical Missionary*, Extra No. 1, March 1893, 10
13. *The Medical Missionary*, Extra No. 1, March 1893, 10
14. *The Medical Missionary*, Extra No. 1, March 1893, 10
15. *The Medical Missionary*, Extra No. 1, March 1893, 11

the love of God in him, no matter what his profession may be, no matter what splendid sermons he can preach, or how zealously he can exhort, or how earnestly he can pray; no matter how diligent he may be in distributing tracts; and doing in various ways what he supposes to be "giving the third angel's message"; nevertheless the love of God is not in him. The apostle adds (verse 18), "Let us not love in word, neither in tongue, but in *deed*." If we profess to have the love of God in us, it will be manifest, not simply by pious talk, but in deeds; and the kind of deeds the apostle has indicated in the preceding verse in which he refers to the needy poor.[16]

Now it's something of a given that Christians should agree with the Bible, but there is the question of *application*. These are all good verses, but what does a person *mean* when he starts quoting them? Kellogg was happy to answer the question:

> We are not to be narrow in our charities, for Paul says to us, in Gal. 6:10, "Let us do good unto all men." It is true he adds, "Especially unto them who are of the household of faith," but this does not excuse us from doing good to those who are not of the household of faith; for he says *all men*, and certainly we cannot hide behind this apology, for we have not been good even to those belonging to the household. For years and years we have been well able to furnish a Home for the aged, the infirm, the homeless; for poor widows, worn-out ministers, aged pilgrims, and helpless children, members of our denomination, old pioneers in the cause, who gave liberally of their property in the early days when the work was just beginning, and whose faith in the truths which we profess has led them to put all their earnings into the cause instead of hoarding up a competency for themselves—all these worthy and deserving ones who appeal to us on fraternal as well as humanitarian grounds, we have neglected in a manner which has become a denominational disgrace.
>
> I have in my possession the positive proof that worthy Seventh-day Adventists are left by their brethren and sisters to become a public charge, and are today in county poorhouses. Worthy old pilgrims, aged men and aged women, have been left to die among strangers who had no care or affection for them, deprived of kindly sympathy as well as common comforts. Even Catholic orphan asylums have been opened to receive Seventh-day Adventist orphans. Yet we claim to be a "peculiar people." Is it not about time we began to be "zealous of good works"?[17]

If misery really does love company, perhaps some of ministers were feeling a bit better than they had the day before. Not that Kellogg wasn't pressing issues uncomfortably close to home, but at least this time it was aimed at the whole church.

---

16. *The Medical Missionary*, Extra No. 1, March 1893, 11
17. *The Medical Missionary*, Extra No. 1, March 1893, 12

A synopsis of the sermon runs the risk of distorting the "feel" of the occasion. Despite some hard-hitting material, Kellogg manages to project a sense of compassion in this talk that seems a bit more heart-felt than the "correctness" of talk number two. There's a reason for that: the historic evidence is consistent—Kellogg truly enjoyed being generous to those he saw as "needy"—and this presentation carries the impression of sincerity as he calls his church to come up higher on this point.

His closing paragraph pretty much sums it all up:

> When one considers how much the Bible has to say about works, it is indeed surprising that there should be those who are disposed to discount the importance of Christian activity in philanthropic and humanitarian work. We are exhorted to be "furnished unto all good works," "rich in good works," to "maintain good works," to be "zealous of good works," and are assured that we shall be blessed in doing the works, and judged and rewarded according to our works. Good works, ministering to others in Christian activity, in acts of charity, sympathy, and benevolence, are really the sum and substance of the Christian life, and are the basis upon which that life is judged, and the measure of its reward determined.[18]

But Wait! There's More!

The fourth talk of the series, "Faith and Works," came at 11:00 Sunday morning, February 12. The Doctor hardly missed a beat as he picked up where he left off on Friday. There were, it turned out, many more Bible verses that encouraged, even commanded, Christians to do good to others, especially to those with the least opportunity to return the favor.

Again, the underlying issue of Kellogg's relationship to the ministers shows briefly, this time in his opening words:

> I feel a good deal of embarrassment in undertaking to expound the Scriptures before an audience of theologians, but I feel safe in doing so, knowing that you are quite competent to set me right if I am wrong, and will do so, and thus I am not likely to lead any of you astray.[19]

In simple fashion, Kellogg told them what he wanted to do—"My purpose is simply to show that there is in the Bible a good foundation for medical missionary work"—and then he set about to do it. It is interesting to note both the advantage and disadvantage he had in the simple fact that he was talking about developments within the memory of nearly everyone in his audience. He need only refer to facts and events with

---

18. *The Medical Missionary*, Extra No. 1, March 1893, 12
19. *The Medical Missionary*, Extra No. 1, March 1893, 13

which they were all familiar. That was the advantage. The disadvantage? Because they had all lived through those events, they had all formed basic opinions and taken basic positions on the issues already. Kellogg was facing the task of changing people's minds, and it often seems that he really had little hope of accomplishing his goal:

> You will easily remember the time when medical missionary work was first talked about, and also that everybody looked askance at it, because, as they thought, it was something foreign to our work. The idea seemed to prevail that we had a special work to spread the third angel's message, and that the Lord did not want our attention to be diverted into foreign channels. For some years I have been studying the Bible with special reference to this subject, and it seems to me that what we call humanitarian work, or medical missionary work, is just as much a part of the third angel's message as any other work connected with it; certainly no one connected with the third angel's message ought to be any the less a Christian than members of other denominations.[20]

As in so many cases from history, much is left to the imagination in terms of the speaker's delivery. Did Kellogg say this with a jab at the ministers, or with Christlike "tears in his voice"?

After a string of pointed verses from Romans, Galatians, Ephesians, and John, the Doctor inevitably ended up in the classic "pro-works" book of James:

> "Seest thou how faith wrought with his [Abraham's] works, and by works was faith made perfect?" This is a very remarkable expression—"by works was faith made perfect." It is not the works that are made perfect, but the faith; faith is perfected by works. If a man professes to have faith, and does not go to work, his faith will never be perfected.[21]

This may seem like a rather unexceptional observation to be made in the course of a Seventh-day Adventist church service, but remember the context. Every evening for the entire course of the Ministerial Institute and the General Conference session, none other than Elder A.T. Jones was speaking on the third angel's message and righteousness by faith. It had been four years since the 1888 General Conference at Minneapolis, but anyone at all familiar with the history of the period knows that the fires then ignited were still smoldering just under the surface.

That there was a conflict going on within the leadership of the church during this time period is obvious from the Spirit of Prophecy. Everyone involved knew it back then, too. What complicated matters then—and

---

20. *The Medical Missionary*, Extra No. 1, March 1893, 13
21. *The Medical Missionary*, Extra No. 1, March 1893, 13

largely defies analysis now—was the difficulty in figuring out exactly what the disagreements were. Even the most cursory examination points to "righteousness by faith" as being near the center of it all. But did that mean that those who opposed Jones and Waggoner were "legalists"? Were "good works" really so unpopular that Kellogg had to defend them before the church's highest leadership?

It would appear that, to Kellogg at least, the question at this time was not so much the place and value of good works, as it was the nature of those good works. His vision of works took a more decidedly hands-on and humanitarian bent than was common in the church:

> "Pure religion and undefiled before God and the Father is this, To visit the fatherless and widows in their affliction, and to keep himself unspotted from the world." James 1:27. One of the worst spots the world puts on a man is selfishness; for selfishness leads into every other sin. A very good way, then for one to "keep himself unspotted from the world," is to take part in the unselfish work of visiting the fatherless and widows in their affliction, ministering to their wants, and thus cultivating the very faculties which tend to keep self subdued. I have sometimes thought that a person might become so solicitous for his own interests, even his own spiritual welfare, that he might become a very selfish sort of saint. I have seen a considerable number of persons who seemed to exercise a great deal of faith, and yet their faith all centered in themselves. You hear such a person talking in meeting; their expressions are altogether in reference to themselves; they "hope to be overcomers"; they are "looking after the great reward"; they "don't want to be lost"; they are very solicitous in their own behalf. I cannot believe that persons can live a Christian life wholly in reference to themselves, and make a success of it.
>
> It seems that many have an idea that to be a Christian means to be very good, to sit up on a moral pedestal, as it were, apart from the rest of the world, and to be very nice and good. I doubt whether there is any religion in that. Religion consists not simply in *being* good, but in *doing* good. If a person is really good, he will do good....
>
> It is not enough to cease to do evil, we must also learn to do well; we are not only to stop doing evil, but to begin doing well. When one ceases to do evil, it is only the beginning of the Christian life, but he is not to stop there; when he begins to do well, then he begins to follow the example of our Saviour, who went about doing good.[22]

Challenging the Basics

One of Dr. Kellogg's gifts, as it were, was his ability to "think outside the box." Today we have a certain appreciation (at least theoretically) for

---

22. *The Medical Missionary*, Extra No. 1, March 1893, 14

this talent. In the real world of business and interpersonal relationships, of course, the one who "thinks outside the box" can be a real pain. Perhaps that's the main virtue of mastering the skill—everyone else gets to deal with your disruption of affairs rather than you dealing with theirs!

It seems unlikely that the mindset of the 1890s was any more inclined toward accepting innovation than what we might see today. And if there is one form of innovation more suspect than another, it has to be theological innovation. Combine that drawback with the ever present challenge of confronting selfishness, and it's obvious that Dr. Kellogg was walking out onto thin ice:

> "He that hath pity on the poor lendeth to the Lord, and that which he hath given will he pay him again." Prov. 19:17.... If a person is really righteous, he does good, he pities the poor. The person who pities the poor man, and helps him, is not simply lending to him, but the Bible says he is lending to the Lord. What a wonderful thought this is! When a man lends to another, he puts him under obligations. The man who receives the loan must pay it again. The poor man may not be able to pay the loan; hence God assumes the debt. God says he will be in debt to the man who gives to the poor not expecting to receive anything again. Try to grasp this thought, my friends, though it is really too large an idea for a finite mind to comprehend. We are plainly told that we can get God in debt to us by pitying the poor. Only infinite love and mercy and condescension could originate such a thought. Just think of it—the Creator going in debt to one of his creatures, becoming bondsman, as it were, for the payment of a poor man's obligations! Surely, God must love the poor, or he would not himself assume their debts in this way.[23]

Next up for consideration was the parable of the Good Samaritan, with its obvious opportunity for irritating the contemporary "priests and Levites" in Kellogg's predominantly ministerial audience:

> The priest and the Levite were on their way up to the temple to do temple service. That was the Lord's work, as they called it. The priest was going up there, perhaps to preach a sermon that morning, the Levite was going to assist about the work of the temple. They had no time to be troubled with this poor brother. They must be engaged in the Lord's cause. They could not stop to bother with this poor fellow down by the wayside; somebody else might help him but they hadn't time....
>
> In Mark 12:33 we read: "And to love him with all the heart, and with all the understanding, and with all the soul, and with all the strength, and to love his neighbor as himself, is more than all whole burnt offerings and sacrifices." This shows very clearly that the service in the temple was nothing compared with the

service of the Lord in caring for this poor man who had fallen among thieves. The Lord did not regard the sacrifices in the temple as of much account compared with the service that might be rendered him in taking care of this poor creature by the wayside. In this same sort of work the Lord gives us an opportunity for the most glorious kind of service, the kind of service which he considers of higher value than the offering of sacrifice. How can we neglect it?[24]

The Doctor continues, and shows no signs of running out of ammunition. The reader today (and one would have to expect the same of the hearer at the time) is left feeling surprised—perhaps a little embarrassed—to find that there are so many verses that speak so pointedly to the subject of benevolence, kindness, charity, or whatever you wish to call it:

There are greater and more direct rewards promised for the performance of acts of mercy and kindness than for any other class of Christian duties described in the Bible. See what a great reward is offered here (Luke 6:35): "Love your enemies, and do good, and lend, hoping for nothing again; and your reward shall be great, and ye shall be the children of the Highest: for he is kind unto the unthankful and to the evil." We are commanded to love our enemies, to do good and lend, hoping for nothing again. If we do that, we shall be the children of the Highest, heirs of the Almighty. And why? "For he is kind unto the unthankful and to the evil." The Lord asks us to do this that we may be like him, and then he becomes our debtor, and will not fail to pay.[25]

Now I don't suppose you will all approve of what I am saying, but I only ask you to read these texts. They are here in the Bible, and whether you believe what I say or not, read these Bible texts and give them their true force and effect....

In all the Bible there is no reward promised for good talk or good intentions; it is only for good works....

"Blessed are ye that sow beside all waters." Is. 32:20. "Cast thy bread upon the waters, for thou shalt find it after many days." Eccl. 11:1. We must not be too particular in our charities. We must not be too careful that none of our good deeds are unworthily bestowed. Just scatter them like the seed of the sower, even if some seeds do fall on unfertile spots. God sees every seed. Every contribution is laid up in heaven's bank, and every seed that grows will bring a reward "according to the fruit."[26]

It was the parables of Christ which seemed to be the mother lode the Doctor was mining that day. When it came to the Unjust Steward, Kellogg introduced his thoughts with a touch of self-deprecation. Was this sincerely said? Or was it a peremptory challenge to the ministers?

---

24. *The Medical Missionary*, Extra No. 1, March 1893, 15
25. *The Medical Missionary*, Extra No. 1, March 1893, 15–16
26. *The Medical Missionary*, Extra No. 1, March 1893, 16

In Luke 16:1–19, is recorded the very interesting parable of the unjust steward. I don't know that I have the orthodox interpretation, but it seems to be very safe to say that the rich man is God, and the steward is every one of us. God has given us our faculties, as well as our money, with which to do good. Now this steward was accused to the rich man as one who had wasted his goods. So we have wasted our faculties and opportunities and money. When he found he was to be turned out of his stewardship (we all know that is the case with every one of us; we are to be turned out of our stewardship sooner or later), he said, "I am resolved what to do, that, when I am put out of the stewardship, they may receive me into their houses. So he called every one of his lord's debtors unto him," (every one who has not been converted and given himself to the Lord is the Lord's debtor. When he becomes converted he is no longer a debtor, but a son, and an heir) and began dividing his lord's property among them. The unjust steward subtracted 50 percent from one man's debt, and 40 percent from another man's debt, and thus gave to the poor debtors from his lord's property.

All the benevolence that we can exercise is simply in giving away the Lord's property. All we can do for any one is in giving them the use of our faculties, our kind acts, or our money; in doing this we are simply distributing the Lord's property. Now that lord complained of this steward because he had wasted his property in his own selfish gratification, but when the steward distributed his lord's property among the debtors, he does not complain of that at all; the lord commended his unjust steward for doing that. That is what his lord wanted him to do. That is the way the Lord wants us, as his stewards, to do.

At this point in the sermon, an unidentified voice from the audience asks, "What lord was it that commended the steward?"

Hello… Is this a trick question? Jesus didn't say anything about multiple "lords" in the story, so where is this coming from? Was this a suggestion that a "false lord" had somehow injected himself into the narrative just in time to deceive the steward?

Kellogg didn't bite that hook. Instead, he went on:

It was the rich man who was the lord of the unjust steward. The Lord is telling this parable; he is not through with it yet, and he says, "The lord commended the unjust steward because he had done wisely, for the children of this world are wiser in their generation than the children of light; and I say unto you, Make to yourselves friends of the mammon of unrighteousness, that when ye fail, they may receive you into everlasting habitations." Now if we will use these faculties, and the means which the Lord has given us, we all may make friends for ourselves who will be ready when the Lord comes to welcome us into the New Jerusalem. This interpretation may be unorthodox. Some of the brethren may give you a better interpretation, but that is the way it reads to me, and it is a very encouraging thought that the Lord will commend us in these very acts of distributing his property to men who are in debt to him; that is the very thing that the Lord wants to have us do.[27]

"Some of the brethren" no doubt had "better interpretations" to offer. This was clearly another of the Doctor's "out of the box" episodes; nothing quite like this had ever been promoted in Adventism before. But that was true simply because *Christ's Object Lessons* was not printed until 1900. Was Ellen White "plagiarizing" Kellogg when she refined her earlier writings on the subject to produce a passage more nearly like his "unorthodox interpretation"? Here is what she wrote seven years later:

> To the unfaithful steward his lord's goods had been entrusted for benevolent purposes; but he had used them for himself....
>
> The servant in the parable had made no provision for the future. The goods entrusted to him for the benefit of others he had used for himself; but he had thought only of the present. When the stewardship should be taken from him, he would have nothing to call his own. But his master's goods were still in his hands, and he determined to use them so as to secure himself against future want. To accomplish this he must work on a new plan. Instead of gathering for himself, he must impart to others. Thus he might secure friends, who, when he should be cast out, would receive him. So with the Pharisees. The stewardship was soon to be taken from them, and they were called upon to provide for the future. Only by seeking the good of others could they benefit themselves. Only by imparting God's gifts in the present life could they provide for eternity.[28]

But if the parables were the mother lode, Kellogg had saved the "glory hole" for last. What could possibly support his thesis more emphatically than the parable of the sheep and the goats? Again, it was the utter simplicity of his point that made it so powerful:

> We have some important lessons in parables, as you all know. I wish to call your attention to the parable of the sheep and the goats. Matt. 25:31–46. I will not read it through, as it is familiar to you all. I only call your attention to the important fact that the test questions which the Lord asks here are not, "What did you believe? What did you profess? How much faith did you have? How many tracts did you distribute?" There is not a word said about that, but he says to those on the left hand, "I was an hungered, and ye gave me no meat; I was thirsty, and ye gave me no drink; I was a stranger, and ye took me not in; naked, and ye clothed me not; sick and in prison, and ye visited me not. Then shall they also answer him, saying, Lord when saw we thee an hungered, or athirst, or a stranger, or

27. *The Medical Missionary,* Extra No. 1, March 1893, 17
28. *Christ's Object Lessons,* 369

naked, or sick, or in prison, and did not minister unto thee? Then shall he answer them, saying, Verily I say unto you, inasmuch as ye did it not to one of the least of these, ye did it not to me. And these shall go away into everlasting punishment: but the righteous into life eternal."

Now who are the "righteous"? Why, the righteous are those that did clothe the naked, and did visit the sick, and did feed the hungry, and gave drink to the thirsty. They are the righteous. ["Amen."] Now, does not this state as strongly as possible that the Lord wants us to do these things, and that we are not righteous unless we do them? No matter how much faith we profess, unless we have done these things, we are not righteous at all. When we come up to the Judgment, the test question will not be, "Did you preach the third angel's message? Did you give Bible-readings?" but, "Did you feed the hungry, clothe the naked?" etc., because these are fundamental things, while the other things are matters which naturally grow out of the doing of these fundamental things.[29]

Totally aside from what the clock on the back wall of the Dime Tabernacle may have said at that point, Kellogg had given quite a sermon and might well have closed with prayer and gone home. The people had heard plenty to think about for a while.

But Kellogg had more to say. He was done with the parables; now he was ready for the Bible passage which—second only to Revelation 14—Ellen White cites most often as representing the work of God's people in the last days. Some might guess Matthew 24, or maybe the "Great Commission." But this one's in the Old Testament....

---

29. *The Medical Missionary*, Extra No. 1, March 1893, 17

Chapter Six

Cry Aloud, Spare Not!

IF we go by the word count, Kellogg was roughly eighty percent through his fourth sermon when he first touched on Isaiah chapter fifty-eight. Was it tact that made him start with verse three, rather than the more electrifying opening words of verse one? Truth be told, not once in his sermons at the General Conference session did he quote, "Cry aloud, spare not, lift up thy voice like a trumpet, and shew my people their transgression, and the house of Jacob their sins."

Still, it would be hard to accuse him of being shy about pointing out the defects of the church. Working his way from verse three through verse twelve, Kellogg offered simple but challenging comments on three points mentioned in the passage: deal thy bread to the hungry... bring the poor that are cast out to thy house... hide not thyself from thine own flesh.

Stressing the practical application of the passage, Kellogg tied it to a command of Christ in the New Testament, pointing out what he saw as a cause-and-effect relationship to the blessing that God has promised to those who follow His counsel:

> "Let your light so shine before men, that they may see your good works, and glorify your Father which is in heaven." Matt. 5:16. The Lord asks us to let our light shine. How shall we let our light shine? "So shine that they may see your good works." Now we are not going to let our light shine by simply talking. Talking is not letting our light shine. I think that many people have an idea that distributing tracts and talking is letting light shine, but the text says, "Let your light so shine before men that they may see your good *works.*" It is the good works

that are the shining light; it is the things that we do, not what we say, that shine. ["Amen."] And the consequence of these good works is this, that we glorify our Father who is in heaven.

You will find the same thought in Isa. 58:10: "If thou draw out thy soul to the hungry and satisfy the afflicted soul, then shall thy light rise in obscurity." That is the way your light will shine; it will rise like the bright sun coming up in midnight darkness. "And thy darkness shall be as the noonday." Is not this plain? The Saviour teaches us that we are to let our light shine by means of good works; that is the way we are to let it shine, and that is the way in which our light will shine. And the prophet tells us that we are to do these good works which are an indispensable part of religion; and if we do them, our light will rise in darkness, and our obscurity be as the noonday. "The Lord shall guide thee continually, and satisfy thy soul in drought, and make fat thy bones." Oh, what a grand promise is this!...

We find the same thought again in Isa. 58:8: "The Lord shall guide thee continually and satisfy thee, and thou shalt be like a watered garden." Now this promise is not for us unless we do the things that the Lord asks us to do.[1]

Earlier in this presentation, when speaking of the parable of the sheep and the goats, Kellogg had asserted that practical Christianity was a determining factor in the judgment. Eternal life and eternal death hinged on matters of unselfish benevolence more than they did on matters of theological correctness. Once again he has come to a point of division: some are blessed and guided, others are not, and the deciding difference is, "If thou draw out thy soul to the hungry and satisfy the afflicted soul, then...." The conditional aspect of the Doctor's message was becoming clearer.

Then he ended the sermon by making it all personal:

"Thou shalt build the old waste places; thou shalt raise up the foundations of many generations, and thou shalt be called the repairer of the breach, the restorer of paths to dwell in." Verse 12. Now to whom does this prophecy refer?

Ans.—"Seventh-day Adventists."

Then this whole chapter refers to Seventh-day Adventists, doesn't it? ["Yes."] So this is a prophecy relating particularly to us, and we cannot expect our light to shine, no matter how loudly we may talk, or how much we may spread our literature, unless we do what the Lord here tells us to do. Before our light shines like the sun coming out in moonlight darkness, we must begin to do these common works of humanity—these common deeds of charity and benevolence that we have so long neglected. We must begin to clothe the naked, to feed the hungry, and not hide ourselves even from our own flesh, as we have been doing. We have turned away our foot from the Sabbath, but we have been hiding ourselves from our own flesh.

1. *The Medical Missionary*, Extra No. 1, March 1893, 18

At the present day there are Seventh-day Adventists in poor-houses in this State, and in other States. There are poor aged brethren living among paupers and criminals, and we have no place for them. We have been trying to get a home ready for these poor people, but as yet we have not succeeded. Can we expect our light to shine, can we hope that God will manifest his power in a remarkable manner through us, can we properly claim to be "the repairers of the breach," until we fulfill the conditions clearly laid down in the prophecy; in other words, until we fast in an acceptable manner, and do the work which God has clearly pointed out to us as our duty to do?[2]

This was not the sort of inspiring, encouraging sermon conclusion that one might expect to hear at a General Conference. This was something more like you might get from someone out in the desert wearing camel hair clothes. Kellogg had just said that the work of the church— God's true, remnant church of the last days—would never succeed until there had been some significant changes in her program, and in the religious experience of her members.

But What About...

Dr. Kellogg had now given four talks. Each had been challenging in its own way; each had been supported by inspired testimony; each had—so far as we can tell—been politely acknowledged.

But there was an *issue.*

How could Kellogg sound these grave warnings, even to the point of saying that the church was neglecting duties that were *essential* for her success, when less than three months earlier the prophet had said the loud cry had begun? If that wasn't an indication of divine approval, what was? Such questions had to be in the delegates' minds; it was only a matter of time before they would come out.

Between the Doctor's fourth and fifth talks, we might guess there was only one significant event—lunch. For reasons unknown, he had the unusual privilege of speaking twice on Sunday, February 12, one meeting at 11:00 and the other at 3:00. The title for the afternoon meeting was "Special Light About Medical Missionary Work." It would prove to be the longest, and clearly the most controversial, presentation of the series. With 10,427 words in the transcript, and assuming a more or less "average" rate of speech (150 words per minute), this afternoon meeting would have gone for at least seventy minutes (special music and all the miscellaneous preliminaries not included). That's about twice as long as his other seven talks.

---

2. *The Medical Missionary*, Extra No. 1, March 1893, 18–19

Seeking Acceptance

Kellogg began his second meeting of the day with a simple statement:

> I wish especially to call your attention this afternoon to the teachings of the Testimonies. I think you will see that they present before us, among our practical Christian duties, the duty of medical missionary work, and there is certainly no Christian duty which is urged upon us more forcibly, more emphatically, and more frequently.[3]

Except for a couple interludes where Kellogg told stories connected with the medical missionary work, that's exactly what he did. In his effort to call the congregation's attention to the teachings of the Testimonies, he used about thirty major quotations, and maybe another fifteen or twenty shorter snippets from various writings and letters of Ellen White. It seems safe to assume that by the time he was done, his audience would have agreed with his "forcibly... emphatically... frequently" description. Again, due to space constraints, we will consider only enough of this material to track the development of the Doctor's presentation.

Despite the occasional touch of sarcasm and criticism (not to defend either), it seems that Kellogg primarily wanted the church as a whole—and the ministers as the most influential element of the whole—to take the medical missionary work seriously. With so many clear commands from both the Bible and the Spirit of Prophecy, why couldn't they—or why *wouldn't* they—just admit the value of this branch of the Lord's work? These first quotations are simply an effort to gain that recognition:

> "When Christ sent forth the seventy, he commanded them to heal the sick, and next to preach that the kingdom of God had come nigh unto them. Their physical health was to be first cared for [that is, the physical health of the people to whom they preached], in order that the way might be prepared for the truth to reach their minds."
>
> Now I want to ask: Has not the present truth, the third angel's message, been presented back-end foremost?
>
> Sister White says that the care of the physical health is to be the first work, in order that the way may be prepared for the truth to reach the mind. Notice this remark:
>
> "The Saviour devoted more time and labor [now I do not say this myself; this comes from an accredited source, and I trust we shall give due heed to it] to healing the afflicted of their maladies than to preaching. His last injunction to his disciples, his representatives on earth, was to lay hands on the sick that they might recover."

3. *The Medical Missionary*, Extra No. 1, March 1893, 19

"The widow, the orphan, the sick, and the dying, will always need help. Here is an opportunity to proclaim the gospel."

This is not "going off on a side line," but "here is an opportunity to proclaim the gospel."[4]

Whatever his faults, Dr. Kellogg did have a soft heart for the truly needy. More than one observer has remarked that he would often get teary eyed when reading material such as this next quotation:

"We have seen the widowed mother with her fatherless children, working far beyond her strength in order to keep her little ones with her, and prevent them from suffering for food and clothing. Many a mother has thus died from over-exertion."

A mother who has the true instincts of self-respect will not go from door to door begging. She will suffer rather than complain; and because people do not complain, because they do not clamor for assistance, we do not stop to think that they may be suffering; we seldom inquire after them.

"How little has been done by us as a people for this class!"

Please think of that! This was said two years ago. "How little has been done by us as a people for this class," for mothers—for widowed mothers. Have we not come far short of our duty?

"We are not doing as much as is done by other denominations."

Now, I don't say this, the Lord says it.

We have set ourselves up on a high pinnacle, and say, "We are God's special people." Our cause is the Lord's cause, and we talk about ourselves as being THE "peculiar people," and yet we are not doing as much Christian work (and Christian work of a very important character) as other denominations are doing!

Again: "It is right that more should be expected of us than of others."

The Bible teaches us the same thing—that we ought to be doing more than others, but we are doing less. Now, can we expect "the loud cry" to begin while we are so neglectful of the needy around us? We may imagine that the Lord is going to work miracles for us, and do this work himself; but he will not. We need not expect that the loud cry will begin until we do what the Lord wants us to do.[5]

Raining on the Parade

Did Kellogg *mean* to say that? Had he thought this all through, or was that an extemporaneous slip of the tongue? Certainly everything he had said up to this time was pointing in that direction, but is that what he had intended to say?

---

4. *The Medical Missionary*, Extra No. 1, March 1893, 19 [*Counsels on Health*, 33–34]
5. *The Medical Missionary*, Extra No. 1, March 1893, 19–20 [*Medical Missionary*, June 1, 1891]

It was a simple, logical statement. "We need not expect that the loud cry will begin until we do what the Lord wants us to do." Isn't that what the last sermon had been all about? Isn't that what the "If... then" of Isaiah fifty-eight meant? How else could anyone interpret the Lord's counsel? Other than imagining "that the Lord is going to work miracles for us, and do this work himself." Kellogg seemed clear that that wasn't happening; did everyone else think it would?

At the time, of course, no one stopped to pose all these interesting questions. Things were happening too fast. Kellogg had barely gotten the words out of his mouth before he was challenged from the congregation:

> Voice—"The loud cry has already begun."

And who was to argue? Ellen White had said so, three months before. We can ponder the details of Kellogg's thinking on this later. For now, let's just follow the story as it happened:

> Dr. Kellogg—We ought to be able to show that we are doing what the Lord says should be done first.
>
> Voice—"It *has* begun."
>
> Dr. Kellogg—Then we shall see this work that the Lord tells us must be done, begin right away. ["Amen."][6]

It's probably a safe bet that the brave soul who gave Kellogg that "Amen" was a doctor or a nurse. We won't speculate as to who the "Voice" might have been.

Dr. Kellogg, who had just executed one of the more skillful and gracious evasive maneuvers of his career, chose to move on. He did not, however, back down from his assertion; he simply took the opportunity to present more evidence that the message of Isaiah fifty-eight was not something to be set aside lightly. Speaking of the promises in that chapter, he said:

> In order that that prophecy may be fulfilled, we must do those works specified in it. There is something for us to *do* before that prophecy is fulfilled. We cannot be "the repairers of the breach, and the restorers of paths to dwell in," unless we do the works that that people are commanded to do. ["Amen."] The Lord says that very thing here. "Is not this the fast that I have chosen?" etc. Now here is the commentary on that:
>
> "Find out what the poor and suffering are in need of, and then, in love and tenderness, help them to courage and hope and confidence by sharing with them the good things that God has given you. Thus you will be doing the very work that the Lord means you to do."

---

6. *The Medical Missionary*, Extra No. 1, March 1893, 20

This is a part of the third angel's message. ["Amen."] Then we will not be sounding the third angel's message unless we are doing this very thing.

Again: "Do not rest till you break every yoke. It is not possible for you to neglect this and yet obey God."

Every one of us who is neglecting this is not obeying God. And every one of us can do something. No one can sound the third angel's message unless he is obeying God, and anybody who thinks he is sounding the third angel's message and is not doing what the Lord so plainly tells him to do, is mistaken about it.

"Is it not to deal thy bread to the hungry?... When thou seest the naked, that thou cover him?" How many of us have been doing this? We have no right to claim the fulfillment of God's promises and the fulfillment of his prophecy unless we are conforming to the conditions of the prophecy.[7]

But... what did all that mean about the loud cry? Ellen White says... But Dr. Kellogg says... Such were, we may hope, the thoughts of most in the audience. But not all. The transcript indicates that someone had a—

Question—"Suppose you live in a warm and uncivilized country?"

Was this guy serious? The class clown, perhaps? Or maybe a seven-year-old? We'll never know, and it's certainly just as well that we don't. Even Kellogg seemed a bit perplexed, but somehow he took this total pointless non sequitur, made the faintest of sense out of it, and dismissed it graciously. Amazing!

Ans.—Where clothes are not a necessity of life? Well, you see, you have several things to do: you must "feed the hungry" as well as "clothe the naked."[8]

The Call to Labor

Kellogg next turned his hearers' attention to the work of the Haskell Home for Orphan Children. At the time, the building was nearing completion, and the story of its funding was only about eight months old. But those happy memories were not where Kellogg went first. Quoting Ellen White, he said:

"A good move was made at the late General Conference [1891] in the representation of the subject to our brethren assembled, and in the decision that an orphans' home should be established. Now that the impetus has been given to the work by those who realize the great need, let every one stand ready to act a part in helping it forward.

"The Lord said to Peter, 'Feed my lambs.' This command is to us, and the orphans' home is to aid in its fulfillment."

---

7. *The Medical Missionary*, Extra No. 1, March 1893, 20–21 [*Medical Missionary*, June 1, 1891]
8. *The Medical Missionary*, Extra No. 1, March 1893, 21

"Workers are needed here."[9]

With that sort of divine endorsement, you might think there would be quite a crowd of promising workers trying to get a position. Apparently not. Kellogg commented:

> It is difficult to find any one who wants to do work of this kind. The good sisters "want to engage in God's cause;" they want to "work for the Lord." We want missionaries to engage in work for the children, but many seem to think this is not the Lord's work. Does not the Lord care for children?...
>
> But our people do not seem to have had precisely that view of this part of the work. They have thought it was a sort of side issue or something of that kind; they must be distributing tracts, canvassing, etc., or else they are not doing the Lord's work.[10]

Though Kellogg started off addressing the issue of staffing, that's not all there was to the story. A shortage of staffing was just a continuation of the whole shortage of enthusiasm for the project. It's an interesting proposition to try putting oneself in Kellogg's place on this orphanage issue. Remember, it was his idea that he had taken to Ellen White two-and-a-half years before. With her approval, one might have expected the project to move forward steadily, if not rapidly. It was an obvious need, unmistakably called for by both Bible and Spirit of Prophecy. But the response from the "brethren" was underwhelming, to say the least. Putting up with a personal disappointment is one thing, but how was he to relate to those who ignored or opposed what he *knew* God was calling for? Can we fault the man for telling the story? Can we fault him for calling the episode a reproach?

The Evidence of Providence

> This matter was presented before our people two years ago, but they did not seem willing to accept this trust. Only a very few thousand dollars have been raised. A year ago, when we were nearly in despair about it, the committee appointed by the General Conference to consider the matter of an orphans' home, studied it earnestly, but they could not see what to do. At last there came along a woman who had known nothing about us, and we knew nothing of her. She came into my office one day, after she had been two days in the institution, and said, "Doctor, I expect you will think it very strange of me to come in here. I am not sick; I just came into your office to have a little talk with you. I don't know but you will think I am crazy, but I have been looking over your work here, and have been thinking that perhaps you would like a little help in it in some way. I

9. *The Medical Missionary*, Extra No. 1, March 1893, 21 [*Medical Missionary*, June 1, 1891]
10. *The Medical Missionary*, Extra No. 1, March 1893, 21

think you are doing a good work here. I would like to leave a few thousand dollars with you, to help it along, perhaps $10,000."

I told her I was glad she was interested in our work and hoped she would
think the matter over, and that we would be glad to receive any help that she
might give us; but really I had no confidence in what she said, because she was a
stranger, of whom I knew nothing. I could scarcely believe the woman was sane;
but the next day she came in to see me again. She said she had been thinking the
matter over, and that she would like to make the amount of her gift $20,000.
Then she wanted to see the plans of the orphanage, and see if that sum would
erect a building according to the plans. I showed them to her.

I was to start for California the next morning, but this lady that very evening
signed a paper by which she gave $30,000 to the committee appointed by the
General Conference for the purpose of building the Orphans' Home, without any
restriction whatever, except that it should be called the Haskell Home in honor of
her husband.

Now, have we ever known such a thing to happen before in the whole history
of this denomination? Was there ever such a remarkable blessing of God bestowed upon any other enterprise this people have ever started? I take it to mean
simply this, that if our people will not do this work, if our people will not accept
this sacred charge, then the Lord will find somebody else who will do it.
["Amen!" "*Amen!*"] That is just what it means.[11]

To answer the Doctor's rhetorical questions, no, nothing like that had
ever happened before in the history of the denomination. The Lord had
blessed in a remarkable way, but this matter of having "somebody else"
who will do the work when we don't accept it seems a perilous approach
to the Lord's work:

We have the orphans' building nearly completed, but not by means which
any Seventh-day Adventist has furnished. Not a single dollar which has gone
into that building was subscribed or furnished by Seventh-day Adventists. It will
stand as a monument of reproach to us so long as we exist as a people, that the
first home for Seventh-day Adventist orphans was furnished by a good woman
who was not a Seventh-day Adventist, who knew nothing about our work, but
who came here and saw our orphans and homeless ones suffering, and furnished
the money to give them a home. We had to wait for a stranger to come to us; instead of offering a home to the stranger, the stranger furnishes a home for us! Is
not that a reproach to us? ["It is."][12]

11. *The Medical Missionary,* Extra No. 1, March 1893, 21–22
12. *The Medical Missionary,* Extra No. 1, March 1893, 22–23

Back in the Mine Field

Next, Dr. Kellogg addressed the (hopefully hypothetical) concern of someone who might be worried that this "doctrine of good works" is a "new doctrine" among Seventh-day Adventists. Starting with a selection from 1859, he showed that the Spirit of Prophecy, at least, had been calling for this kind of ministry all along. Other selections came from 1862, 1867, 1870, 1875, and 1876. Not surprisingly, they are remarkably consistent in their call to practical service.

That much was fine, but along the way, Dr. Kellogg touched again on the question of the loud cry. Speaking of a comment from 1862 that is now found in *Testimonies*, vol. 1, 274—"I was shown that a most solemn duty rests upon the church to have a special care for the destitute widows, orphans, and invalids"—Kellogg said:

> This was in 1862, thirty-one years ago, and we have not paid any attention to it; a whole generation of orphans has grown up, and a whole generation of widows has died, since this testimony was given. How can we expect the loud cry to go until we live up to all the light the Lord has given us? How can we expect any special manifestation before the world until we take hold of the light that has been shining on our pathway for more than thirty years? I don't think the loud cry will ever go until our widows and orphans are properly taken care of, and until we are doing something more than simply to make a propaganda of our peculiar tenets of faith.[13]

No comment was made on this, but it was one more piece of concern, one more perceived slight against the ministry, since there was little doubt about whom Kellogg thought was making "a propaganda of our peculiar tenets of faith."

A second point, viewable as either a poke in the eye or a plea for acceptance, was the Doctor's comment—and the support he got from a minister!—about health reform:

> That was during the year 1867, and the same is true now. Today our people are farther behind in health reform than they were over twenty years ago, when they were pretty thoroughly united in taking hold of health principles. Is not that true, Brother Loughborough?
> *Ans.*—"Yes."[14]

Then it was back to the loud cry. This had to be getting on some people's nerves!

---

13. *The Medical Missionary*, Extra No. 1, March 1893, 24
14. *The Medical Missionary*, Extra No. 1, March 1893, 24

We must not be satisfied with preaching simply, but we must exercise "true benevolence to men." Then we shall have "power to move the world." We cannot get moral "power to move the world" until we get where we will do what the Scriptures and the Testimonies say we must do. We have not done it yet. We have waited for outside people to come in and build our Orphans' Home. The Lord may be ready to start the loud cry, but we are not ready; we have not done our part, and the Lord is waiting for us to do something in the direction of good works.[15]

There are a good many poor, dying mothers praying for homes for their children who are soon to be orphans; and there are a good many fathers and mothers who are lying sick in their beds, needy and suffering, praying to the Lord for help, and the Lord is going to give them help through those who will do his work, and the loud cry cannot go till this work is done that he has commanded us to do; for that comes first in order, as you will see by reading Isaiah 58. How can we expect the Lord is going to use us in the work of illuminating the whole world, when we cannot even show that we are as good as others even in matters of common humanity?

"Said the Judge, 'All will be justified by their faith and judged by their works.'"

We have had faith for some time, and now it is time we went to doing works.[16]

Now I don't know whether the loud cry is begun or not. I do not think that is the most important thing for us to know. I think the most important thing for us to know is, whether we are obeying God doing all that the Lord has instructed us that we ought to do. If we are doing that, then, when the loud cry does come, we will know it, and we will have a part in it. ["Amen."]...

Now the question is, whether Seventh-day Adventists are going to lead in this work, or is it going to be left for some one else to do. The Lord has given us here a very precious work to do; it is not the whole of the third angel's message, but it is a part of it. You read in Isaiah 58, how we can make our light shine:

"If thou draw out thy soul to the hungry, and satisfy the afflicted soul, *then* shall thy light rise in obscurity, and thy darkness be as the noonday."

If we want the loud cry to begin, brethren, that is the place where it is going to begin. The loud cry is going to begin with our doing the things that the Lord in this chapter says come *before* the loud cry. So he says we must draw out our soul to the hungry, and satisfy the afflicted soul. He says *if* we will do this, our light shall shine. This duty, you see, is repeated twice over in this chapter:

"Is it not to deal thy bread to the hungry, and that thou bring the poor that are cast out to thy house; when thou seest the naked that thou cover him, and that thou hide not thyself from thine own flesh? *Then* shall thy light break forth as the morning.... If thou draw out thy soul to the hungry, and satisfy the aff-

---

15. *The Medical Missionary*, Extra No. 1, March 1893, 25
16. *The Medical Missionary*, Extra No. 1, March 1893, 25 [*Testimonies*, vol. 4, 386]

flicted soul, *then* shall thy light rise in obscurity, and thy darkness be as the noonday.... Thy righteousness shall go before thee."

That is the way our light is going to break forth, our righteousness is going before us. Now, by "righteousness" I do not mean that righteousness which consists simply in—I hardly know how to express myself so as not to be misunderstood—but righteousness must mean right doing. "Thy righteousness shall go before thee," the good deeds that the Lord has been telling us we must do—"deal thy bread to the hungry," etc., that is the righteousness that shall go before us; that is the way our light is to shine.[17]

Called to Account

Dr. Kellogg may have thought he could get away with comments like that without anyone noticing. It's obvious he felt strongly on the issue, and it came out quite a number of times, but he never chose to drive the matter to a head. After all the comments given above, he simply moved on to tell the story of the gift from the Wessels brothers and the beginning of the city mission work in Chicago, which he clearly saw as a great blessing from the Lord. Had he said his piece? Was he satisfied with his coverage of the matter? We'll never know, because right in the middle of his comments about Chicago, there was another

> *Ques.*—"Don't you think the loud cry has commenced?"

No avoiding things now. Had Kellogg planned on a head-on collision like this? Is that what he had set out to do? Or had he merely spoken naïvely, thinking that everyone would be understanding of his "unorthodox interpretation"? Whichever it might have been, the time had come for a clear explanation. Characteristically unintimidated, he obliged:

> *Ans.*—I don't know. I am presenting this subject of medical missionary work from my standpoint. There is everything to indicate that the Lord is anxious to have the loud cry begin to sound, but he says these things referred to in Isaiah 58 must first be done, and so far, the things that have been done in this direction have been done by other people, not by us.
>
> The Lord will do wonderful things by us, if we will do his will—in doing those things that he has commanded us to do. Some things the Lord must do but there are things that we can do. We don't need to wait for the Lord to feed or clothe this or that hungry or poorly clad person. The Lord is telling us to do it. He says, if we will do those things that we have neglected (although we may have been doing other things), *then*, when we are in trouble, or persecuted for righteousness' sake, we can claim this promise. But can we claim this promise unless we

---

17. *The Medical Missionary*, Extra No. 1, March 1893, 26–27

do these things? ["No."] But if we do them, we can call upon the Lord, and he will say, "Here I am"; he is then ready to help us. ["Amen."] I know the Lord is ready to do it; he is ready to help us if we will do his work. How can we neglect this kind of work? It is the most blessed work on earth. I tell you there is nothing that has so much *immediate* blessedness in it as this work. Why, the Bible says we are "blessed in the very deed [doing]." We don't have to wait for the blessing to come a long time afterward....

Now we are a small and an obscure people. We are not going to make ourselves heard by any great noise that we can make. Prejudice will be so strong that we cannot be heard for the noise we make; we must do something besides making a noise. People won't hear because they are so prejudiced; they hear physically, but they don't hear intellectually nor spiritually. So we must do these works that are mentioned here, and then our light shall rise in obscurity, the Lord will hear us, and the world will begin to hear us, and the loud cry will begin. We are an obscure people, and no matter how much noise we make, we cannot make ourselves anything but an obscure people. But our light may rise in darkness, by our fruits, by our works. We may make a little stir by our preaching and literature, but that will be all, unless we have made our light *shine* by our good works. Unless we do these things, we shall never be anything but an obscure people.

One reason people look down upon us, is, that they never heard that Seventh-day Adventists have ever done anything in the way of benevolence. Did the world ever hear of us as a people especially interested in the welfare of the widow, the orphan, the afflicted, and the needy? We have no reputation of that kind in the world....

Now if we expect that our light is going to shine, and that the loud cry is going to begin, and that this people is going to begin it—that we are going to be the instruments through which the Lord is going to do this wonderful work we ought to begin to let our light shine by our good works pretty soon.

Brother Jones[18] may be right in thinking that the time has come for the loud cry to begin; but if the loud cry has been begun by our people, it must be because we have just begun to do a little in the way of letting our light shine. But we have done so little in that way that it seems to me that before the loud cry will make any great noise in the world, we will have to let our light shine a great deal brighter than we have ever yet done, because the works come *first*. The light must shine through these "good works," before we can be called "the repairers of the breach and the restorers of paths to dwell in," for that promise comes after all of these conditions, you see....

We had a testimony over thirty years ago, saying that we as a people were to "rise higher and higher," but it does not appear, from testimonies received at diff-

---

18. In A. T. Jones' 1893 talks at the same General Conference Session he used the phrase "loud cry" in 36 paragraphs. See especially February 6, 167; February 7, 183; February 13, 243; February 23, 359.

ferent times since that one was given, that we have risen perceptibly from that time until now—a period of over thirty years. How is the loud cry going to be given through us, when a large part of the denomination are thirty years behind time, and sounding a note altogether out of tune? We must do the work which the Lord has told us to do, and which we have left undone. We must do our duty in relation to health principles and benevolence in connection with other questions. We must heed the light and accept the whole truth before we can expect the Lord to sound the loud cry through us.[19]

And there you have it. That was Kellogg's answer, and the end of his sermon. There seems to be no record of any sort of reaction—official or otherwise—to his comments. But a major thesis of this book is that his position deserves closer inspection, something we have the luxury of doing more than a century after the fact. From our vantage point, we can see not only the theory of what he advocated, but also the playing out of principles since that time.

It's an interesting topic of consideration, but we're not ready for it yet. Why not? Because the next day Dr. Kellogg spoke again, this time on "Special Light on Medical Missionary Work." Perhaps you noticed that the title is exactly the same as the one we just covered. That's right—same song, second verse.

We'll look at that talk in the next chapter, and then try a little analysis of just one aspect of Kellogg's position. The larger picture of what he was saying will require the consideration of much more history before we're ready to evaluate it. But that will come...

---

19. *The Medical Missionary*, Extra No. 1, March 1893, 28–29

Chapter Seven

What Makes a Beginning?

UNDERSTANDING Kellogg's perspective on his sixth presentation is easy: The clock ran out on him the day before! Sometimes that happens to a speaker, and it makes a perfect case for a "Part Two" presentation. And that's pretty much what he said when he stood up to speak:

> The Testimonies seem to be filled from beginning to end with reiterations of the doctrine that works are necessary for the manifestation of faith. Yesterday I read quite a number of extracts upon this point; I want to read a few more this morning upon the same subject.[1]

This talk, given February 13, is only half as long as the one the day before, but since the topic is similar we won't be looking at it in as much detail. Because our interest centers primarily around the question of the loud cry, we will focus on that aspect of his presentation.

Dr. Kellogg began by re-emphasizing a point he had made before—that good works are called for in the life of the Christian. After a few related comments, he used a quotation from Ellen White that touched on Isaiah fifty-eight. He had said earlier, of course, that this chapter's injunctions constitute the prerequisite methodology of the loud cry just as surely as its promises depict the blessings of the latter rain. That is the core of his position, the central issue we are tracking. So now we join the Doctor's sixth session, already in progress:

---

1. *The Medical Missionary*, Extra No. 1, March 1893, 29

Now we must do works, brethren; there is no doubt about that. There are a great many things depending upon this, not only our own souls' salvation, but the success of the work in which we are engaged....

"The Lord has entrusted you with talents of means, to use to advance his cause, and to bless the needy, and to relieve the destitute. You can do a far greater amount of good with your means than you can do by preaching while you retain your means."

Now that applies to every one of us, just in proportion as we have means that we are not using.

"You can do a far greater amount of good by your means than by preaching while you retain your means."

What does that mean? It means that we are to do good with our means in the way described in what I have just been reading—acts of benevolence, charity—good works. I read to you yesterday that works preach louder than preaching. But I read on:

"Look over the history of your past life. How many have you blessed with your means? How many hearts have you made grateful by your liberalities?"

That shows distinctly what is referred to here by doing good with our means.

"Have you loosed the bands of wickedness? Have you sought to undo the heavy burdens, to let the oppressed go free, and to break every yoke? Have you dealt your bread to the hungry, and brought the poor that were cast out to your house? Have you covered the naked?

"If you have been rich in these good works, you may claim the promise given in this chapter."

On the other hand, if we have *not* been rich in these good works, then we cannot claim these promises.

"'Then shall thy light break forth as the morning [this promise, you see, has a condition: *if* we have been rich in good works, then we may claim these promises], and thine health shall spring forth speedily: and thy righteousness shall go before thee; the glory of the Lord shall be thy rereward. Then shalt thou call, and the Lord shall answer; thou shalt cry, and he shall say, Here I am.' 'And if thou draw out thy soul to the hungry, and satisfy the afflicted soul; then shall thy light rise in obscurity, and thy darkness be as the noonday; and the Lord shall guide thee continually, and satisfy thy soul in drought, and make fat thy bones, and thou shalt be like a watered garden, and like a spring of water, whose waters fail not.'"

I never get tired of reading these texts. There seems to be something grand and new and beautiful in every line every time I read them. There is wonderful meaning in these expressive figures. But I read on: "But you are not now entitled to these promised blessings."

Then we are not entitled to have our "light break forth as the morning," our "health [healing] spring forth speedily," and to have the Lord say, "Here I am," when we cry to him; and so of the rest of these promises; we cannot expect them when we have not complied with the conditions upon which the promises are based. Is not this as plain as anything can be? It is right here—the Bible says it, the Testimonies say it. What more evidence do we want?

Here again: "You are not now entitled to these promised blessings. You have not been engaged in this work. Look back over your past life, and consider how destitute it is of good, noble, generous actions. You have talked the truth, but you have not lived it." "It is now high time that you were changing your course, and working diligently to secure the heavenly treasure."[2]

It should be noted that the passage Kellogg is citing here is from a personal testimony written to a specific individual, rather than to the church at large. Thus the applicability of the passage to the denomination as a whole is a debatable point. Some might say that it doesn't fit. Kellogg, obviously, said it did.

Kellogg noted that the testimony just quoted was written in 1871, and made the point that similar counsels had been given through the years right down to that time. As another example, he cited this passage from 1876:

"You do not possess a spirit of self-denial that resembles the great Exemplar. You should cultivate benevolence, which will bring you more into harmony with the spirit of Christ in his disinterested benevolence."

We cannot *cultivate* benevolence by praying for benevolence, or by talking about benevolence. In order to cultivate benevolence, one must go to work; he must be benevolent; even if you don't enjoy it very well at first, keep practicing it, and by and by you will come to enjoy it better; you will thus cultivate benevolence, and in this way you may by God's help get to be benevolent.[3]

Kellogg quoted more of this passage from 1876, which deals with the story of the Good Samaritan. Of course, as one interested in working for the poor, this story had a natural appeal to the Doctor. Ellen White's comments are, as Kellogg would remark, "very pointed" and "very strait."

"Here Jesus wished to teach his disciples the moral obligations which are binding upon man to his fellow-man. Whoever neglects to carry out the principles illustrated by this lesson is not a commandment-keeper, but, like the Levite, he breaks the law of God which he pretends to revere. There are some who, like the Samaritan, make no pretensions to exalted piety, yet who have a high sense of their obligation to their fellow-men, and have far more charity

---

2. *The Medical Missionary*, Extra No. 1, March 1893, 30; [*Testimonies*, vol. 2, 684]
3. *The Medical Missionary*, Extra No. 1, March 1893, 31; [*Testimonies*, vol. 4, 56]

and kindness than some who profess great love to God, but fail in good works toward his creatures."

These are very pointed remarks. We claim to be commandment keepers, because we "turn away our foot from the Sabbath," but "whoever neglects to carry out the principles illustrated by this lesson, is not a commandment keeper."

This is very strait talk indeed. And there is more in the Testimonies on the subject of benevolence and charity, than there is upon any other one question. If you take the subject of Christian benevolence and the subject of health reform and put these two together, you will find there is more said upon these subjects than on any other half dozen subjects, and yet there is less said about them by our ministers, I fear, than on any other subjects in the whole of these volumes. Now can't we let our hearts and minds expand a little?[4]

If Only He Could See Us Now!

Kellogg's emphasis on the passing of time and the repetition of testimonies on the same wrongs is interesting to note, if for no other reason than to ponder what he might say now that we are a further century and more downstream. As to his views on the loud cry, he makes himself perfectly plain in this final selection, taken from near the close of his talk:

Thirty years ago, the Lord gave us a symmetrical system of truth so that we might keep ourselves in health, and be thoroughly furnished unto all good works. If we really believe the Lord is going to use us in doing the great work that he has to do in this world, we ought to be hurrying very fast to catch up, for we are fearfully behind. Certainly the Lord is not going to do this work through us, while we go on ignoring the instruction that he has been giving us during so many years. We must not imagine that we are going to sound the loud cry while we are ignoring these important truths. The Lord has been giving us these truths that we may make preparation for what is before us. Instead of that, we have been going back into Egypt for years and years.

Now listen again: "When the advocates of the law of God [that means us] plant their feet firmly upon its principles, showing that they are not merely loyal in name, but loyal at heart, carrying out in their daily lives the spirit of God's commandments [that is the same as what is said of the good Samaritan], and exercising true benevolence to man [that does not mean to do a little for a man in order that we may present some of our denominational views. We should begin to do good, because we love Christ], then will they have moral power to move the world."

We shall never have the moral power to move the world, we shall never see the loud cry, nor make the third angel's message go to any great extent—we will never see it go so as to move the world, at least—until we carry out these truths in our daily lives.

"It is impossible for those who profess allegiance to the law of God, to correctly represent the principles of that sacred Decalogue while slighting its holy injunctions to love their neighbor as themselves."

It means a good deal to love our neighbor as ourselves. Again: "The most eloquent sermon that can be preached upon the ten commandments is to *do them*."

The words "do them" in this testimony are printed in italics; and what it means "to do them" is plainly taught in the parable of the good Samaritan.

"The singular absence of principle that characterizes the lives of many professed Christians, is alarming. Their disregard of God's law disheartens those who recognize its sacred claims, and tends to turn those from the truth who would otherwise accept it."

That is, the fact that we do not do this work turns people away from the truth. How can we expect to see the "loud cry" drawing people to the truth, when our actions are such as to drive them away from the truth?

"Let the world see that we are not selfishly narrowed up to our own exclusive interests and religious joys, but that we are liberal, and desire them to share our blessings and privileges, through the sanctification of the truth. Let them see that the religion which we profess does not close up nor freeze over the avenues to the soul, making us unsympathizing and exacting. Let all who profess to have found Christ, minister as he did to the benefit of man, cherishing a spirit of wise benevolence. [Now that is pretty large.] We shall then see many souls following the light that shines from our precept and example."

Now the loud cry will not go until we do this. It is as plain as anything can be that the great development of this work is not going to take place until our light shines—until we let our light shine by our good works.[5]

But Ellen White Said...

Dr. Kellogg gave two more presentations at the General Conference session that year. We will look briefly at them in the next chapter, but since neither of them so directly addresses the issue of the loud cry, we'll put their consideration off for a while so we can do a little de-briefing on what we've covered thus far.

There are any number of interesting inquiries that might come out of Kellogg's talks, but they can easily be generalized enough so as to fall into two basic areas. The larger-scope issues center around the validity of his major premise. If he was right about medical missionary work forming a necessary element of the Lord's work in general and of the loud cry in particular, then there are profound implications for Adventist history,

---

education, evangelism, missiology, and eschatology. Given a little reflection, it's hard to imagine any element of Adventism that wouldn't be affected to some degree, and if Kellogg was right, some of these areas could easily be seen as ripe for a major overhaul.

But before embarking on any considerations so vast, there is, as it were, a sentinel issue which must be addressed, a roadblock that can be seen as entirely negating any need for such revisionist pursuits. This, of course, is the obvious discrepancy between Ellen White and John Harvey Kellogg: She said the loud cry had begun; he said it couldn't have because the church wasn't anywhere close to meeting the conditions.

It takes no great imagination to see those two positions as locked in irreconcilable contradiction. For Kellogg's thesis, this is a huge problem, since so much of its supporting evidence is drawn straight from Ellen White. It would be more than a little hypocritical to reject her authority on the one point while building so much of his case on her writings.

Of course, for many people with a cursory knowledge of Adventist history, the whole idea of believing Kellogg is preposterous from the get go. "Come on! The guy was a *pantheist!*"

But this is an example of a little knowledge being a dangerous thing. Another cliché that fits well is "timing is everything." Thhe Kellogg of 1893 was a far cry from the Kellogg of a decade and more later. Plus, there are a few twists and turns to Kellogg's story in the early 1900s that bring "complexity" to the issue. We'll consider these in later chapters.

So we are left with the question of Kellogg's belief in the gift of prophecy through Ellen White. To be blunt in a general sort of way, we might ask whether or not Kellogg believed Ellen White. Or more specifically, as the "voice" in the meeting had said, "Don't you think the loud cry has commenced?"

By the time one has waded through his first six meetings, it's hard to conclude that Kellogg believed the loud cry had begun. But when he was asked point blank whether or not he thought "the loud cry has commenced," his answer was not "No." Instead, his first words were—

> I don't know. I am presenting this subject of medical missionary work from my standpoint.[6]

Making Sense of the Illogical

How could he *not* "know" unless he didn't believe Ellen White's plain statement? Logic would seem to preclude any other conclusion. But we

6. *The Medical Missionary*, Extra No. 1, March 1893, 28

are, after all, talking about a living, breathing, human being; one, probably, with at least as much emotion and pride and prejudice as most of the rest of us. Sometimes logic fails to capture the essence of our positions and decisions, and there is good reason to think that may have been the case here.

For starters, in the 1890s, Kellogg was known as an ardent supporter of Ellen White. None other than former General Conference president George I. Butler wrote to Kellogg in 1906 to remind him of those days, saying "I used to say sometimes, I thought the Doctor believed the Testimonies more than he did the Bible."[7]

A similar testimony to Kellogg's belief in the Testimonies was written many years later by Percy Magan, then the recently elected president of the College of Medical Evangelists (now Loma Linda University). When Magan assumed the presidency in 1928, one of the issues he had to face was the offering of internships to CME graduates by the Battle Creek Sanitarium and Hospital. Kellogg's influence being unacceptable, the practice had to end. Some things are best dealt with in person, so Magan ended up making a trip back to Michigan. He later wrote an account of the interview with Kellogg and Dr. B.N. Colver, a Sanitarium physician. For our purposes, it is only the comments about Kellogg's past that matter:

> *Magan*: I well remember the day when you used to stand on top of a table in the old gymnasium with tears streaming down your face, telling the helpers, of whom I was one, what a wonderful thing God's gift to this people through Ellen G. White was. I have heard you read from her writings by the hour and talk in a most earnest and subdued way about the wonderful spiritual insight that she had and how much it all meant to you. In an earlier day you made impressions upon my life.
>
> *Kellogg*: Well, Magan, whenever I made those statements which you referred to I always qualified them.
>
> *Colver*: No, Dr. Kellogg, you did not always qualify them. You did not qualify them at all. You believed them with all your heart, and there are scores of people who can rise up to witness to that.[8]

When Kellogg said "I don't know," he certainly wasn't implying any total or sudden loss of confidence in Ellen White, after all he had spent

---

7. Letter, G.I. Butler to J.H. Kellogg, March 7, 1906

8. Letter, P.T. Magan to W.A. Spicer, August 6, 1928 (quoted in Emmett K. Vande Vere, *Windows: Selected Readings in Seventh-day Adventist Church History*, 264)

much of that fifth meeting quoting her. And the next day, he went right back at it again.

But how could he "believe" in her prophetic role and say, "I don't know," when asked if he thought what she had said was true? The simple answer is, he was confused. More learned expositions on "cognitive dissonance" and "reality distortion" might be offered, but "confusion" should suffice. Not the momentary kind of confusion that comes and goes, but a deeper confusion, fueled, perhaps, by some of the most basic weaknesses of human nature.

Put yourself in the Doctor's place. The causes he championed—basically "health reform" and "Christian benevolence"—were clearly supported by both the Bible and the Spirit of Prophecy. He had been supported in these two points by Ellen White for years. His case that they were necessary for the finishing of God's work was—at least in his own estimation—unimpeachable. The ministers were, unfortunately, among the most influential elements of resistance to what he knew to be right. And he was supposed to believe that the blessing of the loud cry was being poured out upon the church through their ministration, while they continued to ignore or oppose the genuinely self-sacrificing work that he and his associates were doing?

Ellen White's description of his case, though given at a later date, points back to this time, and helps explain the difficult position he was in. In a letter dated February 22, 1899, she would write this:

> The Lord has greatly exalted and blessed His servant, Dr. Kellogg. He has used him to honor His name upon the earth and to give character to the work. Dr. Kellogg has been obtaining a most precious experience. But there are some who have acted as though they had been appointed to work against him. The Lord has reproved their course of action. They knew not that they were working on Satan's side of the question. As men and women have thus worked out their own attributes, this has been a hindrance to the doctor. His brethren have had evidence that he has been working in accordance with the will of God. But although they have had light on this point, they have not all stood by his side to help him. Some have held up his hands, but others have not heeded the admonitions given....
>
> Those who refused the warnings of God followed a course of action which brought its sure result. These influences have sometimes made the work of Dr. Kellogg doubly as hard as it should have been. They have led him to stand apart to some degree from the ministry. I desire to present matters as they are presented to me. Such a spirit of criticism and fault-finding has done the work Satan designed should be done. Dr. Kellogg has been led to take the course he

deemed it his duty to take. He has not connected with those who were not in sympathy with the work he knew to be of God.[9]

We might surmise that, in 1893, Kellogg had experienced some or all of this already. Of course, this wasn't written until six years later, so Kellogg didn't have the advantage of this insight at the time. (Even then, it should be pointed out, this letter wasn't written *to* Kellogg. He probably had no need to hear this kind of endorsement, or to know that it had been written to others. He was, after all, very human, and had problems enough with pride.)

Notice especially the last two sentences of the quotation. Kellogg "knew" his work was "of God," and so he followed "the course he deemed it his duty to take." Was he wrong in either of these points? It seems extremely difficult to believe that Ellen White would say that he was mistaken in his opinion of his work, and only slightly more likely that he incorrectly "deemed" what was his "duty."

The description given by Ellen White will no doubt inspire some readers with a sense of *deja vu*. The challenge of staying faithful to truth in the face of opposition from one's brethren, without losing all patience with them and leaving the church, is more severe a test than most are called to endure. Biblically, we might think of Job, Joseph, and Jesus as examples of those who passed this test. And it's not only names starting with "J"—Paul wasn't always treated the best by his brethren, either.[10]

In Adventist history, we find another "J"—James White, who dealt with similar struggles. Then, of course, A.T. Jones and E.J. Waggoner both faced "persecution" from the saints, but with less happy outcomes. It's safe to say that this kind of "friendly fire" opposition is one of the hardest tests that God's workers are called to endure.

This is the kind of "confusion" behind Kellogg's "I don't know" response. How well would you have handled it?

If That Was Wrong, What Was Right?

It's easy—and appropriate—for those with no particular grasp of the circumstances to say that, when Ellen White wrote that the loud cry had begun, she meant just that. But the answer of simple faith can still leave us far short of the understanding that God would have us gain. Faith and understanding both play an important role in the Christian life; it is not right for either to banish the other.

---

9. *Battle Creek Letters*, 14
10. See *Sketches from the Life of Paul*, 226; *Acts of the Apostles*, 400–406

Unchallenged faith produces ignorance and intellectual sloth (consider the Dark Ages, for example), while the exaltation of understanding inevitably leads astray (consider the Enlightenment, for example). Christian maturity requires that both be employed in harmony, despite the appearance of mutual exclusivity. And in this case, there were plenty of questions raised by the announcement of the loud cry.

What about Isaiah fifty-eight? Are there no conditions implied by that chapter's two "if's" and three "then's"? What of Christ's example of spending more time in healing than in preaching; is that not for us to follow? What about all the verses talking about widows and orphans; are they just "junk DNA" in the genetic code of Scripture?

And what about Ellen White's *other* comments, the ones calling for the church to take up the medical missionary work? How was Kellogg to reconcile all these unfulfilled duties with the idea that the end of all things was at hand? Did that mean that all those other things were just *options* rather than *necessities*? If so, what would that say about the very nature of the Great Controversy? (More on that in a later chapter.)

Further prayer, study, and thought may provide a better answer some day, but at the very least it's worth pointing out that neither Kellogg nor his questioners seems to have paid close attention to the wording of Ellen White's famous statement:

> The time of test is just upon us, for the loud cry of the third angel has already begun in the revelation of the righteousness of Christ, the sin-pardoning Redeemer. This is the beginning of the light of the angel whose glory shall fill the whole earth.[11]

Notice, "begun" and "beginning." Here is perhaps the core of Kellogg's difficulty. He seems to have never differentiated between the level of compliance with the conditions of Isaiah fifty-eight that would be required to *start* the loud cry, and the level of compliance necessary to *finish* it.

He came close, at least once:

> Brother Jones may be right in thinking that the time has come for the loud cry to begin; but if the loud cry has been begun by our people, it must be because we have just begun to do a little in the way of letting our light shine.[12]

Apparently the "if... because" connection of his comment seemed too remote to take seriously. But why should it have? It actually fit the circumstances perfectly. Ellen White had said the loud cry had begun, but

---

11. *Review and Herald,* November 22, 1892
12. *The Medical Missionary,* Extra No. 1, March 1893, 28

the rest of the world wouldn't have known it. It's not like our evangelistic efforts had suddenly become vastly more successful. Adventists weren't on the front pages of any of the world's great newspapers. The loud cry "had begun"... but only just barely. Proportionately, the medical missionary work had barely gotten going... but it was *beginning*!

The irony of all this is that Kellogg—often accused of self-promotion—was failing to take much credit for the work he had championed. The orphanage, the visiting nurses, the Christian Help Bands started up around the country... they all owed their existence to Kellogg and the workers at the Sanitarium.

Perhaps it was the desire for acceptance from the church that led him to miss the connection. After all, if the church wasn't acknowledging the medical missionary work, how could it be considered effective?

Kellogg had a tendency toward the big and grandiose; perhaps he was just unable to imagine anything as significant as the loud cry coming from such a humble showing as the medical missionary work had produced so far.

Or maybe he felt slighted (he surely had been), and was looking for an apology before he could view the church as worthy of any special blessing. Perhaps it was all this and more. Whatever the cause, Kellogg never followed up on his "because we have just begun to do a little" statement.

Others, of course, never followed up on it either, but that was because they had overlooked Ellen White's use of the term "revelation" and the whole sentence about the "light of the angel whose glory shall fill the whole earth." The loud cry, she intimated, was something that was shown and demonstrated. Many were more comfortable with a gospel consisting exclusively of "proclamation." A gospel of that sort, though, was foreign to the Lord's work and totally inadequate for the need:

> The work that the Great Teacher did in connection with His disciples is the example we are to follow....
>
> It is only by an unselfish interest in those in need of help that we can give a practical demonstration of the truths of the gospel....
>
> The Lord will give you success in this work; for the gospel is the power of God unto salvation when it is interwoven with the practical life, when it is lived and practiced. The union of Christlike work for the body and Christlike work for the soul is the true interpretation of the gospel.[13]

No false or faulty gospel will finish the task at hand. At the end of time, nothing but the unadulterated "true interpretation" will suffice.

---

13. *Review and Herald*, March 4, 1902

And the glory that fills the whole earth?

> We shall see the medical missionary work broadening and deepening at every point of its progress, because of the inflowing of hundreds and thousands of streams, until the whole earth is covered as the waters cover the sea.[14]

Perhaps the care provided at the Haskell Home, the sacrifices of the visiting nurses in Chicago, and the "good works" of the Christian Help Bands *weren't* overwhelming. Neither is a stream; but put "hundreds and thousands" of them together and you're eventually going to end up with an ocean.

Perhaps there was no one, medical or ministerial, who was prepared to accept and promote the final gospel in its simplicity and its humility. Kellogg saw the need for the practical ministry, but wanted a respected corp of medical missionaries based in imposing medical facilities, making a stir in the world. The ministers generally saw no need for any of that, but preferred a sole emphasis on the fine art of preaching.

To use a military analogy, one still had an attachment to fancy uniforms, expensive equipment, and dress parades, while the other wanted to fight a war with only the air force. Time and reality seem bent on teaching us that, along with the proclamation of those flying in the midst of heaven, there is a necessity for boots on the ground, a whole army of Privates in dirty fatigues down in the mud and the blood... fighting the war the same way Jesus fought it.

---

14. *Medical Ministry*, 317

Chapter Eight

Openings and Opportunities

DOCTOR Kellogg had two more meetings yet to go. How it came about that he would speak more than the original schedule called for is uncertain. Nevertheless, the main fireworks were over; these last two meetings seem, at first glance, relatively tame in comparison to the few days before.

In their printed form, they bear the titles "Openings for Medical Missionary Work at Home and Abroad," and "Opportunities for Medical Missionary Work." But before going into all that, Kellogg showed once again that he'd done his homework, and that the inspired writings had still more direction, encouragement, and reproof on his favorite topic. Working primarily from the chapter, "Doing for Christ," now found in *Testimonies*, vol. 2, 24–37, he placed before his audience a string of memorable short quotes:

"Years ago I was shown that God's people would be tested upon this point of making homes for the homeless."

"I have been shown more recently that God would specially test his professed people in reference to this matter."

"From what has been shown me, Sabbathkeepers are growing more selfish as they increase in riches."

"To become a toiler, to continue patiently in well-doing which calls for self-denying labor, is a glorious work, which heaven smiles upon."

"Faithful work is more acceptable to God than the most zealous and thought-to-be holiest worship."

"Prayers, exhortation, and talk are cheap fruits; but fruits that are manifested in good works [please note what kind of good works], in caring for the needy, the fatherless, and widows, are genuine fruits, and grow naturally upon a good tree."

"When hearts sympathize with hearts burdened with discouragement and grief, when the hand dispenses to the needy, when the naked are clothed, the stranger made welcome to a seat in your parlor and a place in your heart, angels are coming very near."

"Every act of justice, mercy, and benevolence makes melody in heaven."

"The Father from his throne beholds those who do these acts of mercy, and numbers them with his most precious treasures."

"Fatherless and motherless children are thrown into the arms of the church, and Christ says to his followers, Take these destitute children, bring them up for me, and ye shall receive your wages."

"This is the special work now before us."

"All our praying and abstinence from food will avail us nothing, unless we resolutely take hold of this work."[1]

Perhaps this is enough of a sample, though Kellogg included many more, and even that didn't exhaust the chapter. By this time, though, the Doctor was ready to move on to show what actually could be done. The work of the Christian Help Bands was an obvious illustration, and probably not well known to the out-of-town delegates, so he described their origin and progress, much as we have already seen. Perhaps to reinforce the message that this was a work almost anyone could do, Kellogg had with him that day some of the Band leaders who each shared briefly about their work.

A Few Words of Experience

First to speak, appropriately, was the leader of Band No. 1, A.W. Semmens, the Australian nursing student whom we met once already. Since he and his group were the pioneers of the project, he was in a good position to answer that common question, "How do you get started?"

The Lord had been moving upon our hearts to go out into the city to see if we could not help some of those who could not help themselves. And when Dr. Kellogg called us together in November last, and laid before us his plan, we recognized it as the very thing the Lord wanted us to do. At first we did not know how to work, as the work was all new to us; but we thought we would start out and learn how. So we

1. *The Medical Missionary*, Extra No. 1, March 1893, 35–36

divided the city up into districts, and we each took a district. We then went out, in-quiring where we could find a sick or suffering needy individual, and we soon had work enough to keep us going all the time. We found sick and suffering poor on every side. As our time was limited, we could not stay with them, but we could tell those who were well how to take care of the sick, and could supply the needy with food and clothing. In about three weeks we had forty families to look after, and our work soon increased so that we found we must have more bands.[2]

Mrs. S.M. Baker, reported that:

The members of Christian Help Band No. 6 have given relief to nine different families in the city, representing twenty-three persons in all. To some of these families our relief has been but very little—sending baskets of food, or giving a little treatment in case of temporary need; perhaps sometimes only a visit of sympathy, where that was all that was needed. At other visits, we have taken reading matter, which has been gratefully received.[3]

The next to speak was Mrs. M.S. Foy, who—like Mrs. Baker—eventually went into this type of work on a full-time basis. She told a story of circumstances which might have ended much differently, had not someone been there to take an interest:

The first case that I was called to, was that of a woman who was very ill with typhoid fever. The physicians had given her up. She lived over one of the stores on ——— street. When I called there, there were ten in a little room about 10 x 12. Three or four men were smoking, and the daughters were greatly alarmed; they feared their mother would not live through the night. A physician was called in, and... we told him what we were doing, and asked him if he would be willing that we should give the patient some treatment.

He said he would be very glad to have us do so, that he thought she would not live, but that anything that we could do to make her more comfortable would be acceptable. We sent her a nurse, who attended her about five nights, and during this time the nurse showed the daughters how to treat and care for their mother so as to tide her over the fever. We visited her at the end of that time, and found her doing well, and very grateful for the help given her just at the time of need, and her daughters have always welcomed me very warmly.[4]

The final voice in that meeting was Mr. G.B. Replogle, the leader of a band who for the last few months had been visiting "about twenty-six families." He seemed to be speaking for the whole group when he gave his assessment of the program:

2. *The Medical Missionary*, Extra No. 1, March 1893, 37–38
3. *The Medical Missionary*, Extra No. 1, March 1893, 38–39
4. *The Medical Missionary*, Extra No. 1, March 1893, 39

During my past two years' experience in nursing at the Sanitarium, I have had no work the results of which I was so well satisfied with, as with this volunteer work that we are doing here in this city.[5]

The Parting Shot

Dr. Kellogg had one last meeting in which to make his case, though he apparently didn't know that in advance. Preparing on short notice, he probably thought back over what he had already said.

He had cited authority "line upon line." Nothing much to be gained by more of that approach. Maybe the salesman in him knew that he needed to close on something a little more upbeat.

What to do? How to spread his vision of medical missionary work before the delegates?

The answer, of course, was "tell stories." Kids of all ages love stories, and Kellogg was good at it. He knew how things work: if you want their attention, switch to a narrative. He began with the story of the visiting nurses program:

Last year I received a letter from a wealthy banker in Chicago who had become acquainted with our work here at the Sanitarium through his daughter's visit here as a patient. The daughter, an only child, afterward died in Chicago from a surgical operation. On her dying bed, she requested her father to promise to support a Sanitarium nurse to do medical missionary work among the poor of Chicago. Her father wrote to me saying, "we must have one of your nurses." We had none to spare at that time, but he kept writing, telling me of the circumstance I have related; finally his wife wrote me to the same effect.

The gentleman promised to support a nurse as long as he lived, and to provide for the support of a nurse after his death. Then I said, "This certainly means that the Lord is opening the way for us." So I selected one of our best nurses (Sister Emily Schranz), went down to Chicago, and got her started there. I said to the gentleman, "We do not wish to interfere with any good work that anyone else is doing; we want to do something that no one else is doing." So a place was selected for the nurse in one of the worst parts of Chicago, in the vicinity of the "stockyards."

She went to work there. When she had gained some experience, she was sent down into the more central and a still worse part of the city; and now for several months she has been working in the very heart of the wickedness of Chicago, where no other nurse has ever dared to go before, where there is no provision for the sick poor, no hospital, no dispensary. There are dispensaries in other parts of Chicago, but in this part of the city no one has ever had the courage to start a dispensary.

5. *The Medical Missionary*, Extra No. 1, March 1893, 40

There are now two nurses there at work. The second nurse who goes down to help Sister Schranz, is a volunteer-nurse. Her expenses down and back are paid by our nurses at the Sanitarium. This is a part of the same volunteer missionary work that you heard about yesterday. The volunteer nurse gives a month's time to the work. It is the hardest kind of physical labor, disagreeable enough and dangerous too, but she does not ask for any pay. The nurses do not take any pay, because they want the work to be their own work for the Lord.

To show you what sort of place these nurses are at work in, I may state that three or four weeks ago, we undertook to find rooms where the nurses could live nearer their work. A thorough search was made, but there could not be found a single respectable house in the whole district. The streets there are thronged with the most wicked characters. Go into one of the houses, and you find a regular pandemonium—such a jargon of rough voices, and harsh sounds, and sad sights as you never met before.

Sister Schranz once told me, "The first thing I hear when I go into some houses is the noise of a great fight upstairs. In one of these places, where there is a poor sick woman up two flights of stairs, in order to get up to her, I have to go through a whole crowd of drunken men. Before I get there, I just have to stop and pray for the Lord to open the way for me, and He does open the way. I go in, and those fighting, swearing, drunken men just stand aside and let me pass between them and then go on with their fighting.

"When I get up in the morning, I get down on my knees and pray, 'Now, Lord, make this a good day for me and give me great opportunities for doing good'; and as I go about my work, the difficulties and dangers disappear."

I go down to Chicago sometimes to spend a day with the nurses, to see how the work progresses, and it is interesting to see how it is appreciated by the people. In some places in that part of the city it is not safe for a man to go alone, so I go behind the nurse. The nurse generally goes behind the doctor, but in this case the doctor goes behind the nurse. I find the way all open before the nurse as she passes along, right into the worst kind of places, where you and I would not dare go without a policeman.

When the nurses first began their work there, a policeman would often come up and touch them on the shoulder, and say, "You don't want to go down there." But when it was explained to him that they were missionary nurses, and he saw their badges, he allowed them to pass on. The very worst characters treat our nurses with courtesy. Sometimes a poor old drunken fellow reeling out of a saloon, unable to walk straight, seeing the nurse passing, takes off his hat as he tries to steady himself, and says, "Good morning, (hic) Sister Emily."

In this way the nurse is received, as she goes into the vilest of tenement houses filled with the vilest of people. Very often in going upstairs the nurse meets a policeman coming down from a search for someone who killed somebody over in another part of the city a few days before. These places are the haunts of the wickedest and most depraved characters in Chicago. I have seen some of these poor creatures whom the nurses have helped in their wretched condition, just get down on their knees and kiss the nurse's hands—fairly overwhelming her with praises and blessings for what had been done for them. They would speak to me aside and tell me how the nurse had helped them; and that no one had ever before come there to help them; that the doctors cared nothing for them, because they had no money; that nobody but the nurse ever said a kind word to them or did anything to help them because they were poor, miserable, drunken wretches.[6]

Thinking Way Outside the Box

Kellogg liked the story about the nurses. He valued compassion, admired courage, and loved success—and that story had it all. Wasn't that enough to engage the saints? Couldn't they all share that vision?

Perhaps not. Perhaps it was just too foreign.

There is an interesting minor detail that shows up here in this talk. As the Doctor makes his case for a humanitarian/medical component in the denomination's evangelistic program, he made an easily overlooked comment that is quite remarkable, really. Here's what he said:

> We are told that the time is coming when medical missionary work will be the only missionary work that can be done. Now isn't it time we were getting ready? Every single Seventh-day Adventist ought to be trained to do something in this work.[7]

Kellogg's "We are told..." comment is an obvious reference to Ellen White, and for most current-day Adventists with any exposure to her comments in this sort of thing, there's nothing new in the offhanded paraphrase. We've heard it before; may even know the reference. It's found in *Counsels on Health*, 533. But when you look at the quotation itself, there's something curious.

The words are a bit different, true enough, but the thought is the same: "soon there will be no work done in ministerial lines but medical missionary work." No, the curious aspect is the source. It's listed as coming from the *General Conference Bulletin* of 1901.

If you check, you'll find that the comment has been re-printed in eight different volumes, but they all stem from that 1901 original. So what was John Kellogg quoting back in 1893? A private letter, perhaps? A personal conversation, maybe?

6. *The Medical Missionary*, Extra No. 1, March 1893, 41–42
7. *The Medical Missionary*, Extra No. 1, March 1893, 43

Whatever the details in this case, it points out that there were things that Kellogg knew that others didn't. It could be that the gap was simply too great for others to share this vision of his. It was a foreign concept to them in many ways, and the lack of unity between the medical and the ministerial branches of the church had long ago become a formidable barrier to communication.

But he wasn't giving up. There was one more thing to try.

Since J.N. Andrews had sailed for Europe two decades before, Adventism had become a worldwide missionary church. Missions was a hot button appeal, and though Kellogg's image of missions wasn't the same as that held by most of the ministers, perhaps there was room for common ground.

He began by describing the spiritual need in Chicago, then amplified it by reminding his hearers that "Chicago contains a population equal to one-half that of the whole State of Michigan." But Chicago was more. Chicago was the perfect training ground for world missions:

Chicago is a cosmopolitan city; its population is made up of Danes, Swedes, Norwegians, Germans, Bohemians, Hungarians, French, Poles, Russians, Jews, Syrians, Arabs, Mexicans, Cubans, Africans, Chinese, Japanese, etc. Almost every country on the globe is represented in Chicago. What a splendid place that is for a missionary school!

It is a part of our plan to train nurses here for a time, then send them down to Chicago to get a practical experience in medical missionary work. There is a field in that great city where all can be trained for work. Those who expect to work in Denmark, among the Danes, can find work in Chicago among the Danish population there. Those who want to work among the Germans, can find them there. Those who want to work among the Jews, can find work in Chicago among Jews, Arabs, and Syrians....

I was talking with a medical missionary the other day, who had been with Bishop Taylor in Africa, and he said, "Many of our missionaries in Africa go back home again; they didn't know anything about missionary work when they came, and had no missionary spirit when they got down there. They found that it was necessary to do all kinds of disagreeable things, such as washing and cleaning an old sloughing sore, or taking some old, filthy garments off from a man and cleaning him up, and putting him into a wholesome condition, sitting up all night sometimes, where the odors were unwholesome and the vermin so thick that it seemed positively dangerous to stay there; and then perhaps to get right down in the dirt and filth and pray for him. Some of the missionaries don't have any taste for doing such work as that, and so many of them come back home again pretty soon."

Now if we should take these missionary students and put them in Chicago at work, it would be a means of trying them. In this way we may find out who has the true missionary spirit, and who has simply a missionary sentiment which he has received from what he has read in books. One who has been tested by such work as we propose to do in Chicago knows what real missionary work is....

The Lord says we must have broader ideas. What we want in Chicago, we want in New York, in Brooklyn, in Albany, in Buffalo, Pittsburgh, Philadelphia, Cincinnati, Cleveland, Columbus, Kansas City, Omaha, St. Louis, New Orleans, San Francisco, Atlanta, Nashville, Detroit, and a hundred other large cities, and a thousand smaller cities. Every one of these cities ought to be occupied right away. There are wonderful fields open for this work. No one else is working in these fields in this way. Now is the time for us to step right into the gap, and do a work for humanity that no one else is so well prepared to do.

While our enemies are preparing to persecute and imprison us, let us prepare ourselves to do the most noble work on earth. When our enemies come to seize us, let them find us at the side of the sick and suffering, let them find us feeding the hungry and clothing the naked. The honest in heart will then see that we are true Christians and not fanatics, and that we are really persecuted. This is an argument which everybody can understand. There must be preaching, of course, and tract distributing, but our works will preach louder than preaching—louder than we can preach in any other way....

Now, brethren, if you want the whole Seventh-day Adventist denomination trained to be medical missionaries within the next two years, you can have it done. Think of what the influence would be upon your neighbors, if you should begin that kind of work....

You can see what a wonderfully large and practical work there is to be done, and this is just as much a part of the third angel's message as is the warning against the beast and his image and the mark of the beast. I hope these ministers and delegates will interest themselves in hunting up the right kind of persons to enter this work.[8]

And there you have it: that's what thinking outside the Adventist ministerial box looked like in 1893. But you couldn't find it in the *General Conference Bulletin.*

Perhaps it was the Doctor's idiosyncrasies and excesses that erected barriers between him and the ministry. That last idea, for instance. How much sense would it make to try and train the whole church as medical missionaries? Doesn't the "division of labor" apply here. After all, that's why we have "health professions," isn't it?

Good questions. Glad you asked. Here's the data; you figure it out:

---

8. *The Medical Missionary*, Extra No. 1, March 1893, 45–47

Let our ministers, who have gained an experience in preaching the word, learn how to give simple treatments and then labor intelligently as medical missionary evangelists.[9]

All gospel workers should know how to give the simple treatments that do so much to relieve pain and remove disease.[10]

In every place the sick may be found, and those who go forth as workers for Christ should be true health reformers, prepared to give those who are sick the simple treatments that will relieve them, and then pray with them. Thus they will open the door for the entrance of the truth.[11]

As the canvasser goes from place to place, he will find many who are sick. He should have a practical knowledge of the causes of disease and should understand how to give simple treatments, that he may relieve the suffering ones.[12]

In the fifty-eighth chapter of Isaiah the Lord tells us plainly what the work is that he requires of us. In order that our young people may be fully prepared to do this work, small sanitariums are to be connected with our schools. The students are to be taught how to use nature's simple remedies in the treatment of disease.[13]

God's people are to be genuine medical missionaries. They are to learn to minister to the needs of soul and body. They should know how to give the simple treatments that do so much to relieve pain and remove disease.[14]

People sometimes see Ellen White's comment that "soon there will be no work done in ministerial lines but medical missionary work"[15] as an indication of things slowing done. It looks more likely that the statement actually describes the first time things really get going right!

9. *Testimonies*, vol. 9, 172
10. *Counsels on Health*, 389
11. *Medical Ministry*, 320
12. *Counsels on Health*, 463
13. *Review and Herald*, September 9, 1902
14. *Welfare Ministry*, 127
15. *General Conference Bulletin*, 1901, 204

Chapter Nine

What Are the Odds?

IT'S time to slow down, take a few deep breaths, and weigh the implications of these ideas. It's one thing to toss out theories, but sometimes quite another to make those theories work in the real world. Harsh reality tells us that sometimes it's impossible. It might be fun to ask, "What would the world be like if there were no hypothetical questions?" but of course we'll never know.

Is that the way it is with Kellogg's dream for Adventist evangelism? And, more importantly, is there any realistic chance that Kellogg's ideas were even approximately what God wanted us to do back then? If so, the next obvious consideration is, what about now?

But that's a huge jump. "Now" can wait. If we're going to get to "now" in all this, there's a great deal of ground that must be covered first. We've already looked at the concern of Kellogg's contradiction of Ellen White's comment on the loud cry. The individual reader, of course, will have to decide whether or not that concern has been allayed enough to warrant giving further consideration to Kellogg's thoughts. If it hasn't been, there's not much practical value in the rest of this book.

But if that issue can be surmounted, others are waiting in line. Let's look at some of them.

For starters, if Kellogg's basic premise that medical missionary work (covering everything from simple humanitarian activities to life-saving surgeries, as appropriately called for) is an *essential* component of the loud cry, then we would have to admit that the great majority of our denominational efforts to re-ignite the loud cry have been fatally lacking.

Stop and think about the gravity of that for a moment, because that's a pretty big deal. Is that a position *you* want to try selling to God's people?

At the same time, let's not make it worse than necessary. If Kellogg's general *technique* was right, and the *techniques* used since have been deficient, it does not necessarily follow that all the *people* who used those deficient techniques were morally flawed. There can be a difference between "mistaken" and "sinful." But still, it's a pretty bitter pill to swallow.

The second point to consider is that there was a living prophet on hand for twenty-two years after this 1893 episode. If God's people had taken a wrong turn away from His chosen plan, one would expect to find frequent and pointed comments from the Lord's mouthpiece.

What would those divine messages be saying? For starters, we might expect something akin to, "No, no! Not that road! Stay on *this* one!" If that didn't get the desired response, we might then expect to hear, "Stop! Turn around!" Eventually, as our route diverged further and further from the original plan, the message might turn to, "It's not worth going back now, but if you take this next corner it will get you on a road that runs parallel to the first one."

In other words, if Kellogg's thesis is even approximately correct, there should be evidence of actual effort—probably through the influence of the prophet—to get the Lord's work back on track. A "Plan B," if you wish, somewhat similar at least to the "Plan A" which was never deployed.

A third point is that if medical missionary work really is tied in to the loud cry, then it should be possible to show that it is also closely related to righteousness by faith and the other theological concepts that we know are related to the loud cry.

In Verity...

The first two points are matters of history and will be addressed in chapters to come. The third issue will be covered in detail in chapter twenty-two, but is important enough that a partial explanation will be helpful here, so let's do that much right now.

Is medical missionary work integrally connected to the loud cry? Let's consider another connection that is directly attested to by divine authority:

> Some of our brethren have expressed fears that we shall dwell too much upon the subject of justification by faith, but I hope and pray that none will be needlessly alarmed; for there is no danger in presenting this doctrine as it is set forth in the Scriptures.... The exceeding great and precious promises given us in the Holy Scriptures have been lost sight of to a great extent, just as the enemy of all

righteousness designed that they should be. He has cast his own dark shadow between us and our God, that we may not see the true character of God. The Lord has proclaimed himself to be "merciful and gracious, long-suffering, and abundant in goodness and truth."

Several have written to me, inquiring if the message of justification by faith is the third angel's message, and I have answered, "It is the third angel's message in verity."[1]

This is a famous quote, but one wonders how much thought has been given it, beyond the obvious use of legitimizing the Jones-Waggoner message of justification by faith. The problem is that we seldom think of justification in any of the terms or images that we find in the third angel's message.

Consider the contrast. Justification by faith is a "most precious message" that brings peace to the soul through forgiveness. By and large, we like the concept of justification (sometimes to unwarranted excess).

The third angel's message, on the other hand, is... shall we way, somewhat more confrontational. We might condense the message something like this: "If you worship the beast or get his mark, it's wrath for you, and you're going to burn." And these two messages are the same thing? Really? In which universe?

Well, this one, actually. It's like "heads" and "tails" are the same coin. And the stuff in the middle that holds them together? That's the conflict between "the Truth" and "the Lie,"[2] and an understanding of authority.

Let's start with an illustration. Suppose you are a private in the army, the absolute lowest guy on the totem pole. When the Sergeant yells, "Soldier! Take this shovel. Dig a ditch. Five feet deep, four feet wide, twenty feet long! Now!" what are you going to be doing?

Digging, obviously. Why? Because that Sergeant could make your life miserable if you get him mad at you.[3] Makes sense, doesn't it?

But while you're digging, a Lieutenant comes up, hands you a paper, and says, "Soldier! Take this message to Major Johnson, headquarters Company C, on the double!"

Now what are you doing? Running, of course, with a paper in your hand. Why? Because a Lieutenant could do even more damage than a Sergeant.

And then when a Humvee skids to a stop beside you, and a guy with four stars on his shirt yells, "Soldier! Get in here!" it's a safe bet you'll be

---

1. *Review and Herald*, April 1, 1890
2. See page 19.
3. This is a little like the first angel's message; "Fear God and give glory to Him."

going for a ride. So far, so good. But what about the ditch, and the message for Company C? Your life is ruined! The Sergeant and the Lieutenant are going to be furious that you didn't obey their orders.

Well... no, not really. Oh sure, they may be mad at you, but the General is your protection. He has suddenly become your best friend. Why? Because when there was a conflict of authorities, you wisely chose to honor him. You showed your faith in him through the act of obedience, and it is universally understood that as the higher authority, his command releases you from the command of lesser authorities—and from the punishment that would otherwise have come for disobedience. He is your protector.

This is exactly the situation brought to light in the third angel's message. The united powers of the world have commanded everyone to worship the beast on Sunday. If you don't, they'll kill you. On the other hand, God forbids you to worship the beast, and if you do, He'll burn you.

You? You're between a rock and a hard place—and the rock is red hot liquid brimstone. So... your move. Now, whom do you trust? Everything you can see, hear, touch, taste, and smell—not to mention watch on YouTube—tells you that your only hope is to fall into line with the world.

And the third angel's message says not a single word of encouragement or promise, just a matter-of-fact statement of the results of doing wrong. Everything hinges on the individual's faith in one authority or the other. Are God's commands *really* for my best good? Even when obedience to Him could get me killed?

Of course, though this test may be more severe than past death threats in some way or the other, this is only the "entry level" challenge. The full test of Christ Himself as the "avenging enemy" is yet future. That will be the ultimate test of faith in His wisdom, power, and love.

The connection that makes justification by faith "the third angel's message in verity" is simple. To do the righteous thing by faith in God is righteousness by faith. And what would we suppose "the right thing" might be, given that Jesus spent His whole ministry doing medical missionary work?

As to the third angel's message, we'll see in more detail later on that the only effective way to *give* the message, is to *live* the message. Living out the principles of self-sacrificing service both strengthens our own faith, and exerts the strongest influence for others to accept—and live— according to the same principles.

Chapter Ten

Kellogg vs. the Ministry

T HUS far in our recounting, a reader with little previous exposure to these matters might easily conclude that Dr. Kellogg was something of an eccentric uncle to the wider Adventist family. A little peculiar, but harmless enough.

Similarly, the contention between Kellogg and the medical workers on the one hand, and the ministerial and administrative employees of the church on the other, may seem fairly insignificant. Indeed, up until 1893, that may almost be accurate. But to assume that matters stayed like that is to drastically underestimate the impact these things would have on the denomination.

What comes to light with a closer investigation is that multiple issues and circumstances, over time, pushed erring mortals on both sides of the conflict to the point of rupture. A common—and not altogether inaccurate—perspective is to sum it all up by noting Kellogg's increasing estrangement from his brethren, and his eventual involvement in genuinely dangerous heresies, and conclude that he regrettably slid away from the faith he once espoused.

There's truth in that. But, as has often been noted, it takes two to tango. We many times shy away from acknowledging the errors of those who "won the battle" against Kellogg, and rightly so. They may have made mistakes, but they did not throw all truth overboard and follow their own wills. That's a vital distinction for which they deserve credit and the decency of historians who have nothing to gain from tarnishing their legacies.

And so we will focus little on individuals in telling this story, but be assured that when mistakes were made in dealing with Kellogg, it was flesh and blood people who made them. Personalities were involved, strongly held convictions were at stake, and human nature was ready to take pride or offense, as the case may be. In short, we are talking about the same kind of people as walk the earth today; it behooves us to be charitable.

Where Did the Trouble Begin?

We've already seen Kellogg's conversion at the time of the Minneapolis General Conference in 1888, his growing interest in the Benevolent Work, and some of his frustration with ministers whom he found less than supportive. But where did the real trouble begin?

Details are scanty as to the origins of some issues, but it's safe to say there were challenges from early on. One of the earlier indications is in a letter to the General Conference president going into the Minneapolis meeting. Those familiar with the history surrounding the 1888 General Conference will remember that there was a great deal of tension between Elders Butler and Smith (based in Battle Creek, Michigan), and Elders Jones and Waggoner (based in Oakland, California). Elder Butler was ill, and unable to attend the Conference, but he wrote a 39-page letter to Ellen White. He might better have spent the time praying.

To her daughter-in-law, Mary, she described his letter as "a most curious production of accusations and charges against me."[1] This letter has been scrutinized closely by those interested in the subjects of 1888 and righteousness by faith. It may come as a surprise that this letter mentions the name of A.T. Jones only once, and Dr. Waggoner three times, but Dr. Kellogg's name appears fifteen times.

It is just one of the ironies of the story that G.I. Butler—whom Ellen White reproved resoundingly for the attitude toward Dr. Kellogg expressed in his letter—would twenty years later be one of the last two Adventist ministers whom Kellogg considered to be his friends. (The other was Elder S.N. Haskell.) But on to the letter:

> It will be seen sometime that our brethren and sisters have not been inspired by the Spirit of Christ in their manner of dealing with Dr. Kellogg.... Your attitude toward him will not bear the approval of God, even if he was the man which you think him to be. You cannot be any help to him while you maintain this position, but you can pursue a course that will so weaken his confidence in his brethren that they cannot help him when and where he needs to be helped....

---
1. *Ellen G. White 1888 Materials,* 66

Like yourself he was taken from among the laboring class, and by his indomitable will and persevering energy and with one object in view, he has reached a position among the honored men of the world. This position did not compel him to sacrifice one principle of our doctrines of faith to make a success. He has signalized himself as a man of wisdom and aptitude to plan and execute them, and his high standing in the medical profession has an influence to remove from a large class the false impressions which have prevailed with regard to Seventh-day Adventists' being an ignorant class of people....

Dr. Kellogg is a finite man and has his errors as well as other men, but God has done a work through him and has been giving him strength. He does not now feel exasperated, as he once did, when he is misjudged....

There is no reason why his brethren should stand away from him and criticize and denounce and condemn him when they have no real knowledge of his work and what they are talking about. They gather from hearing or supposition the idea that Dr. Kellogg is a designing, dangerous man, and acting upon that idea they unjustly and with an unchristian spirit place themselves directly in the way of his efforts, thus counteracting the good work he is trying to do, and their course is not fair and just. It may produce a condition of things to drive him to the very things they condemn. The opposition that has existed in reference to Dr. Kellogg is contagious and is hostile to the health of the soul. This is not the Spirit of Christ and will have no saving influence upon Dr. Kellogg....

If the doctor fails in doing his duty and being an overcomer at last, those brethren who have failed in their want of wisdom and discernment to help the man when and where he needed their help, will be in a large measure responsible, for there have [been] but few [who have] faithfully warned him in kindness and love for his soul, but hurt him with their thrusts behind his back.

Has not Dr. Kellogg shown the greatest respect to our ministers, and has he ever given the least evidence that he was ashamed of his brethren? ... I hope, my brother, that you will no longer cherish such thoughts. They are unworthy of a Christian.[2]

It sounds like Battle Creek may have deserved its name. Some neighborhoods are just tougher than others, but why should it be that way among Christians?

Going further back in time, there is another, more human-interest type of story that may have contributed to the Doctor's strained relations with at least one member of the ministry. It seems that when he was in his early twenties, John had developed an interest in a talented and attractive young woman named Mary Kelsey. How mutual that interest might have been is hard to say, but eventually Miss Kelsey moved to California to work at the Pacific Press, and in 1876 she married W.C. White.

2. *Ellen G. White 1888 Materials*, 99–106

It is said that the friendship between John and Willie was never quite so cordial as before.[3]

The entirely unofficial "verbal history" of the Battle Creek area has suggested that while Mary was still in Battle Creek, Willie on the West Coast, and John attending medical school in New York, letters were traveling back and forth across the country from both directions. But the story is that Willie had a friend who worked in the Battle Creek Post Office, and some of John's letters mysteriously vanished before delivery.[4] If there's any truth to the story, it's not hard to imagine some stress being injected into that particular relationship.

In contrast to that is a well documented sore spot that must have applied to a far greater number of ministers:

> I speak to my brethren in America: Why do some of our ministering brethren manifest so little interest in health reform? We were greatly burdened after the Ashfield camp meeting to see ministers who did not receive and practice the light on health reform, and who were making no advancement in spiritual growth. The messages given on this great and needful subject seemed to be distasteful to some of our ministers. They would put forth some faint efforts to reform, but because they had no mind to practice it, they lapsed into an indifference upon the subject. Then, in order to vindicate their own course of action, they began to pick flaws in the men who advocated this reform. If they could find any excuse for remaining away, they would not attend the meetings where health reform was presented. These men became its bitterest enemies. They were displeased with those who gave it their attention and presented it to the people. Thus those who should have been the first to advocate the principles of health reform in every line of their work, by precept and example, showed that they were not in harmony with it.
>
> What then? They visited with their brethren, and at the table revealed their principles by eating meat and drinking tea and coffee. Then they would make some remark in regard to their not being so "straight-laced" as some of their brethren and sisters. These men were not making that progress in divine things that would make them safe teachers. They were opposed to health reform because instruction on temperance in all things was opposed to their practice of self-indulgence. This was the great stumbling block in the way of our bringing the people to investigate and practice and teach the truth of health reform.[5]

3. Richard W. Schwarz, *John Harvey Kellogg, M.D.*, 149
4. No documentation at all, except the author's memory of a Battle Creek native's account of what someone had told him that he had heard from a long-forgotten source.
5. *Manuscript Releases*, vol. 4, 372

Certain aspects of "health reform" require a level of self-denial that not everyone is prepared to choose for themselves. That's one thing, but attacking the messenger is a whole new level of concern. There were, unfortunately, some members of the ministry in the 1800s who fell into both of these categories.

Human influence is a powerful force, as will become more prominent in this story further along. We've already seen a brief mention of this in the "contagious" opposition to Dr. Kellogg. This force of influence and example is almost Newtonian, sometimes, in that every action tends to result in an equal and opposite reaction:

> It is a fact that our ministers are very slow to become health reformers, notwithstanding all the light which the Lord has given upon this subject. This has caused Dr. Kellogg to lose confidence in them. Their tardy work in health reform has created in him a spirit of criticism, and he has borne down on them in an unsparing manner, which the Lord does not sanction. He has belittled the gospel ministry, and in his regard and ideas has placed the medical missionary work above the ministry. I have seen that in the censuring of ministers remarks have been made which have not been to the honor and glory of God.[6]

It's worth trying to keep a sense of chronology in all this, even though we haven't space to document every change and fluctuation. This last comment, depicting Dr. Kellogg as belittling the ministry, comes from 1898. It isn't hard to see how this attitude could develop, but it will be helpful to keep this aspect of the story in the right time period. Overall, it's safe to say that around the year 1896, Kellogg's irritation with the ministry began to rise notably.

Of course, when we consider the catalog of unsanctified motivations, it would be foolish to overlook jealousy:

> Some have looked upon the medical missionary work with suspicion because of its constantly increasing success. Unless these are baptized with the Holy Spirit they will continue to entertain their jealous feelings, whatever power God may reveal in advancing the truth. They will lose the spiritual blessings they might have had and will bring the divine judgments upon themselves.[7]

When Did We See You Hungry?

And, as a final consideration, there seems to have been a continuing distaste for helping the less fortunate. It does seem likely that the genuinely "poor and needy" might have had even less fashionable clothes than

6. *Manuscript Releases*, vol. 4, 373
7. *Manuscript Releases*, vol. 21, 401

had Miss More some decades before when she visited the Adventist head-quarters. This point came in for special notice from the pen of Ellen White:

> My brethren in America, in the place of questioning and criticizing Dr. Kel-logg because he is doing the class of work he is, when you do your God-given service, you will be heart and soul engaged in doing the same kind of work, which will be of far more account in the sight of God than for so many to flock into Battle Creek, where they become religious dwarfs because they do not do the work God has appointed them.[8]

In fact, this matter of the simplest form of medical missionary work, the kind of thing the Christian Help Bands were doing, was assigned a far higher level of importance than we might have expected:

> Again and again the Lord has pointed out the work which the church in Bat-tle Creek and those all through America are to do....
>
> The medical missionary workers are doing the long-neglected work which God gave to the church in Battle Creek....
>
> The Lord has moved upon Dr. Kellogg and his associates to do the work which belongs to the church and which was offered to them, but which they did not choose to accept....
>
> If the medical missionary workers will carry this line of effort into the churches everywhere, if they will work in the fear of God, they will find many doors opened before them, and angels will work with them.
>
> When the Lord moves upon the churches, bidding them do a certain work, and they refuse to do that work; and when some, their human efforts united with the divine, endeavor to reach to the very depths of human woe and misery, God's blessing will rest richly upon them.[9]

To Ellen White's thinking, this simple medical missionary work is huge. The issues which hinge upon it are stunning. Notice particularly the italicized sections in these next two paragraphs. And, just for the record, those italics aren't "supplied"; they are in the original:

> This work is the work the churches have left undone, and *they cannot prosper until they have taken hold of this work in the cities, in highways, and in hedges.* Then angels of God will co-operate with human instrumentalities, and a religious system will be inaugurated to relieve the necessities of suffering human beings who are in physical, mental, and moral need....

8. *Home Missionary*, November 1, 1897
9. *Testimonies*, vol. 8, 70–72

The very work Dr. Kellogg has been managing is the kind of work *the whole of our churches are bound to do under covenant relation to God.* They are to love God supremely and their neighbor as themselves.[10]

Is it fair to say that these warnings raise medical missionary work to such a level of importance that neglecting it would doom our evangelistic efforts—if not to total failure—to falling short of success?

And what is it that is causing all this? Simple. It's selfishness:

> The Lord gave me light that in every place where a church was established, medical missionary work was to be done. But there was in the Battle Creek church a great deal of selfishness. Those at the very heart of the work indulged their own wishes in a way that dishonored God. Dr. Kellogg was not sustained in the health reform work, the importance of which had been kept before the church for thirty years. This work was hindered because of the feelings and prejudices of some in Battle Creek who were not disposed to conform their course of action to the Word of God regarding health reform principles....
>
> God has not forsaken His people, but His people have forsaken Him. Those in Battle Creek should have worked for the ones who needed their help. Dr. Kellogg took up the work they did not do. The spirit of criticism shown to his work from the first has been very unjust, and has made his work hard. The lack of sympathy his brethren have shown him has prepared the way for the work he has been doing in criticizing them. The Lord has no justification for any such work.[11]

Details, Details...

Several points deserve notice here. For starters, John Kellogg wasn't perfect. Though this section has focused on the unjust criticism and opposition which he received, that's no reason to believe that everything he was doing was free from error.

The issue of his criticizing the ministers, for instance, is a human enough response, but not excusable. As mentioned previously, about 1896 we start to see a notable shift in his relationship both to the ministers and to Ellen White. It seems as though he felt it was hopeless to expect them to treat him fairly, and so he set himself to the task of simply showing them up. It's as if he decided that he was right, they were wrong, and he was going to prove it.

In a previous chapter, we noticed the unfortunate $40,000 donation from the Wessells brothers which started up the Chicago City Mission. As Ellen White said, it would have been better if that money had stayed

---

10. *Home Missionary,* November 1, 1897
11. *Battle Creek Letters,* 11–12

in Africa. It would have been better for Kellogg, too, since it was that money which catapulted him into the high dollar, large scale, institutionalized style of Benevolent Work.

Of course, for the sake of making a flashy public statement and showing up a bunch of financially constrained ministers, high dollar and large scale were fine. So as Ellen White raised objections to this kind of expenditure when other parts of the world field were suffering for funding, Kellogg increasingly turned a deaf ear.

One other confusing aspect of the situation is trying to make sense of what may seem to be conflicting commendations and condemnations written to or about Kellogg and his work. Which was it? Good or bad?

The problem here is that Kellogg had so many things going that it's easy to misapply. In the quotations used in the last subsection, for instance, you will note the references to the Battle Creek Church and its members who weren't doing the work they should. As a result, the Medical Missionaries had taken up the work. The commendation is for the Christian Help work, the simplest and most basic of all Kellogg's benevolent programs.

Ellen White sought to commend wherever and whenever possible, but there were the "tough love" moments too, like this one focusing on the much more expensive work being done in Chicago:

> The Lord has sent you warnings, but you have not heeded them....
>
> Of the work you have taken up in Chicago the Lord inquires, "John, who hath required this at your hands?" You have establishments in America of your own ambitious creating. As you belong to the Seventh-day Adventist people, God has given you another work to do. You have not been called to do this work. Money and talent should not be diverted from the principal work for this time....
>
> The deceptive power of the enemy has led you to leave God's banner trailing in the dust while Dr. Kellogg has committed himself as working "undenominationally" in a work which has taken the money from a people who are decidedly a denominational people....

As Kellogg's involvements in Chicago grew in size and expense, the issue of finances became a sticking point. This leads to another area of easy confusion. Ellen White sometimes wrote comments about the work in Chicago which, taken in isolation, sound like absolute prohibition of certain lines of work. In other settings, though, she endorses the same kind of activity.

The key is understanding the time and circumstances. The statement above continues, and illustrates the sort of prioritized common sense that Ellen White was using in these matters:

In the working of the cause of God for this time the benevolent work should give special help to those who, through the presentation of truth at our camp meetings, are convicted and converted. They become the loyal subjects of the kingdom of God and unite with those who keep the commandments of God and have the faith of Jesus. They are to be laborers together with God as is represented in Isaiah fifty-eight. That chapter does not sustain you in the kind of work you are doing and in expending God's revenue on that class of people found in the slums. There we obtain the least results for labor put forth in true conversions and additions to strengthen the forces of workers together with God.

We must engage in the work of caring especially for those who have the moral courage to accept the truth, lose their situations in consequence, and are refused work to earn means to support their families....

They are not to be left without help and forced to work on the Sabbath... because the means that God designed for His loyal people are diverted into channels that help the most unworthy and disobedient and the transgressors of His law.... What is left for the poor saints who are placed in most discouraging circumstances for conscientiously obeying the truth? God has not vindicated your course for years, and I do not want you to continue in it till the bitter end. Shall the poor among God's people be left without any provision being made for them? Shall it be made as hard as possible for them to obtain means to live?...

The work has been hindered, the cause of God should have a different showing, far different, and who is to blame for this hindrance? You give heed to men not of our faith. You delight to show what you have done, and by a free use of money that was not yours to handle, in a way that God has not appointed, fields have been left barren of the very facilities that could have been furnished them.[12]

Inspired counsel can be confusing. Parts of that last quotation sound very clear-cut and definitive, but it's not a good idea to pretend that we can see more definition in her writings than the prophet herself could. She certainly saw no contradiction between that statement and this next one. If we do, we're seeing something wrong!

Constant work is to be done for the outcasts, but this work is not to be made all-absorbing. This class you have always with you. All the means must not be bound up in this work, for the highways have not yet received the message. There is work in the Lord's vineyard which must be done.[13]

Part of the frustration was that the dynamic Dr. Kellogg was a better fund raiser than the ministers. His tendency to use up the available money for his own projects created a great deal of stress. Ellen White, in particular—and even the church administrators who often came out on the short

---

12. *Manuscript Releases*, vol. 4, 429–432
13. *The Australian Years*, 397 (EGW Letter Letter 138, 1898)

end of the stick when working with the Doctor—didn't want to have to de-nounce him to the church. But he had no hesitancy in using his church connections to raise money that was often needed for other projects.

The Long, Sad Demise

By New Year's Day, 1900, the situation was critical. Of course, for the last nine years Ellen White had been far from the scene of Kellogg's work since she had been in New Zealand and Australia. Letters took six weeks to cross the Pacific, so being an active player in what was going on in Battle Creek had been difficult. But letters were the only thing going, so she sat down to write another one. This one was addressed to Elder G.A. Irwin, president of the General Conference:

> I see that your difficulties are becoming more settled and pronounced be-cause Dr. Kellogg refuses counsel and chooses to do the very things that God has told him not to do. But the Lord God Omnipotent reigneth. If Dr. Kellogg refuses to change his methods of labor, then the sure result will come....
>
> Seek to save Dr. Kellogg from himself. He is not heeding the counsel he should heed. He is not satisfied because the Lord has signified that the mission-ary work does not consist alone in the slum work in Chicago. That work, thought to be the great and important thing to be done, is a very defective and expensive work. It has absorbed the means, and has deprived our poverty-stricken foreign mission fields of the help God designed them to have. The use of means in what is called the medical missionary work needs most thorough investigation. Means have been consumed and will continue to be consumed in a work which is not the greatest or most important to be done in our world....
>
> The Lord has signified that the missionary, health-restorative gospel shall never be separated from the ministry of the word. The Lord Jesus has in His own example shown us the way in which His work is to be done in the restoration of suffering humanity.[14]

The most well known issue with Kellogg was the question of panthe-ism. Our purposes don't require a full review of that issue, so we can suffice by noting that it came to prominence with the publication of Kel-logg's book, *The Living Temple*, in 1902. The Sanitarium had been de-stroyed by fire in February, and funds were needed to rebuild. Kellogg suggested that he could make a donation of a recently completed book, have the Review print it at cost, and encourage the church members to sell it as a fundraising project. The idea seemed good, and got the General Conference go ahead.

---

14. *Manuscript Releases*, vol. 4, 427

But when a review committee read the book, there were concerns that it contained heretical teachings. Years of contention followed. What is of interest to us at the moment is a sermon given by Ellen White on Friday morning, April 3, 1903. The setting was an open meeting of the General Conference, well over a year after the writing of *Living Temple*.

Notice Ellen White's strong defense of Kellogg. Quite remarkable, really, when you consider that she was speaking of one who was clearly confused on the pantheism issue at the very least. And she was blunt, very blunt:

We'll begin with a comment we've seen before:

> After the meeting at Minneapolis, Dr. Kellogg was a converted man, and we all knew it. We could see the converting power of God working in his heart and life.
>
> But as the institution [the Sanitarium] has grown in popularity, there has been danger that the reason for which it was established would be lost sight of. Repeatedly I have given the instruction that was given to me—that this institution should not be conducted after the manner in which worldly medical institutions are conducted....
>
> It was the piety of the workers, not the largeness of the buildings, that was to bring conviction to hearts. Many souls have been converted; many wonderful cures have been wrought. The Lord stood by the side of Dr. Kellogg as he performed difficult operations. When the doctor was overwrought by taxing labor, God understood the situation, and He put His hand on Dr. Kellogg's hand as he operated, and through His power the operations were successful. ...
>
> God does not endorse the efforts put forth by different ones to make the work of Dr. Kellogg as hard as possible, in order to build themselves up. God gave the light on health reform, and those who rejected it rejected God. One and another who knew better said that it all came from Dr. Kellogg, and they made war upon him. This had a bad influence on the doctor. He put on the coat of irritation and retaliation. God did not want him to stand in the position of warfare, and He does not want you to stand there.
>
> [Some] have turned away from the Battle Creek Sanitarium.... because of something that the doctor had said or done that did not please them. This God did not approve. [15]

Thirteen months later, at a meeting in Berrien Springs, the last major effort was made to restore union between Dr. Kellogg and church administrators. In anticipation of the occasion, Ellen White wrote a letter to Elders Daniells and Prescott, two of the ministers Kellogg detested most:

> Yesterday a very strong impression came upon me that now is our time to save Dr. Kellogg. We must now work with determined effort. We must not pre-

15. *General Conference Bulletin*, April 6, 1903

scribe the precise steps he must take, but we must lay hold of the man himself, and let him see that the Spirit of God and the spirit of soul-saving are in us. Satan has worked to bind him up with himself, but shall we stand by, and make no effort to pull him away from Satan? Shall we not, in the name of the Lord, call for Dr. Kellogg to come to this meeting, not that we may make accusations against him, but that we may help him, and all of us draw with Christ?

Not one of us is above temptation. There is a work that Dr. Kellogg is educated to perform as no other man in our ranks can perform it; and if he will draw nigh to God, God will draw nigh to him. We are to draw with all our power, not making accusations, not prescribing what he must do, but letting him see that we are not willing that any should perish, but that every man should have that which Christ died to present to him—eternal life.

Is it not worth the trial? Satan is drawing him, but last night I saw a hand reached out to clasp his hand, and the words were spoken: "Let him take hold of My strength, that he may make peace with Me, and he shall make peace with Me. Satan is striving for the victory. I will help Dr. Kellogg to stand on vantage ground, and every soul who loves Me must work with Me. As he sees Me do, so must he do."[16]

The Lake Union Conference meeting of May 1904 was, by almost any measure that could be used, a total disaster. Recriminations flew from both sides, and events were shaped in such a way that Ellen White found herself trapped and unable to accomplish any of the things she wanted so much to see happen. From then on, it was all downhill.

In 1907, John Kellogg was disfellowshiped from the Battle Creek Tabernacle. He sent a secretary, but did not bother to attend himself.

True to her promise to his dying mother, Ellen White had done all she could to prevent his apostasy. Despite her best attempts, "God's physician"[17] had been lost to the cause.

We may be thankful for those who had the courage to throw out a lot of dirty bath water that really needed to go, but the suspicion remains that there may have been a baby or two that went along with it.

Why did it happen this way?

There's no need for complicated answers, when the normal ones of pride, selfishness, greed, and the occasional hurt feelings are more than enough. The great tragedy of the lost will always be how unnecessary it was, how easily things might have been different. It always has, and will always be, a sad story.

---

16. *Special Testimonies*, Series B, No. 2, 30

17. *S.P.S. Edwards—Memoirs of SDA Pioneers*, 41; *Spalding-Magan Collection*, 366

Chapter Eleven

Meanwhile, Down Under

S INCE John Kellogg's leadership never ushered in a great denomination-wide medical missionary revival encompassing the good works
called for in Isaiah fifty-eight and the blessings of the loud cry, we might
wonder if the whole thing was just his pet theory. Perhaps that particular
vision was misguided and unnecessary for the Lord's work.

Or perhaps it *was* needed, and simply set back to square one through
one or more human imperfections. How would one know? As suggested
back in chapter nine, a good way to judge would be to see whether or not
the prophet began working for a credible "Plan B" to fill the role.

At the end of the 1893 General Conference session, though, Ellen
White was nowhere to be seen, at least not from Battle Creek. If, on the
other hand, you happened to be in Kaeo, New Zealand, you would have
had better luck. It had been fifteen months since she had arrived in Australasia, and it would be another seven-and-a-half years before she put
foot on American soil again.

Our search, then, for a "Plan B" takes us first to the shores of Australia
and New Zealand. How much interest, if any, did Ellen White manifest in
this humanitarian/medical type of ministry while developing the fledg-
ling church in the South Pacific?

The answer, it turns out, is "a great deal of interest."

Not only did she promote that kind of work, but she established a
context for it that remains of interest to us today, because the work Ellen
White oversaw there in its development was intended to serve as a
model for the rest of the world.

The best known of the elements that might be included in this specific purpose is Avondale College:

> The Avondale school was established, not to be like the schools of the world, but, as God revealed, to be a pattern school.[1]

> The light which has been given me regarding the work of the Avondale school is that we must not pattern after the similitude of any school which has already been established.[2]

> The school in Avondale is to be a pattern for other schools which shall be established among our people.[3]

But there are also indications of a broader effort to develop a "pattern" for more than just the educational work:

> It is [God's] purpose that there shall be a true pattern in Australia—a sample of how other fields shall be worked. The work should be symmetrical, and a living witness for the truth.[4]

That comment about symmetry... that's important. The symmetry of the work back in the States was suffering as a result of Kellogg's megalomania. In fact, to a large extent it was Kellogg's ability to attract and expend funds that made the work in Australasia so extremely difficult. Symmetry is key. But what aspects of the work were to be held in this symmetrical relationship? The clearest answer comes from W.C. White:

> It has been presented to Mother that Australasia is a field in which we will do a model work, a work that will show to our friends and brethren in other lands how the evangelistic work and the medical work should be carried forward in perfect agreement, in perfect harmony, blended together.[5]

Given Ellen White's concerns with Kellogg's imbalance, and the intention to create a model of "perfect harmony" between the evangelistic and the medical work, the latter half of the 1890s provides an excellent study of similarities and contrasts between Battle Creek and Australia. It seems as though the prophet *did* have a "Plan B."

Laying the Groundwork

There are a host of "data points" that could be produced in support of this "Plan B" idea. Perhaps the best place to start is the moment

---

1. *Counsels to Parents, Teachers, and Students*, 349
2. *Manuscript Releases*, vol. 8, 150
3. *Manuscript Releases*, vol. 8, 74
4. *General Conference Daily Bulletin*, March 2, 1899
5. Letter, W.C. White to Dr. F.T. Lamb, August 23, 1899, WCW Book 13, 512 (quoted in Bert Haloviak, *Ellen White and the Australasian Ministers, 1893 to 1901*, 5)

when Ellen White seemed to sense the magnitude of what is really a very simple plan. On the 6th of August, 1894, she wrote to her son, Willie, describing one of those "Ah ha!" moments when an idea strikes home with extra clarity:

> Yesterday it all opened before me that in this very line of hospitality, I have been repeatedly shown that we can unite the people with us, and can have twofold influence over them. This was unfolded before me in the first experience in this work, many years back, and we have ever linked our interest with humanity.[6]

Hospitality is not a highly technical theological term, and some people might see great ambiguity in this statement. But some ideas don't require rocket scientists to appreciate their value.

It would be wrong to make it look like this was the first time Ellen White had considered such matters. After all, those statements that Kellogg had read at the 1893 General Conference were all from her pen.

But Ellen White was not the only one thinking such thoughts, since items like this next selection had been running in the *Bible Echo* for a number of months already:

> Our people who are engaging in Christian Help work of various kinds in America are meeting with great encouragement. They find a vast field of labour spread out before them, and they find that their efforts to help the poor and suffering are amply repaid. One who is prominently connected with this line of work writes thus of a visit to one of the cities where a band of workers is located. He says:
>
> "We have a mission Sabbath-school already in Chicago, started three weeks ago with twenty pupils. The next week we had twenty-two, the next forty-five, and at the rate it is increasing, in a month we shall have two hundred children. Our workers go out and gather up children that are found in squalor or fighting on the streets, and bring them into our school and hold them in the most respectful quietness and good behaviour by telling them simple Bible stories, and singing gospel songs.
>
> "I started out with Sister Louise last Sunday morning to visit some of the subjects for the purpose of taking a few photographs to throw upon the screen in talking about this work and to interest people in it. I had no sooner turned the corner than a little girl shouted at the top of her voice, 'O here is Sister Louise!' and ran and threw her arms about her and expressed the greatest delight at seeing her. Her cry attracted others, and soon children were running from every direction, shouting, 'Sister Louise,' and in a few minutes there was such a crowd I had to go out into the middle of the street. They fairly pulled and pushed her

---

6. Letter, Ellen White to W.C. White, August 6, 1894, W135, 1894 (quoted in Bert Haloviak, *Ellen White and the Australasian Ministers, 1893 to 1901*, 17)

along the street, there was such a mob of them. They filled up the sidewalk away out into the street, and before we had gone a block there were more than fifty children in all, all worshiping Sister Louise. I felt very small and insignificant beside 'Queen' Louise.

"Sister Louise had been in their homes and nursed them when they were sick and given up to die, some of them; had nursed their mothers and cared for them, had shown them how to clean up their homes and make them brighter; had given them little picture cards and flowers, and had said kind words to them, and like their parents they were ready to go down on their knees to her. It is no trouble for any of our nurses to gather any number of children together for a Sabbath-school, and no trouble to keep them absolutely quiet, even though they are brought in from the very lowest haunts of vice in the city. It is perfectly wonderful what power there is in the influence of medical missionary work."[7]

Notice, however, that the story is from America. This was a Kellogg export item, but the Australians saw value in the picture. It was something they wanted.

Getting Started

On Sabbath afternoon, May 12 [1894], a special meeting of the North Fitzroy church was held to consider the Christian Help work. Bro. Daniells conducted the meeting, and cited his hearers to the example of Christ, who "went about doing good," ministering to the suffering body as well as to the sin-sick soul. Bro. Semmens, who has had considerable experience in this work in America, told how the work is done there. Sister Ingels gave some examples of practical Christian work in Prahran.

The objects of the Christian Help Bands are, 1. To minister to the sick; 2. To provide for the needy; 3. To comfort the distressed; 4. To uplift the fallen; 5. To lead to Christ the unconverted. This work has been entered upon heartily in North Fitzroy. Between fifty and sixty persons have enrolled their names as volunteers. Five bands of ten persons each (including the leader) have been organized, and have commenced work. Already a large number of needy cases have been found, and there are calls for food, clothing, and bedding. Some of these wants have been met, and others will be promptly.

A committee was appointed to solicit contributions, and encouraging offers of help have been received, including a donation of two guineas from a member of the Fitzroy city council.

We look for good results.[8]

Attentive readers will have spotted the reference to our friend, A.W. Semmens. He had by this time finished his nursing course and returned

---

7. *Bible Echo*, March 18, 1894
8. *Bible Echo*, May 28, 1894

to Australia. And that just happened to put him in the right place at the right time so that his story provides a particularly good illustration of what working in "perfect harmony" was all about. It also put him on the hot seat: he was the one who was supposed to show everyone else how to achieve the "good results" they were all looking for.

Unfortunately, the work in Australasia would be hampered by financial shortages for years to come. It seemed as though they were always a dollar short of those good results they wanted. In the early months of 1893, Australia's banking system had crashed, life savings were lost, and bad times were at hand. Ellen White noted this in the *Review*:

> The failure of banks and the financial pressure make hard times everywhere in this country. It is difficult for students to obtain money to defray their expenses at school, or for our brethren to build even the most humble places of worship. We hear of people starving to death in the cities, and nearly every day persons come to our door begging for something to eat. They are never turned away....
>
> O how thankful I shall be when we can see the work going with power, and many souls compelled to come in from the highways and hedges because of the overwhelming evidence of the truth that the Lord impresses upon the human heart."[9]

Perhaps as a blessing in disguise, the great need of the people provided the opening God's workers needed to reach them. The resulting use of practical service as an evangelistic approach was not new to Ellen White, but she certainly emphasized it during her time in Australasia more than she ever had before:

> We cannot with our wills sway back the wave of poverty which is sweeping over this country; but just as far as the Lord shall provide us with means, we shall break every yoke, and let the oppressed go free.[10]

But Does It Work?

The scrutiny of the Christian Help work was pretty intense; it wasn't more than a month-and-a-half before the first status report on the new program was published. Expectations were high:

> One branch of the work just being entered upon here, is that of the Christian Help Band. Brother Semmens has done good service in this line, and the North Fitzroy church is doing considerable in response to his labors. So quickly have the efforts of the church in this direction been recognized, that already members of the city council have met with the band to give counsel in planning its work.

9. *Review and Herald* , May 29, 1894
10. *Manuscript Releases*, vol. 16, 69

Substantial help is also promised from those outside of our people who desire to see such work go on, as they recognize in it the fruits of practical Christianity.

Other bands will soon be organized in the various suburbs where our people reside. We look for this kind of work shortly to do as much or more for the propagation of the message of truth for these days as the regular preaching of the word.[11]

And the attention didn't let up. This Christian Help work concept had attained significant stature in the church's collective mindset. Thankfully, the news was good:

Some five months ago the Christian Help work was started under the leadership of brother Semmens. Seven bands were organized. The locality around the Echo office for some distance was divided into districts, with one band to each. Each district had two lady visitors, whose duty it was to make investigation and determine what help should be given to the destitute cases reported. Through this means many of the poor and needy have had their wants relieved and the gospel preached unto them.

During the past six months there has been a greater interest manifested in this church in the missionary meetings than for years past, and the attendance has been increased fourfold.[12]

And to fill out the picture a bit more, here two more assessments of the situation. It should be pointed out that Mrs. Semmens was also a trained nurse, and was working closely with her husband:

I am more and more satisfied that the plans on which Elder Corliss is endeavoring to work, are in harmony with Apostolic methods. We have been very much encouraged by the growth in wisdom and in efficiency of the young men who are working with him, and we are much pleased with the results of their labors. There is now such a demand for Bible readings upon the part of the people to whom we have been distributing the printed sermons that we shall arrange to release Brethren Semmens and Pallant from the work of distribution, that they may spend their entire energies in holding readings. They are now carrying six or eight readings each a week.[13]

For some months they [A.W. Semmens and his wife, Emma] have been laboring in Sydney and its suburbs. He combines the work of a colporteur-evangelist and a missionary-nurse, and his labors are very effective. He is becoming one of the best Bible workers we have, and I think he is being much benefited by the course of instruction [in how to give "Bible Readings"] he is receiving from Elder Corliss.[14]

11. J.O. Corliss, *Review and Herald*, July 24, 1894

12. Anna L. Ingels, *Review and Herald*, December 4, 1894

13. W.C. White to O.A. Olsen, August 20, 1895, WCW Bk 8, pp 113-14. (quoted in Bert Haloviak, *Ellen White and the Australasian Ministers, 1893 to 1901*, 35)

This is the sort of news we like. Arthur and Emma Semmens were great additions to the church's working force, and they had won the respect of both administrators and members. What's more, even while learning how to give Bible Readings, they were effectively teaching others how to go about this new Christian Help work approach. One such student was the Elder Corliss mentioned here, whom we'll see again. Things were going well. Everyone should be living happily ever after.

Behind the Scenes

Not unexpectedly, there was more going on than met the casual eye. The idea of a new approach to the medical work was certain to raise a few eyebrows, if not a few tempers. One who had concerns was Dr. Kellogg. And that gave rise to nearly "equal and opposite" concerns on the hearts of others. A good illustration of this is a letter from W.C. White to Elder A.G. Daniells:

> I think I will state briefly a few principles which have been burned in to my memory by our experiences in America, and the discussions that have arisen over them; also by the messages of counsel that we have received from time to time from the Lord.
>
> We have been taught by the example of Christ, and by the Testimonies that have been repeatedly given to our brethren in the ministry, and to the physicians and managers of the Battle Creek Sanitarium and the Health Retreat, that the work of the gospel minister and of the physician should be combined; that the minister should have a care for the physical prosperity of his flock, that the physician should be a true minister of Christ, laboring for the health of the soul as well as for the body. With this instruction in view I have felt that our brethren made a grave mistake when they put a check upon our ministers from teaching health reform, and called for specialists to do that work.[15] It would have been better if the specialists had been employed to teach the ministers, so that their work with the people would have been more effective.
>
> I have felt that it was just as grave an error for Dr. Kellogg to make everything of the health work, and belittle the evangelistic work, as he virtually does by magnifying the one so far above the other. I have felt that his criticisms were largely out of place regarding the work of Brother Semmens during the past two years, because in treating the matter as though Semmens was not fulfilling his

---

14. Letter, W.C. White to Elder Robert Hare, November 20, 1896 (quoted in Bert Haloviak, *Ellen White and the Australasian Ministers, 1893 to 1901*, 30)
15. A reference to the formation of the largely independent Medical Missionary and Benevolent Association perhaps? This was done in 1893, and the records of those proceedings were left out of the *General Conference Daily Bulletin* along with Kellogg's talks. That information was to be published in a second *Extra* edition of the *Medical Missionary*. See page 64. This author has never seen a copy and does not know whether or not it was ever printed.

mission while dividing his time between evangelical and nursing work, he virtu-
ally says that persons trained in the health work must make that their exclusive
business; and thus he does just what the [General] Conference did in putting
asunder that which God has joined together.[16]

It's Not Exactly What We Had In Mind...

But part of what makes the Semmens' story interesting is that they
weren't entirely happy with their job. We can get a look behind the
scenes through a letter written by W.C. White to the Executive Committ-
tee of the Australasian Union Conference:

> You may be familiar with the circumstance which attended the coming back
> to Australia of Brother and Sister Semmens, and with the fact that they have al-
> ways looked forward to the time when they should be principally engaged caring
> for the sick.

Notice what Brother and Sister Semmens wanted to do. That is, after
all, what they had been trained to do in the Nursing course at Battle
Creek.... Well, a lot of people have wanted a change in their first job assignment, so this isn't particularly earthshaking. What makes it more interesting is what Willie White goes on to say:

> Dr Kellogg has never been able to understand why our Conferences should
> not employ them to work in the interests of the sick and suffering, and to in-
> struct our people in the principles of healthful living, the same as many workers
> trained at the Sanitarium are employed by the American Conferences. He has
> been very much dissatisfied that Brother Semmens was so largely employed in
> evangelistic work....

It seems there was a difference of opinion between the Australian
brethren and Doctor Kellogg, and it's important for us to understand it.
Willie continues:

> We have been anxious to make a beginning in some line of work that would
> be largely self-supporting, and that would provide an opportunity for the sick
> among us to have rational treatment, and that would also open the way for the
> training of Christian Help workers....

Willie's goals are, shall we say, proportioned differently than Dr. Kellogg might have expressed them. There is nothing in the Australasian
version that Kellogg would utterly reject, nor anything in his version that
W.C. White and his colleagues would consider heretical. The difference is
balance: the Australasian formulation minimizes expense by striving for

---

16. W.C. White to A.G. Daniells, June 17, 1896. WCW Bk. 10, pp. 81-2. (quoted in Bert Haloviak, *Route to the Ordination of Women in the Seventh-day Adventist Church: Two Paths*, 30)

self-support, while providing a needed service (rational treatment) to church members. At the same time, the plan is to train those members that they are recipients of the Lord's blessings only so that they may be of service to others.

Kellogg's approach tended to absorb the finances of the church (though he would often argue that point) and expend them in a less dis-criminating and controlled manner, forgetting the difference between the "household of faith" and the rest of the world. From what we've covered in earlier chapters, it's easy to see how Kellogg's loss of confi-dence in those who were, in fact, making "war upon him" could have led to such a result.

But Elder White's letter continues:

> From our experience with the health work, and health institutions in Amer-ica, and from the testimonies sent to the managers and physicians at the Sani-tariums, during the last twenty-five years, our brethren came to the unanimous opinion, that it was right, and essential to the highest success of the health work, that our health institutions should be sustained, and directed by the body, acting through properly appointed committees. And that all physicians and nurses should be as fully under the supervision of the general body, as are the ministers and Bible workers....

Willie puts this down as a strongly held conviction. What's more, he attributes the success that they had had in their work to this very policy:

> It is the recognition of these principles, that has led to the rapid growth of our health institutions, and our Medical Mission work in its various branches [in Australia and New Zealand], during the last seven years.[17]

Elder White's comments here are important. His position is that the success of the medical work in Australasia was due to the relationship it maintained to the more specifically "evangelistic" element of the church's work. This may sound simple, maybe even obvious, but conflict was close at hand. Willie had said that the denominationally affiliated health insti-tutions needed to be "directed by the body."

The Question of "Supervision"

Without implying anything more than necessary, it might safely be said that most people who have tried the experiment would agree that telling a bunch of physicians what they have to do is not an easy job.

---

17. Letter, W.C. White, August 11, 1896. WCW Book 10, 328 (quoted in Bert Haloviak, *Ellen White and the Australasian Ministers, 1893 to 1901*, 29–30)

Control of the medical work by unqualified and unsupportive ministers is exactly what Kellogg was opposed to back in the United States. And, given the ministers "tardy work in health reform," it's hard to deny that he had a point.

Were the ministers of Australia and New Zealand more converted than the ministers in America? Where the physicians more subservient than their counterparts in Battle Creek? Such analysis is beyond human computation, and should we undertake it, we would no doubt fail to comprehend all that should go into the case. Perhaps we are best advised to simply acknowledge that there appears to have been enough give and take, enough commonality of purpose, sufficient faithfulness to the teachings of the other group, and enough mutual trust to allow these two groups to unite their sacred callings in a way that furthered both and produced the added benefit of inspiring the laity of the church to take up and vastly multiply the simpler tasks of both spiritual and medical service.

For emphasis sake, let's itemize and expand this last sentence:

1. In Australasia, members of both the ministerial and the medical forces of the church were willing to live and let live, at least enough to enable them to cooperate. Given the basic nature of human interactions, it's safe to say that one side or the other got the short end of the stick now and then. Apparently the scoring on this point was not so one-sided as to lead to rupture.

2. Both groups evidently saw value in the other group's efforts that contributed to their own ultimate goal: the physicians acknowledged the primary importance of the spiritual life, and the ministers valued the unrivaled influence of practical health and humanitarian service.

3. Disrespect shown to the work and tenets of a prospective partner is foolish. If you want the other guy to respect your theology, don't be dismissive of his physiology, and vice versa. This is the basic lack that proved to be the "deal breaker" in the church's relationship with Kellogg. First, a significant percent of the ministers ignored or opposed Kellogg's health teachings; then Kellogg returned the favor as regards their core theological positions. Which was worse? We might lean toward finding greater fault with doctrinal heresy, but remember that Ellen White said, "God gave the light on health reform, and those who rejected it rejected God." So... which is worse?

4. All of the above resulted in at least enough trust to keep the ball rolling. Like so many of the Lord's arrangements, this looks to be a self-reinforcing re-iterative working relationship. Steps one through

three can only be strengthened by each previous episode of unviolated trust.

5. Perhaps the greatest pay-off is the influence that extends beyond the immediate circle of either group. When the evangelical and medical workers are united, their cumulative influence is felt by the wider membership of the church. Maybe this is why Ellen White so frequently wrote comments such as these:

> How shall we reveal Christ? I know of no better way... than to take hold of the medical missionary work in connection with the ministry.[18]

> Successful evangelistic work can be done in connection with medical missionary work. It is as these lines of work are united that we may expect to gather the most precious fruit for the Lord.[19]

> The education of students in medical missionary lines is not complete unless they are trained to work in connection with the church and the ministry.[20]

"God Was Training Us"

It's pleasant to note that, like many other once-frustrated Christians, Arthur and Emma Semmens ended up being thankful for the experience which had troubled them at the time. He later said:

> Our first work began in the Australasian Bible School, located at St. Kilda, Victoria. Here we had many varied experiences.... Later we labored in tent and Bible work in Sydney, under the direction of J.O. Corliss, doing much work among the sick. We did not then understand why we could not enter upon strictly medical work; we know now. God was training us, that we should not be one-sided workers, but have an all-around experience.[21]

So... what did this approach to Medical-Evangelism actually look like? What were they doing? One of the more detailed descriptions is of the work carried on at the "Helping Hand Mission" in Melbourne. This "Mission Evangelist's report" covers one year's work:

> There have been 360 meetings held with a gross attendance of 6,000, or an average of nearly twenty per meeting. Thirty open air meetings have been held, forty prayer meetings, and 233 Bible studies, with an average attendance of six. In these meetings sixty-six men have made a profession of conversion. Of these a goodly number are, to our knowledge, standing well.

---

18. *Medical Ministry*, 319
19. *Medical Ministry*, 26
20. *Counsels on Health*, 557
21. *General Conference Bulletin*, June 2, 1909, 284

Homes have been found for four old men and one baby girl. Fifty-eight men have been found billets, and medical attendance and treatments have been secured or provided for in 800 instances. Visits have been paid to the gaol [jail], hospital, and other institutions, and numerous visits made to the docks and slums. Very many of our principal merchants have been called upon and, brought into touch and hearty sympathy with our work.

One man who has experienced the new birth this year says: "Nine months ago I was a drunkard, my wife had left me, I was hopeless. Today I am a Christian, a sober man, and have my home restored." Another says: "I have learned to trust the Lord this year." Another's testimony is: "Twelve months ago I was friendless in Melbourne, today I have friends, work, and hope."[22]

Now this report was from Melbourne, but there were also "Helping Hand" Missions in Adelaide, Perth, and North Fitzroy. Closely related to this last establishment was the "Helping Hand Wood Yard," where men could work in a firewood business to pay for food and lodging. In addition, a "Hydropathic Institute" was operated in Adelaide, and two "Health Homes" in Perth and Summer Hill.

The published reports about these institutions indicate that they were pretty much "standard" Sanitarium-type operations that did a fair amount of free and reduced-cost charity work. Perhaps the most significant difference between these institutions and their American counterparts was that ephemeral quality of "spirit." With a focus on soul winning, and without the sense of alienation from the ministerial and evangelistic work of the church, these institutions were seen as key assets in the denomination's overall game plan.

This may be seen in a presentation given by Dr. Edward Caro in 1899:

In considering the work to be done here in Australia, we see before us a great destiny. While talking with Sister White recently about this matter she made the following remark, "The medical work in Australia is destined to do more in this field than it has done even in America." Is it possible that we shall have such gigantic institutions and piles of buildings as they have? No; we have been told that this is not the best way to carry it forward.

The remark was also made in that conversation that the medical work here in Australia is to be an example of what the work should be. In what respect? I ask. Evidently in the... harmonious relations existing between the medical work and the other branches of the third angel's message.

22. *Bible Echo*, February 26, 1900, 142

In Newcastle we have tried the experiment of uniting our evangelistic and medical missionary work, and now, Brother Starr, what has been the result, has it been successful or otherwise?

Elder Starr: "Splendid. The people themselves are unwilling that there should be a separation...."

[I have never] seen a community in which our peculiar views had been fully presented where there was less prejudice existing. This is as God would have it. Our work is not to create prejudice but to disarm it. We want nurses who are Bible workers; and we want Bible workers and canvassers who are nurses.[23]

Caro's final sentence is key. This was at the heart of the difference between American medical missionary work under Kellogg and the Australasian model that was being developed as a "pattern" for the world church. Truth be told, it was also the difference between American *ministerial* work and the Australasian model.

But Not Without Challenges...

Now, to be honest, the difficulty with looking at the medical missionary work done in Australia while Ellen White was there is that, while there were a lot of really exciting plans that got written up and tried, often the actual implementation was a bit lack-luster. All of the institutions and workers mentioned here were really struggling financially through this whole time period. Quite a few employees ended up using a fair amount of their own money to try and carry on. Some would call that foolish; others would call it "sacrifice."

With the intention of trying to secure the needed funding for these projects as one of his goals, W.C. White made a visit back to the States. Writing to the church at large through the pages of the *Review* in 1897, he gave a status report and made a plea for support:

About a year ago Brother A.W. Semmens, in accordance with the counsel and advice of his brethren, opened a health home in Ashfield, in a seven-room cottage. There was very little with which to start this work except our knowledge that it was a work greatly needed, and the confidence of the people secured by Brother Semmens during two years of labor as a Bible worker and missionary nurse....

Our brethren in New South Wales highly appreciate the work done at the health home, and that accomplished by Brother and Sister Semmens in giving them instruction in practical hygiene and in Christian Help work in their churches and their homes. Our people in the other colonies, seeing what a good work has been accomplished amid great difficulties, have taken courage, and are pleading for physicians and nurses in Queensland, New Zealand, and Victoria.

23. *Australasian Union Conference Record*, July 2, 1899

We sincerely believe that the time has fully come for us to make an advance move, and establish the medical missionary work in the colonies upon a broad and practical basis. There are physicians ready to go. There are trained nurses from the colonies ready to return.... waiting for funds with which to pay traveling expenses. Who will help?

There are seven trained workers, perhaps nine, ready to go during the next three months. They have used all their earnings in getting a thorough education. They can earn their way in the colonies, and be of inestimable service as helpers there, but ten thousand miles of travel over land and sea lie between them and their field, and by the most economical methods of travel the journey will cost $125 each. Who will help?

Are there not nine persons among those who read this who would esteem it a privilege to pay the passage of one of these trained workers to his field of labor? Are there not those who read this who could give us a thousand dollars each to purchase bath appliances for Brisbane, Christchurch, and Melbourne?...

I need not apologize for these requests, for you know of the financial distress in Australia, and of the limited resources of our brethren there. At one time our situation was presented to my mother in this way: She saw our Australasian brethren standing on a precipice, and across the deep water our American brethren on the cliffs. We in Australasia were asking for help, and our American brethren were reaching out their arms, ready to respond, but there was the separating sea, and the question was asked, "How can we make connection?"

I have hoped that my visit to the States would help to make the connection. Workers have been chosen, and arrangements made; now we ask you to do what you can to make effective these arrangements, so that the blessed and glorious work of the missionary nurse and the medical missionary may be felt in each one of our seven Australasian colonies.[24]

This proved to be a persistent issue. The church in America tended to be slow—or just plain resistant—to see the greater need and opportunity in Australasia at the time. Funds which could have been well used to establish the church down under were, time after time, diverted to other projects. Ellen White was not pleased, and since private letters to key people (most notably, J.H. Kellogg) hadn't accomplished her goal, she wrote to the 1899 General Conference Session:

When the General Conference sent me and my helpers to Australia, our people should have understood the situation, and should have provided us with means and facilities for establishing the work in this country....

Here we are in this new world, with only a very few churches, mostly composed of poor people, who are not prepared to give financial aid to the work.

---

24. *Review and Herald*, June 22, 1897, 397

How can we meet the requirements in establishing churches, schools, and conferences, and in building up the medical missionary work? We have been straining every nerve to meet the most pressing demands of the work just now.... Help must be furnished for the erection of a house of worship... at Brisbane, and... at Newcastle. The Health Food Company must have help.... The school is struggling to provide sufficient accommodation for its students for another term. And there is the work of helping the poor, lifting up the bowed down and oppressed, clothing the naked, and feeding the hungry, all of whom are just as precious in the sight of the Lord as the same class in America. So the work that we desire to do in erecting our hospital is still undone. Directions have come from Battle Creek to push forward the medical missionary work, to start a health institution, to put this work in the forefront. But we can not make brick without straw....

While we have been wading through difficulties, and constantly handicapped for want of means, large institutions in America are continually adding to their already abundant facilities. They are absorbing donations that are sorely needed in missionary fields, and are expending means in lines of work that will not accomplish one hundredth part of what might be accomplished with the same means and facilities in this country....

Again the word of the Lord came to me, saying: "I have spared your life to do my work; and wherever I send you, go, and I will send my angel with you. In no case should you be feeble in your request for the advantage of means. Wherever I send you, go, and speak my words. I will be thy mind, I will be thy judgment. All the advantages are mine. The means and facilities are mine, and there should be no withholding. But selfishness, a desire to control, has kept the advantages in one place, so that everything is overbalanced. Call for the means God designed you to have long ago. Hold up my banner. Give honor to no human instrumentality, but to God, that my name may be a praise in the earth. The Lord, he is God, and before him there is no other. My work in Australasia has been greatly hindered. Money has been used unwisely in America, in the great centers, so that there is distress for means to build up the work in new places. But go not forth in hesitancy. I will be with you. Ask of my people the means that should have gone to advance the work in the Australasian field, the new world to which I have sent you."[25]

And there is much more that might be quoted.

The hard thing in all this is that Ellen White (on God's behalf) was calling for self-denial on both a personal and an institutional basis. Giving a personal offering is hard enough, but anyone who has ever run an institution knows that there is *never* any "extra" money sitting around. Ellen White's frequent calls for funding to Australasia *had* to be getting on some people's nerves. Self-sacrifice can do that.

---

25. *General Conference Daily Bulletin*, March 2, 1899

But this also came to be a real challenge to personal faith in the spirit of prophecy. Requirements that cross our wishes always do. And what has been said of cultures may also be said of individuals and institutions: we tend to create a theology that justifies what we want to do.

By the end of the 1890s, this test was coming very pointedly to John Harvey Kellogg. Steeled against cooperation with those who had opposed him, determined to earn a name for himself, he continued his self-appointed task of building his own "great Babylon" in Battle Creek and Chicago.

The Building in Chicago

Nearly the same time as she was writing her letter to the General Conference just quoted, Ellen White was also writing directly to Dr. Kellogg concerning a particularly egregious example of needless expense which she had seen in vision:

> I was shown a large building in Chicago, which, in its erection and equipment, cost a large amount of money. And I was shown the error of investing means in any such buildings in our cities.
>
> At the time that I saw this representation, scenes that would soon take place in Chicago, and other large cities also, passed before me. As wickedness increased, and the protecting power of God was withdrawn, there were destructive winds and tempests; buildings were destroyed by fire and shaken down by earthquakes. I saw the expensive building above referred to fall, with many others.[26]

The full story of this vision, and of this building, must wait till a later chapter. It was significant in 1899, and remains so today, but more pieces of the puzzle must be put in place before we will be able to see the whole picture.

---

26. *Paulson Collection*, 50

Chapter Twelve

Paying the Bills

ONE of the harsher realities of the Lord's work is that it often costs money. A sub-set of that whole discussion is the question of the support of the ministry and the use of tithe. Generally, it's a simple idea, but as has often been said, "the devil is in the details." Those who have wrestled with the details of these issues know that "simple" can become "complicated" rather quickly.

So it was in the 1890s, and we find that—along with a maturing concept of the role of ministers—there was a maturing concept of the purpose and use of the tithe. Writing to A.G. Daniells in 1897, Ellen White put it this way:

> I send you this morning a letter written for America,[1] and sent there yesterday morning, which will show you how I regard the tithe money being used for other purposes. This is the Lord's special revenue fund, for a special purpose. I have never so fully understood this matter as I now understand it. Having had questions directed here to me to answer, I have had special instruction from the Lord that the tithe is for a special purpose, consecrated to God to sustain those who minister in the sacred work as the Lord's chosen, to do His work not only in sermonizing but in ministering. They should understand all that this comprehends.[2]

So... we "should understand all that this comprehends." But how do we do that? Where do we look for that understanding?

---

1. This is likely the material now contained in *Special Testimonies*, Series A, #10, 16–25; another possibility is the letter to W.C. White (who was then in America) found in *Manuscript Releases*, vol. 21, 183–187
2. *Manuscript Releases*, vol. 13, 281

It turns out that one interesting case history—used by A.G. Daniells to explain the Australasian approach to integrating ministerial and medical work—was that of our medical missionary friend, A.W. Semmens.

In 1901 the whole General Conference structure was re-organized with the addition of Union Conferences, and Elder A.G. Daniells was chosen as Chairman of an expanded General Conference Committee. Daniells was one of the leading participants in that General Conference session. His report of the experimental Australasian Union Conference that had been established a few years before, and of which he had been the president, exerted a strong influence on the work of re-organizing the whole denomination. Here's a part of what he had to say:

> Our medical work [in Australasia] stands in the same relation to the evangel-ical work and organizations that all the rest of the work does. We have no sepa-rate medical organization.... That is a part of our evangelical work; and the lead-ing physician, or physicians, are members of our Union Conference Committee, and they hold licenses to preach the gospel, and we encourage them to be minis-ters of Jesus Christ as well as physicians. We foster the medical work the same as we do anything else.

This raised a question in the mind of one of the delegates; he wanted to know, "Do any of the medical workers receive any support from the tithes?" Here's Elder Daniells' response:

> Yes, when they need it. When we first started out, the first man that came to us was Brother A.W. Semmens, a nurse who graduated from the Battle Creek Sanitarium. When he came out there, I did not know what to do, to get him started in the medical work. Some of our brethren had a little more light, and they said, "Let us make him a preacher and a medical worker combined; let us have him work in the churches, and tell the brethren of the gospel of health, and let us help support him from the tithes of the Conference."
>
> So we gave Brother Semmens some money from the tithes, and we said, "He shall have his living now, and we want him to teach the principles of health and temperance, and of the gospel in all its branches, doing what he can to educate the people in all these things. And so he went right along, like all our Conference laborers, making a report of his receipts, and then the Conference paid him what they ought to pay him to make a fair living."[3]

This was a new level of integration for the medical work, and a devel-opment that must have perplexed many administrators. Because of this lack of comprehension, Ellen White felt a need to clearly lay out her posi-

---

3. *General Conference Bulletin*, April 7, 1901, 91–92

tion on the topic. In fact, she went well beyond the position Daniells had described. Writing four days after Daniells made his comments, she said:

> In the night season I am laboring earnestly with persons who do not seem to understand that in the providence of God the medical missionary work is to be as the right hand of the body. Some utterly fail to realize the importance of missionaries being also medical missionaries. A gospel minister will be twice as successful in his work if he understands how to treat disease.
>
> Continually increasing light has been given me on this subject. Some, who do not see the advantage of educating the youth to be physicians both of the mind and of the body, say that the tithe should not be used to support medical missionaries, who devote their time to treating the sick.
>
> In response to such statements as these, I am instructed to say that the mind must not become so narrowed down that it cannot take in the truth of the situation. A minister of the gospel, who is also a medical missionary, who through Christ can cure physical ailments as well as minister in spiritual things, is a much more efficient worker than one who cannot do this. His work as a minister of the gospel is much more complete.
>
> For many years I have been gathering rays of divine light on this subject. Let those who are being educated for the ministry receive an education in medical missionary lines. It is of great advantage to the minister of the gospel who expects to go to foreign fields that he should have a knowledge of surgery, that in cases of necessity he will know how to handle medical instruments. This knowledge will open doors for the presentation of the truth to the higher classes, as well as to the most lowly.[4]

What she called for is not so much a matter of paying medical missionaries from the tithe, as it is a matter of re-tooling our whole concept of ministry. This is putting the full flesh on her frequent calls for an "all-round education" in ways that few would be prepared to seriously advocate.

But she *was* serious.

As if to underscore what she had written, she stood up the next day and told the delegates at the 1901 General Conference:

> I wish to tell you that soon there will be no work done in ministerial lines but medical missionary work. The work of a minister is to minister. Our ministers are to work on the gospel plan of ministering....
>
> Had you carried the work forward in the lines in which God intended you to, had you done medical missionary work, trying to heal soul and body, you would have seen hundreds and thousands coming into the truth....

4. *Manuscript Releases*, vol. 14, 269

You will never be ministers after the gospel order till you show a decided interest in medical missionary work, the gospel of healing and blessing and strengthen-
ing. Come up to the help of the Lord, to the help of the Lord against the mighty
powers of darkness, that it be not said of you, "Curse ye Meroz, curse ye bitterly
the inhabitants thereof; because they came not to the help of the Lord."[5]

Stop and digest those paragraphs. Some may disparage the significance of the comments on account of the word "soon" needing to be
stretched enough to accommodate a century and more. But might not
that delay actually be the result of the church having so few "ministers
after the gospel order" that the "hundreds and thousands" never did
"come into the truth"? The pointed question remains today: who has—
and who has not—"come up to the help of the Lord"?

She had written much the same thing three years earlier:

Christ attaches great importance to the work of the ministry; but this does not
mean preaching merely. It means personal effort also. The Saviour of the world devoted more time and labor to healing the sick than to preaching. His last injunc-
tion to his apostles, his representatives upon earth, was to lay hands on the sick,
that they might recover. And when the Master shall come again, he will commend
those who have visited the sick, and relieved the necessities of the afflicted. "Well
done, good and faithful servant," he will say; "enter thou into the joy of thy Lord."[6]

But Manpower Isn't the Only Expense...

If there is one thing that Dr. Kellogg had demonstrated—to Ellen
White's dismay—it was that humanitarian programs can be expensive.
But isn't that true no matter who runs them? With all the potential scope
of medical missionary work, how could anyone control the expenses?

Actually, in Ellen White's thinking, four primary factors were to combine to keep the financial burden manageable. We can summarize these
as follows:

1. Attend to specific, "high-priority" obligations before spending resources on less pressing responsibilities.
2. Recognize many obligations as individual responsibilities so as to prevent them from becoming all-absorbing, "institutionalized" matters.
3. Maintain balance and symmetry within the whole of the Lord's work.
4. Operate with appropriate funding constraints.

Unfortunately, Dr. Kellogg had violated every one of these principles,
because in one way or another they interfered with his desire to "seek

5. *General Conference Bulletin*, April 12, 1901
6. *Review and Herald*, February 1, 1898

great things for himself" as retaliation for the shabby treatment he had received from others. Let's illustrate them with examples of the repeated calls from the Spirit of Prophecy. In this first quotation we see the simple truth that some responsibilities come before others:

> Care must be taken that the means needed for this work shall not be diverted into other channels. It makes a difference whether we help the poor who through keeping God's commandments are reduced to want and suffering, or whether we neglect these in order to help blasphemers who tread underfoot the commandments of God. And God regards the difference. Sabbathkeepers should not pass by the Lord's suffering, needy ones to take upon themselves the burden of supporting those who continue in transgression of God's law, those who are educated to look for help to anyone who will sustain them. This is not the right kind of missionary work. It is not in harmony with the Lord's plan.[7]

The second principle is related to the Biblical concept of unity through diversified function. We have hands *and* feet, so let's not try to turn everyone and everything into hand tissue. The obvious advantage of having both hands and feet is the ability to do more things—walking and picking things up, for instance.

Extending the anatomical analogy just slightly, we might point out that many physiological functions are performed by semi-autonomous cells rather than large-scale "organs." In other words, individuals can do a great deal of work for the Lord *as individuals*. It doesn't take an organization, or even a committee, to help a stranded motorist. And one person with common sense and a little experience in the field is a far better tool for deciding how best to help a homeless person than is the most scientifically prepared seventeen-point checklist!

> Many who appear wholly indifferent to religious things are in heart longing for rest and peace. Although they may have sunken to the very depths of sin there is a possibility of saving them. Many can be reached only through acts of disinterested kindness. Their physical wants must first be cared for. They must be fed, cleansed, and decently clothed. As they see the evidence of our unselfish love, it will be easier for them to believe in the love of Christ.
>
> This is a work which concerns all our churches. It is not to be done by expensive institutions. We are not called to centre all our interest and all our means in working in the slums of great cities. The last message of warning must be given to the whole world, and ministry to the poor and neglected is but one part of the great work. This we are to do individually, working for individuals as God gives

us opportunity. He who created all cares for all. Those who have fallen the lowest are not beyond the reach of His love and pity.[8]

Everywhere there is a tendency to substitute the work of organizations for individual effort. Human wisdom tends to consolidation, to centralization, to the building up of great churches and institutions. Multitudes leave to institutions and organizations the work of benevolence; they excuse themselves from contact with the world, and their hearts grow cold. They become self-absorbed and unimpressible. Love for God and man dies out of the soul.

Christ commits to His followers an individual work—a work that cannot be done by proxy. Ministry to the sick and the poor, the giving of the gospel to the lost, is not to be left to committees or organized charities. Individual responsibility, individual effort, personal sacrifice, is the requirement of the gospel.

"Go out into the highways and hedges, and compel them to come in," is Christ's command, "that My house may be filled." He brings men into touch with those whom they seek to benefit. "Bring the poor that are cast out to thy house," He says. "When thou seest the naked, that thou cover him." "They shall lay hands on the sick, and they shall recover." Luke 14:23; Isaiah 58:7; Mark 16:18. Through direct contact, through personal ministry, the blessings of the gospel are to be communicated.[9]

The third principle on the list is the need for symmetry and balance. While Dr. Kellogg obviously lost sight of—or just chose to deliberately violate—this principle, it's interesting to note that the "normal" ministerial/evangelistic branch of the work also failed to maintain proper balance in the Lord's work—by simply doing too little:

I know that God would not have His money absorbed in Chicago as it now is. The money invested in this way, consumes much time and labor. This is pleasing to Satan; for he knows that it will close the door against the support of missionaries in their work, and then the work of the gospel ministry will be held up to ridicule in comparison with the large work done in medical missionary lines. A large amount of money has been used in a way which has accomplished very little. Much has been spent on a class of people who will never be fitted to receive and impart, unless the Holy Spirit shall make them entirely new, heart, mind, and body. The work done for this class has been disproportionately large in comparison with the work that has been done in fields that are waiting and longing for the truth. How many more years will the ways of man counterwork that which God would have done?[10]

Some are worried and perplexed because they see that the medical missionary work is becoming disproportionate, because in receiving so much talent and

---

8. *Australasian Union Conference Record*, June 1, 1900

9. *Ministry of Healing*, 147–148

10. *Manuscript Releases*, vol. 4, 136–137

means, this work far exceeds the work being done in other lines. What is the matter? Is it that the leaders of the medical missionary work are doing too much, or that the leaders in other lines of work are doing too little? It is presented to me that in many lines of work we are doing but a small part of what ought to be done. Faith, zeal, and energy are not manifested as they should be in the work of the ministry. The efforts of many are tame and spiritless. It is evident that light given us by God regarding our duty and privileges has not been acted upon. Men have supplanted God's plans with their own plans. I am commissioned to say that the prosperity of the medical missionary work is in God's order. This work must be done; the truth must be carried into the highways and byways. And ministers and church members should awake and see the necessity of co-operating in this work.[11]

In California, in all our cities in America, in the highways and byways, men and women should go forth as consecrated workers, who will proclaim the message of warning. In Michigan, and Battle Creek especially, it has been thought that Dr. Kellogg was working disproportionately for the poor and wretched ones, in medical missionary lines. Then why does not the General Conference go to work? Why does it allow the treasury which should be kept for the purpose of sustaining the ministry, to be drawn upon, and diverted to common things?[12]

And finally, the fourth item—the one we are always tempted to jump to without considering the first three—the issue of funding:

> The Lord does not lay upon His people all the burden of laboring for a class so hardened by sin that many of them will neither be benefited themselves nor benefit others. If there are men who can take up the work for the most degraded, if God lays upon them a burden to labor for the masses in various ways, let these go forth and gather from the world the means required for doing this work. Let them not depend on the means which God intends shall sustain the work of the third angel's message.[13]

> When all is done that can be done in providing for orphans in our own homes, there will still be many needy ones in the world who should be cared for. They may be ragged, uncouth, and seemingly in every way unattractive, but they are bought with a price, and are just as precious in the sight of God as are our own little ones. They are God's property, for whom Christians are responsible. Their souls, God says, "will I require at thine hand."

> To care for these needy ones is a good work; yet in this age of the world the Lord does not give us as a people directions to establish large and expensive institutions for this purpose. If, however, there are among us individuals who feel called of God to establish institutions for the care of orphan children, let them follow out

---

11. *Testimonies*, vol. 6, 299
12. *Special Testimonies*, Series A, #10, 23
13. *Testimonies*, vol. 6, 246

their convictions of duty. But in caring for the world's poor they should appeal to the world for support. They are not to draw upon the people to whom the Lord has given the most important work ever given to men, the work of bringing the last message of mercy before all nations, kindreds, tongues, and people. The Lord's treasury must have a surplus to sustain the work of the gospel in "regions beyond."

Let those who feel the burden of establishing these institutions have wise solicitors to present their necessities and raise funds. Let the people of the world be aroused, let the denominational churches be canvassed by men who feel the necessity that something be done in behalf of the poor and orphans. In every church there are those who fear God. Let these be appealed to, for to them God has given this work.[14]

Constant work is to be done for the outcasts, but this work is not to be made all-absorbing.... No one should now visit our churches and in the present pressure obtain from them means to sustain the work of rescuing outcasts. The means to sustain that work should come, and will come, largely from those not of our faith. Let the churches take up their appointed work of presenting truth from the oracles of God in the highways.[15]

We are to work along Christ's lines.... We are to be continually laboring together with Christ, seeking to turn the darkness of benighted souls into day.... Every poor, tried soul needs light, needs tender, sympathizing, hopeful words. Every widow needs the comfort of helpful and encouraging words that others can bestow. Orphans who are lent to Christians in trust for God, are too often passed by and neglected, and yet they are bought with a price, and are just as valuable in the sight of God as we are.... When the Lord sees that you are faithful in doing what you can to relieve human misery, he will move upon others to provide means to care for those who need help. Those who enlarge their hearts in this kind of work, do no more than their duty. Christ is our example.[16]

The Wealth of the Gentiles

For many people looking at these items, it's the last one that seems most daunting. "How could we ever get non-Adventists to fund our projects?"

It's a fair question, but one for which the Spirit of Prophecy gives us reason to believe there is a good answer. It may be that things are different now, but it's interesting to note that when the plan was tested in Australasia, it worked... at least somewhat. The "Helping Hand Laundry" of Perth provides a good example:

14. *Testimonies*, vol. 6, 286
15. *Welfare Ministry*, 259
16. *Review and Herald*, January 15, 1895

After the Christian Help Band of the Perth church had been assisting the poor in that city for some months, they began to feel that they were not taking aggressive enough steps. They greatly saw the need of providing something for the poor, whereby they might help themselves. It seemed useless to hand out help week after week to able-bodied people willing to work. They decided to start a Helping Hand Laundry, and later to connect with it a wood-yard. The members, both brethren and sisters, went in companies of two to all the leading iron-mongers and grocers with a written list of what would be required to furnish a laundry, asking them to donate such article, or articles, as they saw fit. It was not all easy work, and there was a great cry of hard times and losses in business, but notwithstanding these things, they were greatly favoured, and almost everything necessary was given, including all the timber needed for fittings. A first-class carpenter offered his time to fit up the laundry....

Cards were printed as follows: "You are invited to patronize the Helping Hand Laundry. Charles Street, West Perth, established by the Perth Helping Hand Mission for charitable purposes.

"Objects: For the assistance of the worthy poor. All profits will be devoted to charitable purposes. To provide employment for needy, destitute girls and women. If they have no money, they will be sent to the Helping Hand Laundry, and given work to the amount of meals or beds required. This is true Christian Help. It is frequently worse than useless to give charity. Charity is often debasing, but work is elevating. To provide means, by the profits of the business, for the carrying on of rescue and philanthropic work in this city."

These cards have been distributed through the city and before the sign of the laundry was put up, work began to come in. Since it was opened, work has steadily flowed in, and there appears to be every prospect that this will be permanent. It will be a self-supporting institution almost from the first. Our brethren and sisters have put very little of their means into it, believing that they should keep them for our denominational work; but they have planned, laboured, and prayed, and have gone to the public for the money, and the Lord has blessed their efforts.

They have had many perplexities in dealing with the people whom it was designed to help. Many would promise to work, and then would disappoint them at the last moment, causing much inconvenience, but they have found many worthy persons among them. They are of good courage in this work, and hope to see it grow to larger proportions.

We now have four institutions for helping the poor and outcasts of Australasia: The Helping Hand City Mission in Melbourne; the Helping Hand Laundry in Perth; the Rescue Home in Adelaide; and the Rescue Home in Napier, N.Z. We hope to see more such institutions springing up in every city in this land. The experience of those who have already started proves that this work can be done, and without any large outlay of means by our own people. What is needed is a deep love for perishing humanity and consecrated energy. The Lord will bless these whenever manifested, and will go before and open the hearts of the public. Which church will be the next to own such an institution?[17]

God Gave the Increase

The Rescue Home in Adelaide was a short-lived enterprise eventually set aside in favor of the Medical and Hydropathic Institute. But in terms of public support, the experience in Perth was essentially duplicated in Melbourne and Napier. This account of the four institutions was dated January 5, 1899. Eight months later we find the following:

> Entering upon the past missionary year with only one medical institution, the Sanitarium at Sydney, thirteen establishments are now under the supervision of the Australasian Association. These are:

1. Medical and Surgical Sanitarium	Sydney,	N.S.W.
2. Home for Orphans	"	"
3. Home for Women	"	"
4. Health Retreat	Cooranbong,	N.S.W.
5. Health Food Factory	"	"
6. Medical Branch Office	Newcastle,	N.S.W.
7. Medical Mission	Melbourne,	Victoria
8. Home for the Aged	"	"
9. Health Home	Christchurch,	N.Z.
10. Bethany Home for Prisoners	Napier,	N.Z.
11. Medical and Hydropathic Institute	Adelaide,	S.A.
12. Helping Hand Mission	"	"
13. Helping Hand Laundry	Perth,	W.A.

> Surely the Lord has worked mightily in behalf of His people.

The author noted that, "The present year will probably not see the establishment of so many institutions; we wish to make the foundations sure of those already established. *Can there not be a large amount of individual work done?* If at the next Association meeting we might hear reports from Christian Help Bands organized in every Seventh-day Adventist Church in Australasia, then we should feel that the Lord had prospered our efforts even more than in the establishment of institutions."[18]

This era of implementing a more complete vision of medical missionary evangelism must have been stressful at times. Reports in the Union

---

17. *Australasian Union Conference Record*, January 15, 1899, 2
18. *Australasian Union Conference Record*, September 1, 1899, 8

paper freely acknowledged that there were more than enough challenges, and even some very serious disappointments, but there was always the assertion that the rewards made it all worthwhile.

They were following the Lord's program. They had His instruction as to methods. They had His promise of success. There were sacrifices to be made, but it was worth it. Between 1894, when the first emphasis on medical missionary work began, and 1900, church membership in the Union had more than doubled.

Chapter Thirteen

After Study Abroad

ONE of the best case studies of the "Australasian" approach to evangelism didn't happen in Australasia. That's good, really, because it shows that the success of those methods didn't come just from some offbeat personality trait of those unpredictable Aussies.

The story centers around a minister whom most Seventh-day Adventists have never heard of. John Corliss probably wouldn't be too worried about his lack of fame, but it's our loss to not know his story. He once wrote, "Many men are not appreciated while in life. Their native reserve prevents open display of noble traits which appear only as those nearest to them happen incidentally to mention them."[1] He was writing about John Byington as a "pioneer reformer" in a "History of Medical Work of Seventh-day Adventists," but the same could easily be said of Corliss himself.

Converted shortly after his discharge from the army in 1865, Corliss ended up living for two years with James and Ellen White. As he put it, "I was called to travel quite extensively with [the Whites], from Maine to California, and from Michigan to Texas." This was during the period of James White's recovery from his first stroke, and also the establishment of the Western Health Reform Institute, the predecessor of the much more famous Battle Creek Sanitarium.

---

1. *The Medical Evangelist*, December 1912, 161

For a short period, Corliss served as "superintendent and chaplain" of the Health Institute, but was soon back in "training," this time traveling and working with Joseph Bates, the original Adventist health reformer.[2]

Whether or not it was these early experiences that were responsible is hard to say, but Elder Corliss maintained an interest in practical, health-oriented ministry all his life. This was especially noteworthy during his service in Australia, and again after his return to the United States.

You may recall that we met Elder Corliss, briefly, two chapters back; he's the one who was teaching A.W. Semmens how to give Bible readings. John Corliss was clearly the elder member in that partnership, but he was humble enough—and smart enough—to learn what he could from this nurse he was turning into something of a Bible Worker. And the obvious fact that Semmens could do things that he could not, did not escape his observation. What's more, Elder Corliss noted that the people his junior partner ministered to in practical ways always seemed to be grateful.

There was something about this whole "relieve the pain, treat the disease, save the life" approach that generated a great deal of gratitude. And that, for an evangelist, is a very good thing. People listened better when they weren't in pain, and especially when it was Semmens who had done something to bring that about.

New Field, New Method

To make a long story short, John Corliss went back to the United States with new ideas in his head and a few new tricks up his sleeve. After a year teaching Bible to the nursing and medical students at the Sanitarium in Battle Creek, he served in Ottawa, Canada, in 1898 and 1899. That's where these ideas started taking practical form. He shared his thoughts on the experiment at the General Conference of 1899:

> I was taught, a good many years ago, that the proper method of carrying on tent-meetings was to explain the symbols of the second and seventh chapters of Daniel: then to run down over the symbols of the book of Revelation; and then dwell upon the Sabbath and the law almost entirely, in order to get people to receive a certain theory. I was long dissatisfied with such methods. I found that while I could get a good many people to acknowledge the theory of these things, some way there did not enter into their lives that which I desired to see. When instruction came, telling us that we should blend the health principles with all these other things in our ministerial work, I began to pray most earnestly that God would enlighten me, so that I might be able to know how to do it.

---

2. *Review and Herald*, October 25, 1923, 19; August 23, 1923, 8

I had not been in a series of tent-meetings for some years until last summer. The superintendent of District 1 asked me to go to Ottawa, and I went there. After pleading with God for help, it came to me that instead of dwelling upon one particular feature of our faith until the people began to feel that that was the only thing we had, I should so preach Christ that these things would all blend in him, and that when people came to Christ, they would accept everything of Christ at once....

It was quite a study, and I prayed over the matter much. I soon announced that we would give a series of Bible health talks in the tent. I was indeed surprised to see the interest manifested in this matter. I have a set of Dr. Kellogg's charts on physiology and hygiene. These are so adjusted on rollers as quickly to show the different phases of this subject. I gave Sunday to the consideration of these topics.

I began with the text, "I am fearfully and wonderfully made." From the charts I was able to show the relation of one part of the human system to the other. You may ask, How did you know these things, if you have never been through a medical school? I have never known anything about the technicalities of medical lore, but I did have the *Home Hand-Book*; and by careful study I found it to supply the very information I needed to give the people. From that, I was able to collate points of instruction, in the same way as we gather Bible points, and crystallize them into doctrine. Then would come the text, perhaps Eccl.10:17: "Blessed art thou, O land, when thy king is the son of nobles, and thy princes eat in due season, for strength, and not for drunkenness!"

From the chart again, the combination of foods and their relation to the stomach could be carefully set forth. I also had a supply of health foods on exhibit. At the close of the discourse, the people were invited freely to sample these foods, and make inquiries. This brought me near my audience. These points were dwelt upon Sundays, when the people could attend in force. During the week, a cooking school was held in order to demonstrate the methods of preparing the foods. The reporters of the city papers visited this school, and the daily papers published the principles taught there; and so the whole city became more or less interested. I really never before had an interest like that one, and I attribute it largely to bringing these things to the front, which made the whole truth symmetrical.

The interest continued for ten weeks; and the last night of the series, we had the largest audience of the whole time. As an evidence of the people's appreciation of these things, those in attendance contributed something over twelve dollars a week to the expense of the meetings for the entire time. You see that was an indication that they had been longing for these things, and were willing to pay for all they received; and not only that, but it made them feel better toward our people. They said, "This people are not talking all the time on one doctrine, but they have something that will help our bodies as well as our souls."

With other things we went about hunting up the poor and distressed. The workers entered upon the line of Christian Help work. Day by day they started out with a little hand-bag containing fomentation cloths, water bags, etc., and wherever they found a suffering person, they treated him and tried to help him on his feet again. Many blessings from those poor persons were heaped upon the heads of the tent workers.

As a result of doing that, those who did come into the truth came with a full understanding of what they were doing; and they understood that there was something practical in all these things, too, as well as doctrinal....

From that effort I was impressed that there is something more to do than we have ordinarily done to bring people to realize what they must do to be saved, to get life in them from the very beginning of their Christian experience; to get them to understand that there is a life power that they must have in order to be saved....

Voice—Will you kindly give us some of the material results?

Corliss—I can not give you the exact number of those who stepped out, but I think there were between twenty and thirty. I believe there is something in teaching health reform as a part of the message, and in trying to help the poor, that is better than mere proselyting. This brings the people nearer to the Lord when these things are shown as parts of Christian doctrine. I believe there is light in this method of labor; and if I were to go into the pioneer field again, I should carry it with me. My only regret is that I have been so long in the work without having before learned these principles; and now my soul longs to make known to the young men my experience, that perchance they may be saved from the mistakes which have befallen me in this thing.[3]

As it turned out, Elder Corliss was headed back into the "pioneer field" faster than he realized. True to his word, he took medical missionary work right along with him. His next stop was the City by the Bay, and a key role in perhaps the most fully developed program of Gospel-Medical Missionary Evangelism ever carried on in modern times.

Reaching Hearts in San Francisco

John Corliss didn't start formal medical missionary work in San Francisco. That distinction would go to the board of directors of the Pacific Press. At a meeting in the spring of 1897—

It seemed to them that it would be in harmony with the mind of the Spirit of God to have a work of this kind inaugurated in this city. We realized that this would require men as well as means, earnest, devoted men, men who were willing to sacrifice and who had had experience in dealing with the particular class of individuals who would come to a mission of this kind.

3. *General Conference Daily Bulletin*, February 22, 1899, 52

We found no such man until last December we learned that Brother B.F. Richards, who had had connection with mission work in Chicago and elsewhere, could be secured. The board immediately telegraphed to him to come to California, and within two weeks from that time, he was with us ready to begin work.[4]

With "evangelistic help" from the California Conference, and "physicians and skilled nurses" from the Saint Helena Sanitarium, the Helping Hand Mission opened its doors on February 27, 1898.

The Mission was a good start, but because of the background and experience of the individuals involved, it was focused solely on the "rescue mission" model—like Kellogg's Chicago City Mission.

Under the general leadership of Elder Corliss, who came in 1899, the medical missionary work blossomed out into many additional forms.

In early December 1900, Ellen White visited San Francisco for a week of prayer. Writing for publication back in still-dear-to-her-heart Australia, she painted quite a picture of the work:

> From Elder J.O. Corliss, who is pastor of the San Francisco Church, we learn that there are many lines of Christian effort being carried forward by our brethren and sisters in San Francisco. These include visiting the sick and destitute, finding homes for orphans, and work for the unemployed; nursing the sick, and teaching the love of Christ from house to house; the distribution of literature; and the conducting of classes for healthful living and the care of the sick. A school for the children is conducted in the basement of the meeting-house. In another part of the city a workingmen's home and medical mission is maintained. On Market Street, near the City Hall, there is a bath establishment, operated as a branch of the St. Helena Sanitarium. In the same locality is a depot of the Health Food Company, where health foods are not only sold, but instruction is given as to reforms in diet.
>
> Nearer the centre of the city, our people conduct a Vegetarian Cafe, which is open six days in the week, and is entirely closed on the Sabbath. Here about five hundred meals are served daily, and no flesh-meats are used.
>
> Dr. and Mrs. Dr. Lamb are doing much medical work for the poor in connection with their regular practice; and Dr. Buchannan is doing much free work at the Workingmen's Home. At the Medical and Dental schools in the city, there are about twenty of our young people in attendance.
>
> We earnestly hope that the steps taken in the future in the work in San Francisco will still be steps of progress. The work that has been done there is but a beginning. San Francisco is a world in itself, and the Lord's work there is to broaden and deepen.[5]

---

4. *Bible Echo*, May 23, 1898, 165
5. *Australasian Union Conference Record*, March 1, 1901

Point of Reference

Notice her assessment: "the work that has been done there is but a beginning." That's *it*? Just "*a beginning*"? What was she *thinking*?

Truth is, she was probably thinking of what we should all be thinking of—the loud cry and "this gospel" to "*all* the world." Next to that, her words sound like an overly optimistic exaggeration.

Writing once again of that same visit, she said:

> We have every reason to believe that the work carried on in San Francisco by Brother Corliss and his brethren is the work that needs to be done. San Francisco is a center, and must be thoroughly worked. A much more extensive work should be done in this great and wicked city.[6]

"A much more extensive work," she said, and it seems as if Elder Corliss took those words to heart. Four months later, he described the work in San Francisco at the General Conference of 1901. Unfortunately, we only have space for excerpts from his fascinating talk:

> I have been struck with the thought that in every instance where the Saviour has given the gospel commission, and sent out his workers, he told them to heal the sick.... Thus the Saviour gave his ministers just the same authority to heal the sick as to preach the gospel. He has united the two things in gospel work, so that it would seem almost impossible to separate them.
>
> There is no one thing which has all the elements of success in it for city work. We used to think that an eloquent preacher was required to go into a large city; that he must stir the multitudes with his eloquence, and with his method of uniting the different points of doctrine, so that people would be charmed by it. But from my observation, and in fact from my own experience of many years in city work, I have learned that it is not the eloquent minister who succeeds in such work: in fact, a minister is but a single factor in the work. The great thing necessary is to have a competent and united force of consecrated workers....
>
> We may think, when we enter a place, that there are none there who have talent, but upon investigation one is surprised to find the amount of talent that is rusting in our churches today. We do not want to get the idea that because a man is not accredited by the Conference with credentials, that he can not do anything in such work. I have found that when a person comes into the truth, he makes a better laborer than some who have been long in the church, because everything he has received, is fresh in his mind, and he knows better how to utilize it than do those who have been longer in the way, but have let the definite things of the truth fade in their minds. Besides, new converts are more easily instructed in methods than our older people are. The older ones criticize methods that the

---

younger ones readily receive and act upon. It is therefore well to commence training young converts as soon as they receive the truth. In San Francisco, our best workers, outside of the Conference laborers, are those who have recently embraced the truth, and they do the most work....

Describing a printed card that they handed out to people in the city, Corliss pointed out—

Then it says, "If you know of any sick or in distress, please inform the pastor." And so they come....

Among the listeners at the General Conference session was one who raised a question:

G. F. Watson—I would like to ask if you count this kind of work where we have a church in existence, hovering over the church?

J.O. Corliss—No, sir; not if we do the work of reaching out for the lost. A man can hover over, and simply preach to a church until it depends entirely upon his preaching; but our church does not do that. Our church is at work. We try to get every member of the church at work....

How is the work done? We have, in the first place, our regular Sundays at the Seaman's Home.... Then we have jail services every third Sunday....

But we have another preparatory work that I have come to consider one of the greatest factors we have in training workers. Every Thursday night, just as regularly as the weeks come, we have a doctor occupy the pulpit. There are two of them, in fact, who divide the time between them. There are Drs. Coolidge and Buchanan. They take up the most common diseases, and tell them how to know the symptoms of these. They do not talk in technical terms, but give popular talks, that a common person can receive. The people are then taught how to give simple treatments. There are many poor unfortunates in that city who need help that they are not able to procure in any other way. Our people are instructed to go out, and wherever they find a soul that needs such work done, to take hold and do it free....

The doctors in their practice in the city come across cases that they treat as charity cases. But in order that they may show interest in such people, they offer to provide a nurse. Then the doctor comes to some one who has been sitting under his Thursday night teaching, and says: "I want you to take a case and nurse it for three or four days or a week, and do it for charity's sake, do it for the love of Christ." That individual takes the case, and nurses it through the extreme condition. One can not, after that, make such a patient think that Seventh-day Adventists are not Christians. In this way we may get hold of many....

Another branch of the work is that of the Christian Help band. Although that is rather old, and has died out in some places, it is not so with us.... [Through this work] many are led to say, "Do not tell me that Seventh-day Adventists are not good people; if there's any religion in the world, they have it."

We have also committees to visit old people.... Others visit the sick and poor. Our people contribute regularly to a poor fund. All these committees report at the regular weekly workers' meetings....

We have also a Chinese work in the city, Brother and Sister Brand, members of our church, are doing the best they can for the Chinese who are in the city. They have a small work, but we do not overlook it....

We have workers' meetings once a week, on Wednesday evening. We pray together, and talk over the situation, ask and give counsel, so that everything may be understood for the week to come....

We have also a Japanese school. We have one Japanese brother, who works all he can in behalf of the truth. Not long ago he brought three Japanese, and said, "Sie wants baptism." We got these three Japanese brethren together, noble looking men as you ever saw, and baptized them. They stayed in the church for two or three months, when they got to feeling a burden to go to Japan, and every one of them has gone back to Japan, to assist in the work there. I hope the brethren in Japan will find them, and set them to work; for they know what it means to work.

It is not eloquent preaching in the pulpit, or anything of the kind, that is needed in city work, so much as solid, earnest work to be carried on every day. My candid convictions are that to be most successful in city work, we must have men who will keep their eyes open, and will not feel that their work is done when they have preached a sermon on the state of the dead, the Sabbath question, or something of the kind.... During my nearly two years' work in San Francisco, I have not preached one entire sermon on the Sabbath question.

David Paulson—And yet people have been accepting the Sabbath right along, have they not?

J.O. Corliss—Yes, and we have had as many as three baptisms in a month. We have never failed to have a baptism every month, of people coming into the truth. It is done by working outside. The minister gets no credit for it, and deserves none. The earnestness of the workers, and their careful methods recommend the truth to others. It is not long before they begin to inquire about the Seventh-day Adventists, and what they believe, saying, "I have always thought that the seventh day is the Sabbath." You do not have to argue with such people. We preach Christ, and let everything cluster about him, and center in him. In every discourse Christ is the theme, and the Sabbath is put in in a way without saying very much about it, so that when people accept Christ, they accept the Sabbath with him.[7]

7. *General Conference Bulletin*, April 21, 1901, 370–372

That was the picture of the work in San Francisco in 1901. Quite impressive, actually. Heaven will one day show how many souls will enjoy eternal life because of the work done there. But it was not to last. Nearly everything we've seen in these portrayals of a multi-faceted, Gospel-Medical Missionary Evangelism came crashing to the ground, or went up in smoke, or both, on the morning of April 18, 1906, when the ground under San Francisco shook.

Today, we have the memory of what once was.

Chapter Fourteen

Trying It at Home

ELLEN White probably never had to endure dire warnings that she had been watching highly trained professionals and should never think to try some ridiculous stunt at home. But the odds of success when she tried to bring the medical missionary model of ministry home to the United States were daunting enough to deserve some kind of warning. Back "in country" in September 1900, she had just about enough time to get settled at Elmshaven before the 1901 General Conference the next spring. The big story there would be "re-organization," with sub-plots of moving Battle Creek College out of Battle Creek, and dealing with the "Holy Flesh" fanaticism that had come up in Indiana.

Her efforts to advise and reform the church's approach to ministry were largely drowned out by other events. The next year started off with the complete loss of the Sanitarium by fire, became more complicated with the controversy over *The Living Temple*, and ended with the Review and Herald plant following in the smoketrails of the Sanitarium.

Did she wish she were still in Australia?

The General Conference of 1903 was another contentious occasion; relations between ministers and doctors were at loggerheads; the Review and the General Conference were both moving to Takoma Park; against all her counsel, Kellogg was building an even more extravagant Sanitarium in Battle Creek; and he and his lieutenants pressed a continual fifth-column attack against her prophetic authority.

Did she wish she were dead?

Maybe she did... but she didn't write it down for us to read, and she never stopped working, sometimes multi-tasking toward goals which she herself probably did not understand at the time. In this chapter, we look at this transition time, during which she fought an eventually unsuccessful rear-guard action in an effort to reclaim Dr. Kellogg, while simultaneously setting into motion the developments that would take the place of the Sanitarium's influence and Kellogg's control of the medical work.

Why did she try so hard? For one thing, she had promised Dr. Kellogg's parents she would do all she could to save his soul.[1] We could believe that was reason enough. But even more deeply held than her longing for his salvation was the call for God's people to work as Jesus worked when He was here. Only in that way could they portray His glory to the world in the loud cry.

Patience and Perseverance Personified

We haven't space here for play-by-play coverage of all that Ellen White did in trying to reach John Kellogg's heart. But, as a minimum, we must notice her defense of him at the 1903 General Conference session. Remember, this was a year *after* he wrote *Living Temple*, and all these comments were made in public sessions. Those who like "straight shooting" speakers will enjoy this—far more than she enjoyed saying these things.

Of course, mingled with her defense of Kellogg were many pieces of instruction. Some may have been specific to Kellogg-related issues, but many were laying the groundwork for things as yet undeveloped. Here is a sampling, some of which we've seen before, but it's worth considering again in the context of its time and place:

> Here is the medical missionary work—a wonderful work. God gave us this work thirty-five years ago, and it has been a great blessing. It is to be to the third angel's message as the right hand is to the body. The gospel and the medical missionary work are one. They can not be divided. They are to be bound together. Medical missionary workers should be encouraged and sustained. And let them remember that they are working for the Master. Unless they do this, they can not exert a strong influence for good in the world. And they must ever keep clear and distinct the line of demarcation between worldlings and those who are carrying the gospel of the kingdom to the world.
>
> In the place of erecting large sanitariums, we should establish smaller sanitariums in many places. A few patients in a small institution can be helped and educated to much greater advantage than a large number gathered together in a

---

1. "I have lain awake night after night, studying how I could help Dr. Kellogg. His father and mother, before they died, begged me not to give him up, but to stand by him till the last. I said, 'I will try, if he will listen to me.' I have spent nearly whole nights in prayer for him." —*Sermons and Talks*, vol. 1, 346

large institution. God help us to let the light shine forth. It must shine forth, and God will make us channels of light, if we will let Him.[2]

And let me say that God does not design that the sanitarium that has been erected in Battle Creek shall be in vain. He wants His people to understand this. Now that the building has been put up, He wants this institution to be placed on vantage ground. He does not want His people to be looked upon by the enemy as a people that is going out of sight.

We are now to make another effort to place our institutions on solid ground. Let no one say, because there is a debt on the sanitarium in Battle Creek, "We will have nothing more to do in helping to build up that institution." The people of God must build that institution up, in the name of the Lord. It is to be placed where its work can be carried on intelligently. One man is not to stand at its head alone. Dr. Kellogg has carried the burden until it has almost killed him. God wants His servants to stand united in carrying that work forward. Because one man is one-sided, and another man is one-sided, this does not show that the work of God is to be one-sided.

God's people are to place the sanitarium in Battle Creek on vantage ground. How is this to be done? I can not tell you. But I know that just as soon as the Holy Spirit shall come upon hearts, there will be unity in voice and understanding; and wisdom will be given us.[3]

God has given Dr. Kellogg the success that he has had. I have tried constantly to keep this before him, telling him that it was God who was working with him, and that the truth of God was to be magnified by His physician. God will bless every other physician who will yield himself wholly to God, and will be with his hand when he works.

This was the light given. God worked that the medical missionary work might stand on the highest vantage ground; that it might be known that Seventh-day Adventists have a God working with them, a God who has a constant oversight of His work.

God does not endorse the efforts put forth by different ones to make the work of Dr. Kellogg as hard as possible, in order to build themselves up. God gave the light on health reform, and those who rejected it rejected God. One and another who knew better said that it all came from Dr. Kellogg, and they made war upon him. This had a bad influence on the doctor. He put on the coat of irritation and retaliation. God did not want him to stand in the position of warfare, and He does not want you to stand there.

Those who have turned away from the Battle Creek Sanitarium to get worldly physicians to care for them did not realize what they were doing. God established the Battle Creek Sanitarium. God worked through Dr. Kellogg; but

2. *General Conference Bulletin*, April 1, 1903
3. *General Conference Bulletin*, April 2, 1903

men did not realize this. When they were sick, they sent for worldly physicians to come, because of something that the doctor had said or done that did not please them. This God did not approve. We have the authority of the Bible for our instruction in temperance....

You were surprised to hear me say that we are not to let the Battle Creek Sanitarium go into the hands of the world; that we are to make another effort to place our institutions on solid ground. If you will trust in the Lord, this institution can be placed on vantage ground. When the sanitarium is placed on its proper foundation; when our people can see it as it was when it was first established; when they can understand that the institution belongs to the work of the Lord, and can see that no one man is to have the control of everything in it; then God will help them all to take hold with courage to build it up. Today you do not know just where it is. God wants us to know every timber of the foundation, where it is, and what it is; then He wants us all to put shoulder to shoulder, and labor understandingly. The Lord wants us to do our duty. He wants us to understand that Dr. Kellogg shall not be pushed out of his place, but that he shall stand acknowledged and supported in his God-given work. This he will be if his feet are planted on the truth of the living God. If they are not planted on this truth, specious temptations will come in, through scientific problems and scientific theories regarding God and His Word. Spurious scientific theories are coming in as a thief in the night, stealing away the landmarks and undermining the pillars of our faith. God has shown me that the medical students are not to be educated in such theories, because God will not endorse these theories. The most specious temptations of the enemy are coming in, and they are coming in on the highest, most elevated plane. These spiritualize the doctrines of present truth until there is no distinction between the substance and the shadow.[4]

I wish that a portion of the work of this institution had been taken elsewhere. But the sanitarium has been erected in Battle Creek, and it must be helped. God will institute ways and means by which it can be helped....

There are small sanitariums to be established in various places. Medical missionary work is the helping hand of God. This work must be done. It is needed in new fields and in fields where the work was started years ago. Since this work is the helping hand of God and the entering wedge of the gospel, we want you to understand that you are to have a part in it. It is not to be divorced from the gospel. Every soul before me this morning should be filled with the true medical missionary spirit.[5]

Ellen White's position here is remarkable. While pointing out the wrong of building up a new, bigger Sanitarium, she wasn't saying to trash the place. Instead, it was, "OK, we're in a mess; so what do we do to make the best of it and get back on track." That will be a good approach to remember.

---

4. *General Conference Bulletin*, April 2, 1903
5. *General Conference Bulletin*, April 7, 1903

Pressing On

As detailed in chapter ten, there was no effective reversing of Dr. Kellogg's downward slide. Free will is a precious blessing, or a terrible curse. Though Ellen White put more time and effort into working for John Kellogg than for anyone else (with the possible exception of her own sometimes-wayward son, James Edson), she was also taking steps for the future.

As Battle Creek and Dr. Kellogg fell from usefulness in the Lord's work, attention shifted toward southern California. Fortunately for us, the story of the transfer of the denomination's medical interests from Battle Creek to Loma Linda is fairly well known, at least in its major features. But there is confusion as to the exact goal of the new institution. Was God's purpose simply to re-establish the church's medical work, or to re-establish the medical work specifically to fuel a denomination-wide medical missionary revival?

In other words, our interest is not so much the *fact* of the new institutions, as it is the *purpose* of the new institutions.

Due to space constraints, we will not be covering every aspect of the purchase and development of the Sanitarium and the College. It is a great story, though, and if you're not familiar with it, you should look into it. In this account, we will only sketch the major outlines of the story, and focus on a subset of particular points which address the issue of the college's goals.

The Background

Ellen White had been urging the establishment of sanitariums in southern California for some years. Her calls, and John Burden's perseverance, led to the purchase and development of Paradise Valley and Glendale. But she was insistent that there was another property to be found. In time Burden's attention was drawn to the Loma Linda property, and when the price dropped to $40,000 Ellen White told him to secure it immediately.

True, Burden's conference president told him not to touch the place, and that any commitments he made would be his alone, as the conference had no interest in more debt. But the most noteworthy thing about John Burden was his trust in the Spirit of Prophecy. When Ellen White gave him clear direction, he simply did as he was told. This shows in the correspondence he received from Ellen White: it has been said that she never wrote one word of reproof in her eighty-three letters to him.[6]

---

6. As counted from the E.G. White Letter file on-line listing. Those who received the greatest number of letters from Ellen White are as follows: Edson White (580), Willie White (574), S.N. Haskell (290), J.H. Kellogg (184), A.G. Daniells (125), James White (118), G.I. Butler (93), J.A. Burden (83), and Uriah

One point of Ellen White's instruction that led to the purchase of Loma Linda stands out—her reason for favoring that general location:

> From the light which was given me when I was in Australia, and which has been renewed since I came to America, I know that our work in southern California must advance. The people flocking there for health must hear the last message of mercy.
>
> God has not been pleased with the way in which this work has been neglected. From many places in southern California, the light is to shine forth to the multitudes. Present truth is to be as a city set on a hill which cannot be hid.
>
> Southern California is world-renowned as a health resort. Every year thousands of tourists go there. These must hear the last warning message. We are called upon by God to explain the Scriptures to these people. We are not to build hotels for the accommodation of tourists, and we are not to establish sanitariums in the cities. We are to establish our work where we shall be able to do the most good to those who come to our sanitariums for treatment.[7]
>
> Here in this small territory, where the climate is so favorable, and where thousands are coming in search of health, Christ would have His people establish everywhere memorials for Him—institutions to which they may be drawn and learn of His healing power; places in which the laws of life and health shall be lived and taught in such simplicity that all may receive their benefit.[8]
>
> The Lord would have brave, earnest men and women take up his work in these places. The cause of God is to make more rapid advancement in southern California than it has in the past. Every year thousands of people visit southern California in search of health, and by various methods we should seek to reach them with the truth. They must hear the warning to prepare for the great day of the Lord, which is right upon us.[9]

Not every detail is filled in, perhaps, but there was definitely something of interest to the Lord in those thousands of tourists.

First Impressions

When Ellen White first visited Loma Linda, she examined the buildings and property happily in company with several others. With her that day was Elder John Burden. Here is his account:

> As Sister White stepped from the express wagon to the ground, she said to her son, who was with her, "Willie, I have been here before." He said, "No, Mother, you have never been here."

Smith (48).

7. *Loma Linda Messages,* 481
8. *Loma Linda Messages,* 473
9. *Review and Herald,* June 21, 1906

"Then this is the very place the Lord has shown me, for it is all familiar."

Addressing another who stood by, she said, "We must have this place. We should reason from cause to effect. The Lord has not given us this property for any common purpose."

As she walked about the grounds and the buildings at Loma Linda, she frequently remarked, "This is the very place shown me in vision."

We entered what was then known as the Amusement Building on the top of the hill. Here in one room was a billiard table, and in another a bowling alley. In another room were card tables with the cards scattered about. Mrs. White sat down in a chair, and looking about, began to talk. As nearly as we can remember her words, she said, in part:

"This building will be of great value to us. A school will be established here. Redlands will become a center, as also will Loma Linda. The work at Battle Creek is going down. God will re-establish His medical work at this place. We are farther from the true picture of medical missionary work than when we first began. God never designed that our work should blossom out in the great professional and commercial way in which it stands before the world today. We have educated bedside nurses. He intended that we should educate missionary nurses to go into the homes of the people of the villages, towns, and cities, ministering to the people, singing gospel songs, and giving Bible readings. Those who do this work will reap a rich harvest of souls both from the higher and the lower walks of life. We must have men here who have had an experience in the early development of our work, such men as Elder Haskell, to help us build this on the right foundation."[10]

Legal Limbo

Once the Lord had miraculously provided the funds to purchase the property, the question of development came to the fore. What, exactly, was the church going to do with this place? The beautiful hotel building could obviously be turned into a sanitarium, but anything beyond that was subject to widely varying opinions. The complications came from a number of issues, but the most significant was the question of relating to the requirements of medical licensing laws.

As it turned out, Adventists weren't the only ones confused. It seems that this branch of California law was in a bit of turmoil just then, and lots of people were trying to get a handle on it. Here's the back story on all that:

In the late 1800s, American medical practice was becoming more sophisticated, striving to actually deserve being called a "science." Remember, just forty years before it was still possible for almost anyone to earn an M.D. after their name in six months to a year. But "American

---

10. J.A. Burden, *The Story of Loma Linda*, 91

medicine" was far from a monolith. In California at the time, there was competition between the American Medical Association, the Osteopathic Medical Society, the Homeopathic Medical Society, the Chiropractic Medical Society, and the Eclectic Medical Society.[11]

A short side-note is needed just here to point out an interesting idiom of the day. Through some means or the other, the public had become accustomed to speak of the kind of medicine advocated by the AMA as "regular" medicine. Along the same linguistic lines, there were "regular" physicians who followed the "regular" practice. It was somewhat like teachers graduating from "normal school" when most of them really aren't.[12] This piece of trivia will be helpful in interpreting comments that come later in our story.

In the five-way race for professional influence in the Golden State, one group found the inside track. The American Medical Association was organized in 1847 and—as one generally sympathetic MD/historian put it—had "promoted educational reforms that tended to promote its own type of medical practice as the only legitimate one." This may have been from sincere conviction and a desire to prevent suffering and death, or it may have been from less noble motives. We are talking about people, after all.

Through the end of the 19th century the AMA "continued to fortify its position by exerting increasing influence on the educational and licensing regulations" until their "control over the licensing boards... brought the pluralistic system of medical care in the United States to an end."[13] In California, the first major step in this direction came in 1901 with a new law defining medical licensure.

Until then there had been three licensing boards—a State Medical Society Board (aligned with the AMA), an Eclectic Medical Society Board, and a Homeopathic Medical Society Board. The new law established a nine-member Board of Medical Examiners and fixed its membership at five AMA MD's, two Homeopaths, and two Eclectics. As a check against complete monopoly, a super-majority of six votes was required to take any action.[14]

---

11. The Eclectic Medical Institute (later, College), operated in Cincinnati, Ohio, from 1845–1942. This school of medical thought emphasized the use of herbal remedies, but was open to adopting any other techniques that proved advantageous. Though little known today, Eclectic medicine was very much a part of the mix in the late 1800s and early 1900s. Ellen White comments on this kind of practice in three different manuscripts, now found in *Manuscript Releases*, vol. 20, 364, 373, and 380. Her comment that "Eclectic was less dangerous," is pretty high praise as compared to most of her comments on the systems of medicine in existence in her day.

12. As one who spent twenty years as a classroom teacher, the author hopes his colleagues will take this comment as a hat tip to their creativity!

13. Ober, Patrick K. "The Pre-Flexnerian Reports: Mark Twain's Criticism of Medicine in the United States." *Annals of Internal Medicine* 126 (1997): 157-163

14. *The Statutes of California, 1901*, Chapter 51, 56–64

But not everyone was pleased with the new law, and in mute testimony to the ability of someone to pull strings in a smoke-filled room (or possibly something more noble), a second new law came into being a mere ten days later. This second bill established a separate examining board for osteopathic physicians, and explicitly exempted that approach to medicine from the jurisdiction of any other California law.[15]

That made the osteopaths happy, but left the AMA, homeopaths, and eclectics feeling jealous. Still, that was a much better situation than those wanting to practice chiropractic found themselves in. Their chances of getting a medical license were nearly nonexistent under that system.

Unsurprisingly, there was a great deal of discontent, and many people who wanted to change the law. But with multiple entrenched special interest groups, that wasn't an easy thing to do. In 1903, six different bills addressed the regulatory quagmire; they all went down to defeat. In 1905, five more failures left the situation unchanged. And in 1907, six assemblymen and four senators tried again.[16]

Well into the legislative session, when four competing bills were under consideration, the Senate Committee on Public Health and Quarantine proposed a "Committee Substitute" bill in lieu of all submitted bills. Starting so late in the session, this new legislation needed to find a fast track to enactment, or it would never make it. Apparently, all the right people were in favor, because the bill moved rapidly forward.

In the next twelve days, the substitute bill was adopted, sent to the printer, engrossed, read a third time to the Senate, amended slightly, sent back to the printer, re-engrossed, amended again, re-engrossed again, voted on, and passed to the Assembly. If anything, the bill was even more popular in that chamber. On February 28 the bill was in and out of committee with a recommendation "do pass." The next day, the bill was read to the Assembly, and made a special order for its third reading the next day. March 2, 1907, the bill was read to the Assembly the third time, voted on, and returned to the Senate for enrollment. March 18, it was approved by the Governor and became the law of the State of California.[17]

This is the law that existed in California during the formative years of the College of Medical Evangelists. This is the law that defined the legal

---

15. *The Statutes of California, 1901*, Chapter 99, 113–115
16. The bills mentioned here are as follows: 1903—Assembly Bills 129, 193, 206, 486; Senate Bills 365, 388. 1905—Assembly Bills 267, 528, 996, 1164; Senate Bill 712. 1907—Assembly Bills 61, 241, 367, 646, 769, 813; Senate Bills 238, 665, 710, 846.
17. 1907 *Final Calendar of Legislative Business*, 97

opportunities for the new institution. And this was no ordinary law. Was it providential? Some thought so; others, apparently, did not.

What Should We Write on a Blank Check?

There were several interesting features to this new law. The Board of Medical Examiners was increased to eleven members and composed of five MD's, two homeopaths, two eclectics, and two osteopaths. A super-majority of seven votes was now required to get anything done. But the most significant change came in the matter of the certificates granted to allow physicians to practice medicine. The law stipulated that—

> Three forms of certificate shall be issued by said board under the seal thereof and signed by the president and the secretary: first, a certificate authorizing the holder thereof to practice medicine and surgery; second, a certificate authorizing the holder thereof to practice osteopathy; third, a certificate authorizing the holder thereof to practice any other system or mode of treating the sick or afflicted not referred to in this section.[18]

How did this happen? What sort of anti-establishment, libertarian, free-for-all mindset was in play when this language found its way into law? Who, exactly, was in need of such a provision? The chiropractors, homeopaths, and eclectics could all have been included by name. Who was needing a provision for a kind of medicine that hadn't even been named yet? Other than the Adventists out there at Loma Linda, of course.

No wonder John Burden saw the hand of providence at work, especially so when he saw the other major revision in the law. But we'll let Burden explain the situation. The following comes from a letter he wrote in April 1908:

> Our understanding of the Testimonies is that, while thousands are to be quickly qualified for thorough medical-evangelistic work, some must qualify to labor as physicians. We have been instructed again and again to make the school as strong as possible for the qualification of nurses and physicians; and the opening of a way for its recognition, with no thought or effort on our part, and especially in view of the fact that California heretofore had been one of the most difficult states for medical practitioners to gain recognition in, seemed to us a divine providence, coming as it did the next year after we had started our school.
>
> The battle was fought by the osteopaths, but the Legislature then threw the gate wide open for any school whose requirements for entrance to the medical course were equal to a high school preparation on the ten fundamental branches that underlie medical education. Materia medica and surgery are both thrown out,

---

18. *The Statutes of California*, 1907, Chapter 212, 252

so that a good, thorough school of hygiene or rational practice of medicine would have no difffficulty in being recognized in this state. And should our school be recognized here, its students would have a vantage ground from which to secure recognition in other states, the same as the osteopaths are being recognized....

It certainly was a great misfortune that the American Medical Missionary College was launched under cover of the regular schools rather than under the banner of the healing art embodied in the third angel's message. And it seems to some of us that we shall make the same mistake they did if we undertake to follow their example in establishing a medical school whose very standard, if it is at all maintained, means commercialism from first to last, or else the students who graduate from the school will lose their caste and standing with those who are following the medical practice of the present day.[19]

Thinking Things Through

Let's do a quick point-by-point analysis of Burden's remarks:

1. While Burden knew the Lord wanted thousands of medical missionary evangelists trained, he was working hardest to find a way to convince the church that they could operate a college to train "some" as physicians. Why? Because the Spirit of Prophecy was calling for many institutions, and there would always be a need for "some" licensed physicians.

2. But the Lord had opened a door that would make it much easier to operate a school to train licensed physicians in a manner consistent with the principles of the Adventist health message.

3. The law specified the test areas required for a medical license, but did not include "materia medica" (now referred to as pharmacology) or surgery. This greatly simplified avoiding the prevailing practice of "drugging," and opened the door for a medical degree more focused on lifestyle issues rather than acute care. Not that surgery is sinful; it's just not as well adapted as a general evangelistic tool.

4. The American Medical Missionary College (Kellogg's school in Battle Creek) was a "regular" school (AMA affiliated). Burden felt the AMA approach to medicine was intrinsically geared toward "commercialism from first to last," and that following their model would be a mistake in terms of the church's evangelistic interests.

One of the major factors that made this law unique was the issue of testing. Simply put, when you change the entrance test to a profession,

---

19. *Loma Linda Messages*, 368–369
[Note that since this material is not Ellen White's writing, it can not be found on the CD-ROM from the White Estate. It is still available in the hard copy editions.}

you change the profession itself. While we might have a hard time imagining such a thing in our day, it was no imagination in 1907. Here is the text of the law itself:

> The examination shall be conducted in the English language, shall be practical in character and designed to discover the applicant's fitness to practice his profession, and shall be in whole or in part, in writing on the following fundamental subjects, to wit: Anatomy, histology, gynecology, pathology, bacteriology, chemistry and toxicology, physiology, obstetrics, general diagnosis, hygiene. Examinations in each subject shall consist of not less than ten questions, answers to which shall be marked upon a scale of zero to ten. But all applicants must obtain not less than a general average of seventy-five percent and not less than sixty percent in any one subject.[20]

Burden was right; no pharmacology, no surgery. The way forward seemed much simpler than when they first started looking into opening a medical college. There was no prohibition against teaching additional skills, surgery perhaps the most obvious, but this law created an opportunity for a whole new category of health professional. They didn't have names for Physician's Assistants or Nurse Practitioners back then, but the concept was similar. Just a century ahead of the industry.

Opinions May Vary...

Not all Adventists agreed with John Burden, though. There were a number of different ideas, apparently, and Willie White sketched out a list of four in a letter he wrote a few days after reading Elder Burden's thoughts. Here's how he saw things:

> During my recent visit to Southern California I found that there were four plans in the minds of various brethren which I would describe as follows:
>
> 1. That the Loma Linda School modify its present plans, giving up most of its special work and operate simply as an ordinary sanitarium nurses' training school.
>
> I think this proposition would be favored only by a very few. I do not know who they are. I supposed we had left that proposition way behind, but I am told there are a few, probably those connected with rival institutions, who still hold to it.
>
> 2. That the Loma Linda School be developed along the lines of the recommendation in the resolutions adopted at the October convention held at Loma Linda. These recommendations, I am told, were fully endorsed at the Pacific Union Conference.

---

20. *The Statutes of California*, 1907, Chapter 212, 252

3. That the Loma Linda School carry out the resolutions, adopted at the October convention, and in addition to this that a legal corporation be formed under the California act which would permit graduates of the school to practice their special lines [of medical work] in the State of California.

4. To work toward the end of some day establishing a regular medical college.[21]

In times past when I have heard Mother endeavoring to outline to our brethren things that have been presented to her regarding what might be done at Loma Linda if we advance in the opening providences of God, I have supposed that we would probably work for a few years on plan number 2 and then develop plan number 4.

Elder Burden and some of his associates think that plan number 3 would be a more correct working out of the pattern shown to Mother, and they think that we need not wait several years, but that it could be done without much delay.

The "resolutions adopted at the October convention" that are mentioned in item number two can be found in hard copies of *Loma Linda Messages*, on page 304. Since this material was not written by Ellen White, it is not included on the CD-ROM of her writings. Basically, they say that the school at Loma Linda should teach students what they need to be medical evangelists, ask the General Conference Medical Department to study into what such a school should be doing, and invite the Pacific Union Conference and the General Conference to help with funding.

There may not have been anything more definite that anyone could do at the time, but without clarity on the first two items, and certainly no guarantee on the third, those resolutions are a classic case study of what comes out of a committee when the way forward is looking blurry. So the resolutions may have been "fully endorsed at the Pacific Union Conference," but that didn't ensure much.

The Heart of the Question

Observant readers will have noticed Elder White's expectation of eventually carrying out plan number four, and may remember the significance of the term he used, "a regular medical college."

In many ways, this is what the issue came down to, and the question which kept everything tied up in knots of indecision for the next six or seven years—should the College of Medical Evangelists be affiliated with the AMA?

At the Pacific Union Conference Medical Convention just mentioned, this question came out quite clearly, immediately following the presentation of the resolutions. The account reads:

---

21. *Loma Linda Message*, 373–374

Question—on medical school resolution by Elder [A.G.] Daniells:

I would like to inquire what this contemplates. Does it contemplate a college that will grant medical degrees and diplomas to be presented to State Boards and be used by our missionaries in their endeavor to qualify for foreign lands to practice there? Does it contemplate the establishment of a full-fledged medical college that will be recognized—that will give students a preparation for graduation that will be recognized by legal bodies such as the American Medical Association? You know it must have such recognition to be worth a nickel.[22]

And so it was that a difference of opinion existed amongst those making the decisions and setting the tone of the institution. There were a number of aspects and ramifications to this issue, but it came to a fairly simple focus in one pointed question: Should the College of Medical Evangelists be affiliated with the AMA?

To represent the situation and the individuals fairly, it should be said that all parties showed some evidence of vacillation back and forth on the question over time and as circumstances varied. But, by and large, the representatives of the two opinions can most easily be thought of as John Burden being hesitant to affiliate with the AMA, while W.C. White and A.G. Daniells tended to favor such a relationship.

Commenting on the difference of perspective held by these men, Dr. Owen Parrett, a member of CME's second graduating class (1915), put it this way:

The differences between Elders John Burden and Arthur Daniells focus on the question, Was a *special* training to be given to those desiring a *regular* training, or was a *regular* training to be given to those desiring a *regular* training? Did God desire at the College of Medical Evangelists to offer a "*special* preparation for those of our youth" who "feel it their duty" to "practice as regularly qualified physicians" (CT 479-481), or did God desire CME to prepare "regularly qualified physicians"? *Ordinary*? or *Unique*? Here it focused.[23]

How were they to know what to do?

22. *Loma Linda Messages*, 304–305
23. Quoted in David James Lee, *The Story of Loma Linda*, 1693

Chapter Fifteen

What to Do?

HISTORY is most interesting when you can "get into the guy's head" enough to start seeing *why* things were done, rather than just knowing that something *was* done. The story of charting the course for the College of Medical Evangelists is a classic in this regard. Why did *he* do *that*? What was the other guy *thinking* when he said such-and-such? It's a fun game, at least for those who enjoy it.

But it's not a science, and speculation on the thoughts of those long-dead is an uncertain business. Thus it behooves us to be cautious and charitable in our evaluations of all concerned, even though there may be times when we think we can see mistakes that were made.

Well... one would hope so! After all, given the fact that people have made millions of mistakes over thousands of years, how hard should it be to look back and find something that they might not have seen clearly—since they were fighting that perennial challenge of having to look forward?

There's a Haystack on Top of this Needle!

Our focus right now is determining the proper role of medical missionary work in the loud cry. Specifically, we are asking if medical missionary work is a *necessary* element of the loud cry. With that as a focus, we can simplify our task in this chapter somewhat. The one needle in all the hay that has meaning for us at the moment is the possibility that Loma Linda was intended to foster an evangelistic form of medical service and thus contribute a make-or-break element to the loud cry.

That's the needle. If it's in the haystack, we need to look at it. If it's not, then let's just be thankful for all the hay!

Most readers will have guessed by now that this book argues that such a needle exists. True enough, but to present the evidence for that hypothesis requires that some of Loma Linda's history be fresh in memory.

The Situation on the Ground

The property had been purchased; the sanitarium was in operation; the nurses' program had started; they even had the medical missionary course up and running. As we saw in the last chapter, not everyone was necessarily happy about all this, but it was what it was. The next big question had to do with what the school was going to be in regard to medical education.

Some feared the expense of developing a medical college. That was sensible. Medical education was changing, and there were powerful forces determined to close down scores of smaller medical schools. The assumption was that size and money influenced quality. Shut down the "one-horse" schools and quality goes up. It seemed simple.

But at the same time, there was a clear call from the Spirit of Prophecy for a medical school. On October 30, 1907, while Ellen White was talking, Elder John Burden spoke up:

> Elder Burden—I want to ask a question. Is this school that you have spoken of simply to qualify nurses, or is it to embrace also the qualifications for physicians?
>
> E.G. White—Physicians are to receive their education here. Here they are to receive such a mold that when they go out to labor, they will not seek to grasp the very highest wages, or else do nothing.[1]

That point blank answer should have settled the question as far as the training of physicians. Unfortunately, it didn't.

The issue of whether or not to accept that goal set up battle lines that would be fought over repeatedly for years to come. Perhaps it was the heat of that battle which somehow kept most everyone involved from asking the other simple question that John Burden raised in his letter of April 1908. The *other* question was, Which *type* of medical school should we operate? The law of California, you may recall, allowed for fully legal medical certificates to be issued to the graduates of appropriately chartered schools, "authorizing the holder thereof to practice any other system or mode of treating the sick or afflicted not

---

1. *Loma Linda Messages*, 304

referred to in this section,"[2] provided he meet other reasonable and non-objectionable requirements.

It seems, in hindsight, that this option would have been a welcome alternative to the mandated expense of AMA affiliation.

Of course, the "go or no-go" for such a plan shouldn't be the matter of finance. The Lord still owns the soybeans on a thousand fields (though in our day we might suspect He favors non-GMO varieties). God could supply the money if that's what He wanted, so the decision really should be made on other grounds.

Like what?

The Lord's counsel, obviously. Which strongly implies that anyone interested in knowing which course to take on this largely overlooked issue might have benefited from checking to see what Ellen White had to say at the time. As it turns out, she was saying and writing a great deal, and much of it had a common thread.

Seeking Counsel

The following Ellen White comments are selected from the record of an interview with her son, Willie White, and John Burden on September 20, 1909. When asked if she saw anything inappropriate about getting a state charter for the college, she said:

> We want none of that kind of "higher education" that will put us in a position where the credit must be given, not to the Lord God of Israel, but to the god of Ekron. The Lord designs that we shall stand as a distinct, sanctified, and holy people, so connected with Him that He can work with us....
>
> I must state that the light I have received is that we are to stand as a distinct, commandment-keeping people....
>
> As God's peculiar people, we should not feel that we must acknowledge our dependence upon men who are transgressing God's law, to give us influence in the world. It is God that gives us influence....
>
> [God] will give us advantages that are far beyond all the advantages we might receive from worldlings, by uniting with those who do not recognize the law of God....
>
> There are some who may not be able to see that here is a test as to whether we shall put our dependence on man, or depend upon God. Shall we by our course seem to acknowledge that there is a stronger power with unbelievers than there is with God's own people?...
>
> Your success depends upon the blessing of God, not upon the ideas and views of men who are opposed to the requirements of the laws of God....

2. *The Statutes of California*, 1907, Chapter 212, 252

> We need not tie to men in order to secure influence. We need not think that we are dependent upon the knowledge and experience of men who do not recognize the Lord as their Master....
>
> Jesus Christ is our Saviour today, and He is willing to work in our behalf if we will not put our dependence upon some other power....
>
> Shall we unite ourselves with those that are full of error, who have no respect for God's commandments, and shall our students go forth to obtain the finishing touches of their education from men who, unless they are converted, will not be honored with a place in the councils of heaven?

As Ellen White herself often commented, sometimes certain thoughts made a strong impression on her mind. So much so on this occasion that Willie tried to direct the conversation back to the particular points of interest to the college administration team. He asked, "What is the final outcome? Will all our medical missionaries be simply nurses? Shall we have no more physicians, or shall we have a school in which we can, ourselves, give the finishing touches?" His mother responded:

> Whatever plan you follow take your position that you will not unite or be bound up with those that do not respect God's commandments.

Unfortunately for Willie and Elder Burden, it was precisely this matter of deciding between various plans that they were struggling with. There wasn't much help for them in having that issue dismissed so easily, so Willie tried again: "Does that mean that we are not to have any more physicians, but that our people will work simply as nurses or does it mean that we shall have a school of our own, where we can educate physicians?"

> We shall have a school of our own, but we are not to be dependent upon the world. We must put our dependence upon a Power that is higher than all human power.

Well, that was a bit more concrete. She had definitely reaffirmed the idea of a school. But the charter was still a question. This time Elder Burden spoke up: "Would the securing of a charter for a medical school, where our students might obtain a medical education, militate against our depending upon God?"

> No; I do not see that it would, if a charter were secured on the right terms. Only be sure that you do not exalt men above God. If you can gain force and influence that will make your work more effective, without tying yourself to worldly men, that would be right. But we are not to exalt the human above the divine.

We don't have space for all of this interview, but we may find some-thing of value in noting a few more selections:

> I do not see anything wrong in that, as long as you do not in any way lift men above the Lord God of Israel, or throw discredit upon His power. But enter into no agreement with any fraternity that would open a door of temptation to some weak souls to lose their hold on God....
>
> God desires us to be separate, and yet it is our privilege to avail ourselves of certain rights. But rather than to confuse our medical work, you had better stand aloof, and labor with the advantages that you yourselves can offer....
>
> God is dishonored when His people go to any worldly power, or put their trust in a worldly power. That is where God's people, again and again, became ensnared, and spoilt their history. You must arrange this matter the best you can, but the principle that is presented to me is that you are not to acknowledge any power as greater than that of God....
>
> I have had very distinct light, however, that there is danger of our limiting the power of the Holy One of Israel, in connection with certain plans for con-necting our schools with worldly methods.[3]

Are We Missing Something?

Elders White and Burden must have been grateful for a clear answer to the question of the charter. It may be that they had wrestled with the issue for so long that their minds were focused on only that one issue, and they didn't take a lot of time to think over the rest of what Ellen White had said. But we aren't pressured with those other things just now, so at our leisure we can reflect back on the instruction from the prophet. What do you, gentle reader, see in her comments? Is there any-thing that stands out at all?

It will seem to be a higher percentage here because selections have been lifted from their context, but by actual count, of the sixty-four sen-tences from Ellen White in that interview, twenty-six of them contained warnings about creating ties or establishing inappropriate relationships with those who do not obey the commandments of God. Another twenty sentences contained admonitions to depend on God, or promises of bless-ings for those who do. Only eighteen sentences of the whole fell outside those two categories.

---

3. *Medical Practice and the Educational Program at Loma Linda,* 75–78.
   [This largely forgotten publication was prepared by the White Estate in 1953, and provides insights into the formative years of Loma Linda that are available no where else. Although it has not been included in the EGW CD-ROM, a PDF is available from the White Estate's "Digital Research Cen-ter" at http://drc.whiteestate.org/openpdf.php?file=786.pdf]

Now the question that arises is, Whom could this be a warning about? In just the selected comments printed here we find quite a range of terms used to designate the dangerous relationships she describes:

> ...the god of Ekron... men who are transgressing God's law... worldlings... those who do not recognize the law of God.... men who are opposed to the requirements of the laws of God.... men who do not recognize the Lord as their Master... those that are full of error, who have no respect for God's commandments... men who, unless they are converted, will not be honored with a place in the councils of heaven... those that do not respect God's commandments... not to be dependent upon the world... do not exalt men above God... without tying yourself to worldly men... we are not to exalt the human above the divine... do not in any way lift men above the Lord... enter into no agreement with any fraternity... any worldly power... you are not to acknowledge any power as greater than that of God... plans for connecting our schools with worldly methods.

What individual, informal group, or corporate entity of any kind could possibly be spoken of in all that?

There is no value in hasty answers, so let's look at another piece of evidence. The very first of the designators she used is of particular interest because she spoke of the "god of Ekron" again, twenty-one days after this interview, in a letter to Brother Burden:

> I am instructed to say that in our educational work, there is to be no compromise in order to meet the world's standards. God's commandment-keeping people are not to unite with the world, to carry various lines of work according to worldly plans and worldly wisdom.
>
> Our people are now being tested as to whether they will obtain their wisdom from the greatest Teacher the world ever knew or seek to the god of Ekron. Let us determine that we shall not be tied by so much as a thread to the educational policies of those who do not discern the voice of God, and who will not hearken to His commandments....
>
> Shall we represent before the world, that our physicians must follow the pattern of the world, before they can be qualified to act as successful physicians? This is the question that is now testing the faith of some of our brethren.[4]

If this "god of Ekron" is the same as the "god of Ekron" mentioned in the interview three weeks before, then we have more clues to work with. Who could this possibly be that apparently sets the world's standards, offers "plans" and "wisdom," and has a "pattern" that seems to promise the qualifications "to act as successful physicians"? Getting this right is

4. *Loma Linda Messages*, 447

important; this question has tested the faith of some brethren, and we don't want to fail such a test ourselves.

As an even further piece of evidence for consideration, we may turn to a story from the days when Ellen White was living in Australia.

A Lesson from the Past

When the subject of establishing a college came up, one obvious question was the location. After quite a bit of looking, the attention of the "locating committee" was directed to the Brettville estate near Cooranbong. Naturally the members of the committee wanted to make a wise choice, and there was some concern about the quality of the soil. It didn't look at all like the rich loamy soil of Iowa that Elder Daniells and Elder Rosseau were used to.

But the look of the soil wasn't all there was to the matter. Ellen White had already said she was satisfied they had found the right spot. Elder McCullagh had been healed of his tuberculosis in answer to Ellen White's prayer for a sign of encouragement. The mysterious six-foot furrow had already been found and commented upon. But Elders Daniells and Rosseau were concerned about the soil....

Perhaps there were other issues as well, for Ellen White says the two men had already held up the school project by two years, and that seems difficult to understand if the soil was the only concern. Whatever may have been at the bottom of it all, it evidently grew into a serious problem. Ellen White describes the situation like this:

> Nothing we could say made the least impression on their minds. They would not accept the land. My testimony was of no account with them. They were so strong and firm, that W.C. White was afraid to venture. This union of sentiment between those two men brought upon us a great burden and hindrance.
>
> If the work had been carried forward according to the light God had given, if the place had been purchased, and the deeds made out in my name, as I had told them, we should not have had to sustain the losses that have come to us.[5]

On top of all that, there was the matter of the "land inspector" that A.G. Daniells and W.C. White hired to share his opinion. His name was A.H. Benson, and he's the one who came up with the memorable line about a Bandicoot needing a sack lunch if he wanted to walk across the property. His extremely negative report troubled Daniells and W.C. White.

Finally, when these two Elders came to her with the "expert opinion" of the agricultural agent, the prophet calmly dismissed their concerns

---

5. Letter, EGW to My Brethren, February 2, 1898

with a single question—"Is there not a God in Israel, that ye have turned to the god of Ekron?"

In this case—obviously quite a few years before these same gentlemen would be considering what kind of medical school to establish—who or what was "the god of Ekron"? If there is any consistency to the symbolism, the god of Ekron would seem to be some sort of worldly authority that sets itself up in opposition to the counsel of God. It is dangerous to exalt any such authority to a position "above God." Who could that be in the Loma Linda circumstances?

Contact!

Just now we may find value in an old cryptanalyst's trick called "contact analysis." If one is trying to break a coded English message, it is helpful to know that the letters "t" and "h" commonly occur together as "th." "Qu" is another such "contact" combination. If we take that idea one notch up the ladder of language, we find an interesting "contact" of words in Ellen White's usage. A simple search of the Ellen White CD-ROM shows twenty-eight "hits" for the word "fraternity" that Ellen White used when responding to Willie and Elder Burden.

Two of those hits are from accounts of the interview itself, so they may be ignored, leaving us with twenty-six. Eighteen uses of the word are in the phrase "medical fraternity," and one is in a context that would imply that it is the "fraternity of doctors" to which she refers. That's slightly more than seventy-three percent of the cases.

Six of the hits are more general, speaking of the brotherhood of the church or the ministry, and the one remaining instance is in an explanatory note supplied by the compilers of the book, and not actually written by Ellen White.[6]

---

6. This final, non-EGW instance is of passing interest, nonetheless. In a letter of April 6, 1899, written to Dr. Kellogg, Ellen White used the term "fraternity" twice. The compilers comment following the Ellen White text is where the last instance of the term occurs:

"But according to the light the Lord has given me, something of the spirit of Freemasonry exists, and has built a wall about the work. The old, regular practice has been exalted as the only true method for the treatment of disease. And to a large degree this feeling has leavened the physicians connected with you....

"Dr. Kellogg, God has given you favor with the medical fraternity, and he would have you hold that favor. But in no case are you to stand as do the physicians of the world to exalt allopathy above every other practice, and call all other methods quackery and error; for from the beginning to the present time the results of allopathy have made a most objectionable showing. There has been loss of life in your sanitarium because drugs have been administered, and these give no chance for nature to do her work of restoration. Drug medication has broken up the power of the human machinery, and the patients have died. Others have carried the drugs away with them, making less effective the simple remedies nature uses to restore the system. The students in your institution [Battle Creek Sanitarium] are not to be educated to regard drugs as a necessity. They are to be edu-

From all this, we may consider whether or not a seventy-three percent frequency of association between "medical" and "fraternity" can help us as we try to determine who or what it was that Ellen White had in mind when she repeatedly warned the Elders about establishing working relationships for the College of Medical Evangelists.

Seeking Clarity

In yet another attempt to resolve the matter, a letter was placed in the hands of Ellen White on January 26, 1910, asking for clarification. Unfortunately, the letter only asked if the school should be such that the graduates would be "able to take state board examinations and become registered, qualified physicians." An answer to that question would clearly distinguish between a nursing school and a medical school, but it didn't do any good at all for distinguishing between two kinds of medical school. It would appear that the brethren were diligently studying out a question that had been answered in 1907.

Still, the answer Ellen White gave at this time *is* instructive:

> The light given me is, We must provide that which is essential to qualify our youth who desire to be physicians, so that they may intelligently fit themselves to be able to stand the examinations required to prove their efficiency as physicians. They should be taught to treat understandingly the cases of those who are diseased, so that the door will be closed for any sensible physician to imagine that we are not giving in our school the instruction necessary for properly qualifying young men and young women to do the work of a physician. Continually the students who are graduated are to advance in knowledge, for practice makes perfect.

> The medical school at Loma Linda is to be of the highest order, because those who are in that school have the privilege of maintaining a living connection with the wisest of all physicians, from whom there is communicated knowledge of a superior order. And for the special preparation of those of our youth who have clear convictions of their duty to obtain a medical education that will enable them to pass the examinations required by law of all who practice as regularly qualified physicians, we are to supply whatever may be required, so that these youth need not be compelled to go to medical schools conducted by men not of

---

cated to leave drugs alone.

"The medical fraternity, represented to me as Freemasonry, with their long, unintelligible names which common people cannot understand, would call the Lord's prescription for Hezekiah quackery."

The explanatory note inserted by the compilers addresses the term "Freemasonry," and suggests that "apparently Ellen White saw a parallel between the spirit of the close-knit medical fraternity and that of the Freemasons," which the explanatory note went on to describe as "a secret society based on the principles of brotherliness, charity, and mutual aid." (*Manuscript Releases*, vol. 16, 288)

Though it would be easy to see Ellen White's use of "fraternity," both in this letter and in her 1909 interview, as a negative term, fairness would find little to fault in "brotherliness, charity, and mutual aid."

our faith. Thus we shall close a door that the enemy would be pleased to have left open; and our young men and young women, whose spiritual interests the Lord desires to safeguard, will not feel compelled to connect with unbelievers in order to obtain a thorough training along medical lines.

(Signed) Ellen G. White[7]

This certainly answers the question they asked!

It's interesting, though, to look closely at what Ellen White wrote. It's clear that she recognized the importance of relating to legal requirements, but she actually aimed higher than compliance as outlined by worldly authorities. "The medical school at Loma Linda is to be the highest order," she said, and attributed that to "the privilege of maintaining a living connection with the wisest of all physicians, from whom there is communicated knowledge of a superior order."

This raises an interesting question as to the point of comparison. This "knowledge of a superior order" from "the wisest of all physicians" must be superior to something inferior, but what might that be?

The second sentence of the final paragraph, at sixty-nine words, is somewhat long and complex, at least by our modern grammatical standards. But there are two very interesting words in this one sentence that invite our thought. The words are "special" and "regularly."

In standard usage, it's hard to envision something "special" as being the numerical majority, let alone the only option available. In a restaurant where the "daily special" is the only thing on the menu... perhaps?

But a "special preparation" isn't the routine course that everyone takes in college. What is it that was to make this preparation "special"? The rest of the sentence actually tells us—it's what was needed for the "some" students who were convicted that they had a duty to prepare for the tests required to practice as *regularly* qualified physicians. These are the "special" ones.

And, of course, we've noted in earlier chapters the implications of the term "regular" in the context of the times. It seems Ellen White believed that students who came to the College of Medical Evangelists with "clear convictions" that they needed to qualify as "regular physicians," would require a "special preparation." What were all the rest of the students to be studying.

All those questions aside (or, perhaps, never raised), this reply was read to the delegates gathered for the fifth biennial session of the Pacific Union Conference. At a special meeting called for the purpose, on Saturday night, January 29, 1910—a meeting A.L. White described as "The Great Decision... which determined the destiny of the College of Medical

---

7. *Loma Linda Messages*, 484–485

Evangelists"—the vote was taken to support the formal recommendation for the establishment of a medical school at Loma Linda.[8]

Exactly what *kind* of medical school was not addressed.

So... what did all this mean for the development of CME?

Answers to Questions Often Unasked

Ellen White, despite a decline in vigor due to advancing age, was far from silent on the development of the college. In 1909 she wrote, "I feel a deep interest that careful study shall be given to the needs of our institutions at Loma Linda and that right moves shall be made.... With Christ as our educator we may reach a high standard in the knowledge of the true science of healing."[9]

Because of her "deep interest" in the school, she did what she could to help in every way possible. In her unique position, of course, the greatest help was often writing out counsel from the Lord. A particularly interesting example of this comes from April of 1910. As she mentions in the article, she received instruction about "many things" during the night of April 26. She wrote the article on April 27, not quite three months after the "Great Decision" vote had been taken. It contains a lot to think about, and altogether too much to comment on, so with a minimum of interruption, here are excerpts:

---

8. An interesting perspective on the time period of this conference has been preserved in *Loma Linda Messages*, 590. Written by Clarence Crisler, one of Ellen White's secretarial assistants, the account raises—but does not fully answer—some important questions. Crisler wrote:

"Shortly after I reached the office on Tuesday, February 13, 1912, Sister White came into my room, and told me that she had had a strange experience the night before, an experience somewhat similar to that which she passed through during the session of the Pacific Union Conference held at Mountain View in January 1910, when it had seemed as if she were being torn to pieces by the powers of darkness. She said that she had been struggling all night with unseen agencies that were striving to oppress and discourage and thus defeat the purposes of God. The struggle had been a long and wearing one, and at times had seemed as if the enemy might obtain the mastery; but finally, toward morning, the Lord had helped her to gain a decisive victory. The trying experience had left her, however, very weak, and she feared that during the day she would not be able to do much writing.

"Sister White went on to say that it had seemed during the night as if some of the brethren were misrepresenting matters by placing unfair interpretations upon her writings. The counsels she had given, were being misapplied. Several times, in the course of our conversation, she used the words, misinterpret and misapply; and she brought out clearly the thought that some were making an unwise and an unwarranted use of isolated passages in her writings which, taken out of their original setting, seemed to vindicate and uphold their own policies."

That there was a serious spiritual battle going on at the Conference in 1910 is obvious. Ellen White said it was "somewhat similar" to her experience the night before (February 12–13, 1912. What that similarity consisted of, is not specified. The words "misinterpret and misapply" seem to be used to describe the later event; to what extent they may properly be applied to the event in 1910 is not clear.

9. *Testimonies*, vol. 9, 177

The Lord has shown us the evil of depending upon the strength of earthly organizations. He has instructed us that the commission of the medical missionary is received from the very highest authority. He would have us understand that it is a mistake to regard as most essential the education given by physicians who reject the authority of Christ, the greatest Physician who ever lived upon the earth. We are not to accept and follow the view of men who refuse to recognize God as their teacher, but who learn of men, and are guided by man-made laws and restrictions.

During the night of April 26 many things were opened before me. I was shown that now in a special sense we as a people are to be guided by divine instruction. Those fitting themselves for medical missionary work should fear to place themselves under the direction of worldly doctors....

Efforts should be made to secure teachers who will instruct after Christ's manner of teaching, regarding this of more value than any human method....

Teachers who are not particular to harmonize with the teaching of Christ, and who follow the customs and practices of worldly physicians, are out of line with the charge that the Saviour has given us.

It is not necessary that our medical missionaries follow the precise track marked out by the medical men of the world.... their dependence is upon God and not upon the professedly wise men of the world.

Some of our medical missionaries have supposed that a medical training according to the plans of worldly schools is essential to their success. To those who have thought that the only way to success is by being taught by worldly men and by pursuing a course that is sanctioned by worldly men, I would now say, put away such ideas. This is a mistake that should be corrected. It is a dangerous thing to catch the spirit of the world; the popularity which such a course invites will bring into the work a spirit which the Word of God can not sanction....

At Loma Linda... and in many other sanitariums established for the promulgation of the work of the third angel's message there are to come to the physicians and to the teachers new ideas, a new understanding of the principles that must govern the medical work. An education is to be given that is altogether in harmony with the teachings of the Word of God....

It is a lack of faith in the power of God that leads our physicians to lean so much upon the arm of the law, and to trust so much to the influence of worldly powers. The truly converted man or woman who will study these words of inspiration spoken by the apostle Paul may learn to claim in all their depth and fullness the divine promises.

I am charged to present these Scriptures to our people, that they may understand that those who do not believe the Word of God can not possibly present to those who desire to become acceptable medical missionaries the way by which they will become most successful. Christ was the greatest physician the world has ever known; His heart was ever touched with human woe. He has a work for those to do who will not place their dependence upon worldly powers....

A time will come when medical missionaries of other denominations will become jealous and envious of the influence exerted by Seventh-day Adventists who are working in these lines. They will feel that influence is being secured by our workers which they ought to have.

It seems obvious that the "lines" of work that the Seventh-day Adventist medical missionaries were to be working in must be something unique. Whatever the Lord is calling for here, it must be different from the methods being used by other health professionals.

The last three paragraphs of the article, quoted below, deserve careful thought. Is she speaking here about "special" students who have been trained to "practice as regularly qualified physicians"?

In any case, the closing sentence has clearly been fulfilled:

We should have in various places, men of extraordinary ability, who have obtained their diplomas in medical schools of the best reputation, who can stand before the world as fully qualified and legally recognized physicians. Let God-fearing men be wisely chosen to go through the training essential in order to obtain such qualifications. They should be prudent men who will remain true to the principles of the message.

These should obtain the qualifications and the authority to conduct an educational work for our young men and our young women who desire to be trained for medical missionary work.

Now while the world is favorable toward the teaching of the health reform principles, moves should be made to secure for our own physicians the privilege of imparting medical instruction to our young people who would otherwise be led to attend the worldly medical colleges. The time will come when it will be more difficult than it now is to arrange for the training of our young people in medical missionary lines.[10]

More as a matter of curiosity than of newsworthiness, we include here a comment from the Los Angeles *Times* of November 9, 1924. The medical college had, by that time, become a major player, and the *Times* ran a human interest story on the school's history. Was it intrepid reporting, or mere coincidence, that resulted in this summation of the early years?

First they had to have the sanction of the State Board of Medical Examiners and they also wanted the approval of the American Medical Association.

---

10. *The Medical Evangelist*, April 1, 1910.
  [This is the date as listed on the EGW CD-ROM. The paper itself simply says "Vol. 2, No. 2." Since Ellen White was writing on April 27, it's safe to assume that the paper didn't actually come off the presses on April 1.]

Chapter Sixteen

One Thing Thou Lackest

D URING the years 1910, 1911, and 1912, the school at Loma Linda carried on, but just barely. In general, the mood of the Church's administration seems to have solidified in the direction of aligning the school
with the American Medical Association, and its educational branch, the
Association of American Medical Colleges.

It is difficult to tell if anyone was considering the option once discussed, and still a part of California law, that might have provided some
much-needed latitude. Mostly what shows up are signs of discomfort
with the requirements of the AMA. Occasionally these "discomforts"
were philosophical, such as when W.C. White wrote:

> In our contact with various medical systems, we shall find a great tendency to
> give honor to men, but it should not be so with the Seventh-day Adventist people....
>
> Our medical missionaries should be given the opportunities to know the very
> best things done by the allopaths, the eclectics, the homeopaths, the osteopaths,
> and the water-cure doctors, but none of these systems should be adopted as
> comprising that which our physicians need to know; nor should the name of any
> of these systems be adopted as "the sign of our order." Neither are our medical
> men to give the credit or honor of the results of their labors under God, to any
> man or group of men, or to any locality, or to any system.[1]

---

1. *The Medical Evangelist*, vol. 3, Nos. 8 and 9 (Oct.–Nov. 1911), 132; The lead article in this issue is "The
Fallacies of Sectarian Medicine," by George K. Abbott. The point of the article is that of the then-
prevailing "sects" of medicine (Abbott lists "Allopathy, Homeopathy, Eclecticism, Osteopathy, Chiropractic, Hydropathy, Naturopathy, and Christian Science), none is an adequate embodiment of
what the Lord was asking of Seventh-day Adventists.

More common than these philosophical issues, though, were matters of finance. The first stipulation of the medical authorities was the construction of laboratory facilities and the purchase of equipment. This requirement—a significant strain on finances—was largely met by early 1912.[2]

The bigger issue was the need for clinical practice opportunities for the final two years of the medical course. Some administrators felt that working in the Sanitarium was the most appropriate training for doctors whom they hoped would soon be... *working in a sanitarium!* Others saw validity in the AAMC's position that the Sanitarium did not provide enough variety in the conditions treated.

A system of affiliations with area hospitals was cobbled together so that medical students could gain experience in these other facilities, but it was far from optimal. Note the reasons given in early 1913 by the president of C.M.E., for his dissatisfaction with the affiliation program:

> The patients are entirely under the management of the Medical Superintendent, who has full control of the treatment administered. This differs greatly from the treatment which we wish to demonstrate before our students. There is no way of teaching physiological therapeutics without having a goodly number of patients upon whom to demonstrate.
>
> The last two years of our medical course are the most important years because they are the years when the principles of healthful living and physiological therapeutics are emphasized and taught in detail.... The last two years are given entirely to the application of therapeutic measures and are the most important in teaching the principles for which the health work of the denomination stands. If we had access to all the county hospitals in California this would not at all suffice for giving the education which must be imparted to our students.[3]

The idea of a distinctive Adventist medical practice was still alive, hence the frustration with clinical settings that contradicted what had been taught in the classroom. Apparently the interference of a hospital Medical Superintendent with a different concept of health and healing was recognized as a problem to be worked away from, while a regulatory organization with a different concept of health and healing was not.

Misalignment

One aspect of the developing program which is hard to understand today —and may have been just as hard back then—is the question of the school's focus. The Spirit of Prophecy had clearly called the college to train—

---

2. *Medical Practice and the Educational Program at Loma Linda*, 123–124
3. *Medical Practice and the Educational Program at Loma Linda*, 152–153

nurses who, in addition to their acquirement of more than ordinary skill in the care of the sick, had also learned to labor as evangelists in soul-winning service.

It is for the training of such workers, as well as for the training of physicians, that the school at Loma Linda has been founded. In this school many workers are to be qualified with the ability of physicians, to labor, not in professional lines as physicians, but as medical missionary evangelists.... The cause is in need of hundreds of workers who have received a practical and thorough education in medical lines, and who are also prepared to labor from house to house as teachers, Bible workers, and colporteurs.[4]

Indeed, as we saw on page 177, in 1908 Elder Burden anticipated "thousands" trained for medical-evangelistic work, and "some" trained as physicians. This concept was evidently still current in 1912. On the fifteenth of July, W.A. Ruble, president of CME, met with the General Conference executive committee in Takoma Park. According to the minutes of the meeting:

The college management, he says, expects but few youth to take the medical course, while the many will take the evangelistic medical missionary course....

Considerable time was given to the discussion of the original idea of Loma Linda, the training of medical evangelists (not physicians), and Dr. Ruble explained that while few had presented themselves for this three years' [medical missionary] course, the school aims to keep up the course and desires more young people to enter this department.[5]

With this as the goal of the school, it is a puzzle to see that the largest share, by far, of the time, discussion, fund raising, brain storming, and agony were all over the medical course. Perhaps the effort put into securing this portion of the program—increasingly defined by the desire of some of the administrators to gain the recognition of the AMA and the AAMC—was sending somewhat mixed messages. Somehow, the part of the program that was to encompass "thousands"... just never did.

One Thing Thou Lackest

Despite a growing understanding of the deficiencies plaguing the available options, the medical course's clinical practice problem wasn't going away, and the AAMC was concerned. From their perspective it was clear what CME was lacking: a two hundred-bed hospital in downtown Los Angeles. Only there would they find the scope and number of cases called for in the AAMC model.

---

4. *Counsels to Teachers*, 471
5. General Conference executive committee minutes, July 15, 1912

At Loma Linda, this was cause for concern. Large buildings in large cities were not a priority in the Adventist mindset, particularly not in southern California where a similar idea had been floated back in 1901. Floated, that is, until it was torpedoed by Ellen White.[6]

But *something* had to be done. On March 29, 1912, the CME constituency voted to solicit $15,000 to begin constructing a clinical hospital on the college grounds at Loma Linda. By May 27, plans had been drawn up for a single-story building, forty-six feet by seventy-two feet, with two wings to be used as patient wards. Construction began in late fall, then stopped in early December when the $2,000 raised for the project ran out.[7] More fund raising was required.

A year later the hospital was a near-reality, and cause for rejoicing. Speaking to the Constituency of the college on March 25, 1914, Dr. Ruble pointed out its importance to their plans:

> The addition of the new hospital, which was opened in December, has been a most important acquisition to our college. From a temporal standpoint the matter of therapeutics is the most important reason for conducting a medical course. This new hospital makes it possible for our students to have under their own supervision different diseases which they may treat according to the system of physiologic therapeutics which has been accepted by this denomination."[8]

How much of this was actually accomplished is in doubt. Later in his presentation, Ruble explained that the hospital "has not been fully completed. There are no treatment rooms, dining room, or kitchen."

But the bigger disappointment was yet to come. Just hours later, a line of reasoning never clearly specified in the available minutes of the Constituency Meeting led to the conclusion that the hospital was, after all, unacceptable:

> We find quite a difference of opinion as to how the building should be utilized, all agreeing that it cannot be used for the clinical work of the college as was first thought necessary for the work of the school....
>
> Owing to the great diversity of opinion concerning the best use to which the building should be put, we do not feel competent to advise, except that as it cannot be used as originally designed for the college clinical hospital, endeavor should now be made to turn it so far as possible to the financial profit of the sanitarium.[9]

---

6. *Manuscript Releases.*, vol. 1, 250–253. This story of the 1901 episode will come up again and be dealt with in more detail on page 210.

7. *Medical Practice and the Educational Program at Loma Linda*, 131, 143, 145

8. *Medical Practice and the Educational Program at Loma Linda*, 158

9. *Medical Practice and the Educational Program at Loma Linda*, 161

What had happened? How could they reverse their thinking so suddenly? The clue is in the next sentence:

> It is now conceded by all connected with the college that the clinical work, or most of it, will have to be done in Los Angeles.

Though full details are lacking, it is clear that the major factor was the AMA's opinion that the Redlands/San Bernardino area did not provide sufficient population to fill the hospital with a wide enough variety of medical conditions. It was, after all, primarily a tourist area.

It was a sad and challenging day for the constituency. The minutes of the meeting include a section with the depressing title, "General Discussion of CME Problems." Among the concerns: Lack of finances, the allotment of General Conference tithe funds for the school, the influence on Adventist medical students should they be forced to finish their training at non-Adventist schools, and a general concern that the school might be struggling for a goal other than the Lord's approval.

Characteristic of this last item were the comments made by several that day. The minutes record:

> J.A. Burden emphasized the need of following out the plans laid down by the Lord, that it is merit and not recognition that counts. We have a work to do and need not ask the world for its sanction. He stated that our sanitariums should be the best hospitals in which our students could gain experience in association with God-fearing physicians; that we have been viewing things in a wrong light; that our students should be trained as soul winners.
>
> The question was again repeated by the Chairman [E.E. Andross from the General Conference] as to whether or not the five-year course should be continued. Are medical men needed in this message? Is the Lord calling for such a school as we have been trying to carry? When we know for what the Lord is calling, we will know better how to work to attain that end.

It is not a good sign when the chairman of an enterprise is uncertain about the Lord's calling for the central mission of the organization. Yet Elder Andross was hardly alone:

> S.E. Wight expressed the need of strong ministers and medical men. He thought perhaps if the school was devoted to the medical evangelistic course more would be accomplished. He is in sympathy with having fully qualified physicians, but longs for the day to come when the force of the denomination will be for soul-saving....
>
> B.G. Wilkinson said that he was troubled on the question of standards. Are we struggling to meet the standard of the world or are we not?...

R.S. Owen reminded us that God's recognition should be first sought. That while we should train those to do the work of a physician, a larger number should be trained as Medical Evangelists....

C.W. Flaiz thought that in view of the nearness of the end of the history of this world, we needed men to go out quickly into the field and bring men to a knowledge of the truth. He spoke of the limited funds, and that workers are not being sent out as in times past. He felt that perhaps more results would be attained with a three-year evangelistic course than to follow the five-year [medical] course....

W.A. Spicer felt that we were to choose between two ways, either to equip the school to meet the standard of the world, or not to seek for their recognition. [10]

Needless to say, there were some dark days in sunny California. Central to the issue was the goal of meeting the requirements of the American Medical Association. But what other option did they have?

It was now 1914, and the generous provisions in the law of 1907 no longer existed. The legislative session of 1913 had replaced them with a more limited choice between only an AMA sanctioned "physician and surgeon certificate" and a more restrictive (and arguably less prestigious) "drugless practitioner certificate." The curricula for each was spelled out in detail: The first required both materia medica and surgery, and a total of 4,800 hours' instruction in specified subjects, while the latter required only half as many hours, but forbade the use of drugs and procedures which involved "in any manner severing or penetrating any of the tissues of human beings except the severing of the umbilical cord." [11]

In short, there was still an alternative independent of the AMA's requirements, but there is no evidence that any consideration was given to it. That other groups availed themselves of this option (or circumvented AMA control through some other means) is evident from the continued existence of chiropractors, homeopaths, naturopaths, and osteopaths. While these practitioners were undoubtedly marginalized in the public mind for many years, [12] we should remember that they were working without the benefit of divine promises such as this:

---

10. *Medical Practice and the Educational Program at Loma Linda*, 163–164

11. *The Statutes of California*, 1913, Chapter 354, 722–737

12. An illustration of the acrimony between the AMA and other schools of medicine may be found in an event from the early 1930s. When a Los Angeles-based school of osteopathy sought the use of some facilities at the Los Angeles County Hospital, the Council of Education of the AMA, the American College of Surgeons, and the American Hospital Association all threatened to revoke the County Hospital's accreditation, thus disqualifying it as a "teaching hospital." The only solution, they were told, was to construct separate facilities to house the "irregular" practitioners. (Loma Linda University School of Medicine Alumni Association, *Diamond Memories*, 78)

There are some who may not be able to see that here is a test, as to whether we shall put our dependence on man or depend upon God. Shall we by our course seem to acknowledge that there is a stronger power with unbelievers than there is with God's own people?... When people see that God blesses us, and gives success to our work, as we make Him supreme, then they will be led to give consideration to the truth we teach. Many will be compelled to recognize that our methods are superior to those employed in the schools of the world, as they are commonly conducted. We need not tie to men in order to secure influence. We need not think that we are dependent upon the knowledge and experience of men who do not recognize the Lord as their Master.[13]

Like so many other issues of the past, this is a fun subject for the unproductive game of "What Might Have Been." But reality bids us continue examining what actually was....

The Ellen G. White Memorial Hospital

If CME was to secure AMA approval they must find a way to provide greater clinical experience for their students. The records indicate that the faculty sought out every possible means of filling this need. Working relations were established with the San Bernardino and Los Angeles county hospitals and the Glendale Sanitarium, an out-patient clinic was started in Los Angeles, and students gained additional experience doing "visiting nurses' work." In the final analysis, however, it just wasn't enough to meet the requirements. Something more was needed, and the AMA once again strongly suggested that it be a hospital in downtown Los Angeles.

The influence of Ellen White's 1901 rejection of the plan to build a sanitarium "out at one side" of Los Angeles put the brethren in a hard spot. What were they to do?

In *The Story of Our Health Message*, D.E. Robinson comments that, "It was felt by some of the brethren that the Testimony of 1901 had reference to 'a sanitarium,' and not to a clinical hospital such as the needs of the medical college now required." What the *rest* of the brethren felt Ellen White's instruction meant is not recorded.

What appears to have been the decisive influence in the minds of the brethren was W.C. White's account of his mother's reaction on the ninth of May, 1915, to news of a "very liberal gift to the College of Medical Evangelists for the establishment of a students' home and a hospital in Los Angeles." Years later, at a time of sharp dispute on the location and future of the College of Medical Evangelists, it would be pointedly observed that the

---

13. *Loma Linda Messages*, 443

conclusion Elder White drew from this conversation was not clearly supported anywhere in his mother's writings.[14] But that was far in the future; in 1916, sixteen months after the event, W.C. White described it as follows:

> Mother's lips quivered, and for a moment she shook with emotion. Then she said: "I am glad you told me this. I have been in perplexity about Loma Linda, and this gives me courage and joy."[15]

Out of all these considerations came the action taken by the Constituency of CME on June 17, 1915. Since they included a comprehensive statement of their aims and goals, we quote it here at some length:

> In view of the fact that the College of Medical Evangelists is established with the avowed purpose of giving a medical missionary training to large numbers of nurses who are to be trained with unusual ability as nurses, also for numbers to be trained with the ability of physicians but without legal qualifications, as well as to educate a smaller number as legally qualified physicians; in our opinion, it is necessary, in order to successfully accomplish this purpose, that the College be provided with hospital and dispensary facilities, where a combined evangelistic and medical training can be given along the lines of health reform and rational therapeutics, in such a locality where a larger volume of clinical material can be reached and wider experience in evangelistic lines can be supplied than is possible with the present facilities. In order to accomplish these purposes, therefore, be it
>
> Resolved, That in harmony with suggestions made by Elder I. H. Evans, we ask the North American Division Conference of Seventh-day Adventists to inaugurate a movement to provide property and erect a building for dispensary purposes, also a hospital building to be known as [the] "Ellen G. White Memorial Hospital," at a cost for grounds and buildings not to exceed $50,000.[16]

To pass such a motion did not accomplish the fact. There was still a great deal of time, effort, money, and prayer that went into seeing that building erected and outfitted. In time, the college gained the recognition of the AAMC, and thousands of nurses and medical students became proficient practitioners in that facility. For all that they have done to further God's work, we may be truly grateful.

But just now there is a loose thread that must be picked up. It has been dangling mysteriously since 1899.

---

14. See, for instance, the August 3, 1960, letter of Glenn Calkins to the Officers of the General Conference, 2; and G.A. Roberts' 1960 compilation entitled "Messages on Location of Families and Institutions," 1. Calkins was a member of CME's Board of Trustees for twenty-five years, and a local, union, and division conference president. Roberts was a nurse, pastor, local, union, and division conference president, and General Conference Medical Extension Secretary.

15. *Review and Herald*, September 28, 1916, 2

16. *Medical Practice and the Educational Program at Loma Linda*, 171

Chapter Seventeen

An Object Lesson
for Our People

B RIEFLY mentioned back in chapter ten was the story of a vision and
a building. Sixteen years had passed since 1899, and there had been a
lot of water under a lot of bridges. Back then, the General Conference
was in Battle Creek, Ellen White was in Australia, and John Kellogg was
in the Seventh-day Adventist Church. None of those were true in 1915.

Our story starts with a problem that had consumed a great deal of
Ellen White's time and energy while she lived in Australia. We've seen it
before in this volume—John Kellogg's penchant for raising and spending
money in large amounts, all out of proportion to the needs of the work:

> I had a view of the work which you have been doing for several years. I was lost
> to everything around me. I saw the large work established by you in Chicago, and
> the money that was invested. There was presented before me a long roll of paper,
> having upon it figures of a startling character, while in large letters was inscribed,
> "Consumers, but not producers." The figures showed the amount of God's money
> that had been invested in that enterprise in Chicago, and the results to the work all
> over the world. The representation was most disheartening.
>
> The whole vineyard of the Lord has been robbed to carry on a work that is
> never-ending. It has consumed means that should have supplied the necessities
> of foreign fields. The means spent in Chicago would have given to new fields ad-
> vantages for doing the very work that God has designed should be done. Look at
> the destitution that exists in portions of the field in foreign countries, and in con-

trast see the investment made in one great city. It shows that there has been a misappropriation of means which is not yours to do with as you please....

I have no hesitancy in saying that God did not set you at that work in Chicago....

All this work in Chicago was presented in a vision given to me at midday. It laid upon me a burden which none could understand. I could not understand it. I was overwhelmed with the things presented.

When I came to myself, I was like one stunned. Night after night the picture was before me. I saw the investments you were making, the money you were consuming; and what would the end be? I will not say.

"Who has required this at your hands?" was the question asked. "Sister White," you bemoan, "somebody has set things before you in a wrong light." No, no; things that no one knows have been presented to me.

I have been made to understand the ambitious projects that have bound up in one wicked city means which should have helped the work in this new world and put us on standing-ground. But all the necessities of this field, which were kept before you, seemed to you of less importance than the great things you were creating.

All our entreaties, all our poverty, which you knew, all our inability which was indeed an impossibility, was before you, but the things of your own creation closed your senses to our great need. The Lord signified that we should make a center here, that in this country should be established the very same work that we had started in America by the greatest self-denial and self-sacrifice at every step....

Should you carry out your own way, means would be drawn from the treasury to support the enterprises of your creation, until the missions to which God has appointed a special work would be destitute of every facility for carrying on that work.[1]

The Building in Chicago

This sad state of affairs had been going on "for several years." But one very particular event is our focus. In 1899, Ellen White had been shown "a large building in Chicago, which, in its erection and equipment, cost a large amount of money."

Scenes that would soon take place in Chicago, and other large cities also, passed before me. As wickedness increased, and the protecting power of God was withdrawn, there were destructive winds and tempests; buildings were destroyed by fire and shaken down by earthquakes. I saw the expensive building above referred to fall, with many others.[2]

1. *Manuscript Releases*, vol. 4, 138–144
2. *Paulson Collection*, 50

Alarmed at the loss of this expensive building, Ellen White "wrote [Dr. Kellogg] immediately in regard to the matter."[3]

As it turned out, Dr. Kellogg was in Europe at the time. Whether the letter was addressed to him there, or perhaps forwarded on from Battle Creek is not clear. What is clear is that Dr. Kellogg was not happy with what he read. And he was more certain than ever that he had good reason to be annoyed. It was one thing to be faulted for something he had done that someone else thought was wrong, but being blamed for an expensive building that had never existed was just too much!

And he said so, over and over again.

Ellen White had no explanation to offer. What could she say? She knew what she had seen in vision; she had assumed the building was actually there; beyond that, she had nothing to offer. But there never was such a building. Did that mean that her vision was inaccurate? Or had she made up the vision, all from some baseless gossip? Kellogg was not slow to suggest this as a possibility.

It was all quite confusing, even to the prophet herself. For three years....

A Break in the Case

In June of 1902, there was a Pacific Union Medical Missionary Council at St. Helena, California. During the course of the meetings, Ellen White felt called upon to "make a clear statement of the principles that should be followed in our medical missionary work."

It just so happened that Judge Jesse Arthur, a lawyer and former judge from Michigan who had become an Adventist some years before, was in California for the meetings. Judge Arthur was a close friend of Dr. Kellogg's and worked with him in an administrative capacity on certain projects, most significantly, the American Medical Missionary College, Kellogg's medical school in Battle Creek.

Ellen White recounts events at that time:

> On the third morning Judge Arthur came in a little late. After I had finished speaking, he rose and bore his testimony. He said that he had felt very tired that morning, and had told his wife that he would not attend the morning meeting. But afterward he felt impressed that he must attend, and he did. During his remarks, he said, "I could not rest till I had come to this meeting, and I am so thankful that I did not miss it. This message will be a great blessing to me. I have heard the very things I needed to hear." He bore an excellent testimony, and we were all very much pleased with the words spoken.

---

3. Intriguingly, Kellogg seems to have lost his copy of this letter, and in 1906 it could not be found in the Ellen White files either. See Letter, W.C. White to Dr. Charles E. Stewart, April 10, 1906.

Shortly after the meetings closed, Judge Arthur and his wife spent part of a day at my home. We had much pleasant and profitable conversation. Among other things discussed was the matter of the representation that had been given me of an expensive building in the city of Chicago, used for various lines of medical missionary work....

As I... described the building that had been shown me, Judge Arthur said: "I can tell you something in regard to that building. A plan was drawn up for the erection of just such a building in Chicago. It seemed necessary to our work. It would have cost considerable money. Brother William Loughborough of Battle Creek, drew up the plans, and several men occupying responsible positions in the medical work met together to consider the matter. Various locations were considered. One of the plans discussed was very similar to what you have described."[4]

This was the first time she had ever heard of these plans, and it no doubt helped make some sense out of the experience. It had been three years with no good explanation, and it was probably a real satisfaction to be able to put some of those questions behind her.

Still An Issue...

But, sadly, none of that meant the issue was going away any time soon. For one thing, God brought it back up to her:

Some time after this, I was shown that the vision of buildings in Chicago and the draft upon the means of our people to erect them, and their destruction, was an object lesson for our people, warning them not to invest largely of their means in property in Chicago, or any other city, unless the providence of God should positively open the way and plainly point out duty to build or buy as necessary in giving the note of warning. A similar caution was given in regard to building in Los Angeles. Repeatedly I have been instructed that we must not invest means in the erection of expensive buildings in cities.[5]

All that was well and good for Ellen White, but not everyone was as impressed. Dr. Kellogg, for one, was not interested in object lessons just then. He had other things going on:

Repeatedly it has been shown me that in many cases you have worked upon minds to undermine confidence in the Testimonies. The evil leaven that you have placed in these minds has destroyed their faith in the principles of the truth and in the Testimonies.... After receiving a Testimony of reproof from me, you have said, "Somebody has told her these things, but they are not so."

Over and over again you have told others how I once sent you a testimony reproving you for erecting a large building in Chicago, before any such building

4. *Paulson Collection*, 50
5. *Paulson Collection*, 50

had been erected there. In the visions of the night a view of a large building was presented to me. I thought that it had been erected, and wrote you immediately in regard to the matter. I learned afterward that the building which I saw had not been put up.

When you received my letter, you were perplexed, and you said, "some one has misinformed Sister White regarding our work." But no mortal man had ever written to me or told me that this building had been put up. It was presented to me in vision. If this view had not been given me, and if I had not written to you about the matter, an effort would have been made to erect such a building in Chicago, a place in which the Lord has said that we are not to put up large buildings. At the time when the vision was given, influences were working for the erection of such a building. The message was received in time to prevent the development of the plans and the carrying out of the project.

You should have had discernment to see that the Lord worked in this matter. The very feature of the message that perplexed you should have been received as an evidence that my information came from a higher source than human lips. But instead, you have over and over again related your version of the matter, saying that some one must have told me a falsehood.[6]

Of course, Dr. Kellogg's point wasn't that someone had told Ellen White a falsehood; it was that she had believed a falsehood and written it out as a testimony. In other words, Ellen White's inspiration was a myth. She was just plain wrong and John Kellogg was right. As you may imagine, some people believed Kellogg, and some people believed Ellen White. What no one seems to have noticed was that the whole episode was an "object lesson for our people."

It's a little unusual to call such a testimony an "object lesson." A "warning," obviously; a "reproof," maybe; you might even call it a "preemptive strike," but why call it an object lesson?

The strange thing is that object lessons traditionally have two parts— the visible, acted out part, and the usually larger-scale circumstance that the object lesson is illustrating.

Ezekiel, for instance, was told to take two sticks, label one for Joseph and the other for Judah, and then join them together.[7] But the sticks weren't the real story. They were just the object lesson. So, if the warning about the building in Chicago is an object lesson... what is the real story that it illustrates?

6. *Paulson Collection*, 50
7. Ezekiel 37:15–22

Looking through the comments that Ellen White wrote about the experience, it's all about Chicago... except for one minor comment that just sort of shows up in the middle of things:

> A similar caution was given in regard to building in Los Angeles.

Well, that's sort of odd. What has L.A. got to do with any of this Chicago building stuff?

The Chicago–L.A. Connection

To understand the object lesson aspect of all this requires a little more history. It has already been mentioned that Judge Arthur and his wife stopped by Elmshaven to visit with Ellen White in June 1902. Willie White was also there for the visit, and they spent several hours in pleasant conversation.

When the judge told of the plans for a new building, Willie asked him if he could write out the details for him. The judge said it would be best for him to do that when he got back to Battle Creek, that way he could make sure of dates and the like. It took a while, but the letter of explanation eventually came, dated August 27, 1902:

> My Dear Brother White:
>
> I find it possible at this time to make for you the long-promised statement in reference to the action of the Board of Trustees of the American Medical Missionary College in the spring and early summer of 1899, looking to the erection of a large medical college building in the city of Chicago. The facts are as follows:
>
> During the last of May, 1899, Dr. A.B. Olsen, who was then Secretary of the Board of Trustees of the American Medical Missionary College, prompted by Dr. Bayard Holmes of Chicago, urged upon the Board the necessity of the Medical College becoming a member of the Association of American Medical Colleges in order to give it an assured standing and position among the medical institutions of this and other countries.

Before we go further, perhaps a couple of introductions would be in order. Dr. A.B. Olsen, the son of former General Conference president, O.A. Olsen, was a Seventh-day Adventist physician who worked with Kellogg's medical school. Dr. Bayard Holmes was a non-Adventist surgeon, quite respected and well known, who seems to have had a soft spot in his heart for small, struggling, medical schools and their students. Because he was a nice guy, he donated his time to teach surgery at the AMMC. That was quite a deal, because his expertise as a surgeon helped boost the school's credibility.

And he did it for free! What a nice guy! But nice guys don't always understand what Adventism and its principles are all about. That was probably particularly true of Dr. Holmes, since he didn't believe in Christianity at all.[8]

And just a note to help head off serious confusion: We will be discussing two different entities with confusingly similar names. Kellogg's medical school was the American Medical Missionary College, the AMMC; and the organization Dr. Holmes was recommending the college affiliate with was the Association of American Medical Colleges, the AAMC.

Now, with that all straight, on with the letter:

> In furtherance of this object, Dr. Olsen was appointed a delegate to attend a meeting of such Association which was shortly afterward to take place in the city of Columbus, Ohio, and make application in behalf of our medical college for membership. This he did, and such application was laid over to be acted upon at the next regular meeting to take place a year from that time.
>
> Upon Dr. Olsen's return, he reported that the principal objection urged against admitting our medical college to membership was the want of a suitable building in the city of Chicago. It was then determined by the Board to take steps at once looking toward the erection of such building. A building committee was appointed and consisted of A.B. Olsen, W.K. Kellogg, and myself. Dr. Olsen was chosen secretary of such committee and I selected chairman.
>
> The committee met and immediately formulated plans for the purchase of a site and the erection of such a building. I was instructed, as chairman of the committee, to open negotiations looking either to the sale or mortgaging of No. 28 thirty-third Place which the College owned, and otherwise taking steps to raise the necessary funds to purchase the site and erect the building contemplated. Dr. Olsen was instructed to procure suitable plans for the College building, which he did. The cost of the site and improvements was to be somewhere in the neighborhood of $100,000, or possibly more.
>
> The committee went to Chicago, looked over several sites, and finally settled upon one on Thirteenth Street, and negotiations were opened for its purchase.
>
> All this took place while Dr. J.H. Kellogg was absent from the United States in Europe. After our plans were quite well completed for the going on of the work, it was thought advisable to await Dr. Kellogg's return to this country before proceeding further with the matter.
>
> I learned through others that after the Doctor did return and was advised of what had been done, that he discouraged going on with the project. Just what reasons he assigned for doing so I don't think I ever knew.[9]

8. *General Conference Bulletin*, April 17, 1901, 290
9. *Response to an Urgent Testimony from Mrs. Ellen G. White*, 33–35

It wouldn't be polite to make the judge look silly, of course, but the reason for Kellogg's lack of enthusiasm is actually very simple to figure out—he got a letter in the mail from Ellen White talking about a building in Chicago!

There is another document that has a bearing on this story as well. It is the record of the official minutes from a meeting of the Board of Trustees of the American Medical Missionary College held on June 19, 1899.

A Favorable Basis and a Desirable Recognition

> The meeting was opened by prayer by Dr. H.F. Rand. Dr. Olsen then made a brief statement of his visit to the meeting of the Association of American Medical Colleges and stated that the [application from the] American Medical Missionary College was not voted upon at the meeting, but action was deferred until another year. He then emphasized the importance of securing a suitable building for the College to be located in Chicago; he stated he believed that this would aid greatly in putting the College on a favorable basis before the world and secure a desirable recognition.
>
> [Dr. Olsen said] that it should be remembered that the chief reason why the Board of Health of Illinois did not recognize our school fully was because it had not a suitable building for clinical work and instruction.[10]

So it turns out that the building that wasn't built, the one Kellogg used as his favorite attack on Ellen White for the next thirty years, was a pretty specific item. It was supposed to provide for "clinical work and instruction."

What sort of a building might this be? It seems to have been something familiar to both the Illinois Board of Health, and the Association of American Medical Colleges. But what, exactly, would it have been? And what connection does it have to Los Angeles?

The only answer to these questions seems to be in the experience of denominational leaders about fifteen years later. As mentioned previously, the best account of this comes from *The Story of Our Health Message:*

> By this time it had become evident to all concerned that a clinical hospital was needed to provide the advanced classes of medical students with the practical experience necessary to meet all the requirements for graduation....

[This volume is a dishonest attack on Ellen White which was published by Dr. Charles E. Stewart, one of Kellogg's lieutenants, about the time the Doctor was dropped from church membership. The history is presented meticulously in the book, because it was believed to be a piece of "irrefutable evidence" against Ellen White. What all this history actually ends up showing is that not only was Ellen White correct about the building in Chicago, but God really did give that vision in the way He did so that it would remain as an "object lesson for our people." It is happily ironic that the anti-Ellen White contingent have done us the service of so faithfully preserving this information!]

10. *Response to an Urgent Testimony from Mrs. Ellen G. White*, 41–42

Loma Linda and its environs did not have population enough to supply such a clinical hospital with the required number of patients. So, in looking around for an area that could serve the need, the eyes of some of the brethren turned toward the city of Los Angeles.

However, it was remembered that in 1901 Mrs. White had received instruction "that it would be a mistake to establish a sanitarium within the city limits" of Los Angeles. Would the establishment of a clinical hospital in that city... be a move contrary to that counsel?

It was felt by some of the brethren that the testimony of 1901 had reference to "a sanitarium," and not to a clinical hospital such as the needs of the medical college now required.[11]

For the sake of clarity in all this, there are a couple observations which ought to be made concerning this account. The first is in regard to the idea that the "medical college now required" a 200-bed clinical hospital in downtown Los Angeles. At the time, there were no such requirements established by either state or federal law. The "requirements" in question were only those of the Association of American Medical Colleges. Coincidentally, though pointing it out may not be needed, these were the same folks who had been pressing the same "requirement" upon the administrators of Kellogg's medical college back in 1899.

The second item worth noting is the instruction given by Ellen White in 1901. In August of that year she was in Los Angeles for a camp meeting. The proposition of building a combination sanitarium/vegetarian restaurant on Hill Street was being considered at that time, and it was in that context that she wrote "it would be a mistake to establish a sanitarium within the city limits." This comment may now be found in *Testimonies*, vol. 7, 85.

But it turns out the account reproduced there is not all she wrote on the subject. A more detailed account of the experience is now available in the first volume of the *Manuscript Releases*:

The complete plan in regard to the purchase of the Hill Street property was not laid before me till my last visit to Los Angeles. I was then taken to see this property, and as I walked up the hill in front of it, I heard distinctly a voice that I well know. Had this voice said, "This is the right place for God's people to purchase," I should have been greatly astonished. But it said, "Encourage no settlement here of any description. God forbids. My people must get away from such surroundings. This place is as Sodom for wickedness. The place where my institu-

11. *The Story of Our Health Message*, 398

tions are established must be altogether different. Leave the cities, and like Enoch, come from your retirement to warn the people of the cities."

The words were spoken: "The divine hand is not guiding in the steps that have been taken in regard to this property. The spiritual vision of men has been darkened. Plans have been made that the Lord has not inspired."

I was afterward instructed that the whole matter was inspired by human wisdom. Men have followed their own wisdom, which is foolishness with God, and which, if they continue to follow it, will lead to results that they do not now see. The spiritual eyesight has been blinded.

"The light of the body is the eye: if therefore thine eye be single, thy whole body shall be full of light" (Matthew 6:22). The Lord calls upon those in charge of His work in Southern California to have their eyes anointed with the heavenly eyesalve. This is their only safety.

I am astonished that our brethren should have thought of purchasing the property on Hill Street.... After I had seen its situation, I knew that I could not for a moment give my consent to the establishment there of an institution of any kind.[12]

The wording of this quotation presents a stronger opposition to establishing an institutional presence within Los Angeles than does the statement in volume seven. Words and phrases such as "settlement... of any description"; "institutions... altogether different"; and "institution of any kind" paint a broader application than the more narrow idea of "a sanitarium." If one were to go by the "letter of the law," that final comment about an "institution of any kind" would preclude *both* "a sanitarium" and "a clinical hospital."[13]

But before we jump to conclusions concerning the integrity of the administrators in 1915, or even of the author of *Story of Our Health Message*, we should note that this quotation is from "Letter 182, 1902," addressed to

---

12. *Manuscript Releases*, vol. 1, 251

13. Given the tendency for human beings to push to one extreme or the other on almost any issue, when the Lord would have us occupy a sensible middle ground, it was perhaps a necessity that Ellen White specifically exempt restaurants and churches from the "institutions" that were not to be in the cities.

   "The trades unions and confederacies of the world are a snare. Keep out of them, and away from them, brethren. Have nothing to do with them. Because of these unions and confederacies, it will soon be very difficult for our institutions to carry on their work in the cities. My warning is: Keep out of the cities. Build no sanitariums in the cities. Educate our people to get out of the cities into the country, where they can obtain a small piece of land, and make a home for themselves and their children....

   "Our restaurants must be in the cities; for otherwise the workers in these restaurants could not reach the people and teach them the principles of right living. And for the present we shall have to occupy meetinghouses in the cities. But erelong there will be such strife and confusion in the cities, that those who wish to leave them will not be able. We must be preparing for these issues. This is the light that is given me." *General Conference Bulletin*, April 6, 1903.

"Dear Brethren." Who all might have been included in that salutation is not clear. What is clear is that the letter was not re-printed in any other form until it was included in Manuscript Release No. 56, probably in November 1953.

In other words, those of us who enjoy the convenience of push-button searches of the Spirit of Prophecy have reason to be patient with those who have gone before us. Incidentally, we also have reason to expect that we will be held to a higher level of accountability.

On the other hand, it can't be said that the evidence in favor of a Los Angeles hospital was so strong that everyone was agreed. W.A. Ruble, the first president of CME, went on record—somewhat hesitantly—as thinking there was a better plan:

> I have never been convinced that much of an effort in the way of providing hospital facilities in Los Angeles should be made. I believe that the school should be complete at Loma Linda; that the hospital there should be built up and strengthened; that close affiliation should be brought about between the college and the local county hospital and the dispensary may be discontinued in the city.... As soon as a fairly large hospital is established in Los Angeles, surgery will naturally drift there and the tendency will be to build up the work in the city rather than at Loma Linda. This has always been my conviction. I was loathe to express it very freely while at Loma Linda because I felt it was your firm conviction that the work should be greatly strengthened in Los Angeles."[14]

Now Then, to Make It All Happen

The action of the CME Constituency, in June 1915, authorized the construction of a hospital, but "ask[ed] the North American Division Conference of Seventh-day Adventists to inaugurate a movement to provide property and erect a building for dispensary purposes, also a hospital building to be known as [the] 'Ellen G. White Memorial Hospital,' at a cost for grounds and buildings not to exceed $50,000."[15]

Thus the decision—and the financial responsibility—were largely shifted to that body. Obviously, this meant more deliberations. They would take place in November, at the Autumn Council.

When it became apparent that a quick decision was not forthcoming, Percy Magan—

> Talked to Mrs. [Josephine] Gotzian [who had helped start Paradise Valley Sanitarium], Winnea Simpson [daughter of a leading evangelist], and Mrs. Haskell re[garding the] L[oma] L[inda] situation and re[garding the] women [of the

14. W.A. Ruble to Newton Evans, January 20, 1916
15. *Medical Practice and the Educational Program at Loma Linda*, 171

church] raising $61,800 for Los Angeles [hospital]. They saw light.... Got a lot of women together in parlor of [the women's] dormitory.... Mrs. Haskell presided.[16]

A little later that evening, a group of the General Conference brethren were continuing their discussion about Loma Linda when Dr. Florence Keller led a small group of women into the room.

Many years later, Dr. Sanford Edwards would write his memoirs of this time period. A close friend of nearly all the key players in upper echelon Adventism from the 1880s till the 1920s, Edwards offers a fascinating perspective on many key events (though, like the rest of the race, he no doubt falls short of perfection in both his recollection and his understanding). He was present at the meeting when the ladies walked in. This is his memory:

> When asked by Elder Daniells what was their errand, Dr. Florence said, "There is a portion of Los Angeles called Boyle Heights that is highly populated by Mexicans, Japanese and Negroes, and they have no adequate medical attention, and are in much need of help. Will you plan for a small hospital there which will help them and provide clinical facilities for our students after their two years here [at Loma Linda]? We ladies wish to volunteer to raise the money to build the buildings if you give permission."
>
> W.C. White was a member of the General Conference Committee and Elder Daniells turned to him and asked what Sister White would say about that. W.C. [White] replied that it had never been discussed by her, but he thought that she would approve of a small hospital for the purpose stated if it was not in a densely populated part of the city. From my personal talks with Sister White and studying of her writings, that is the nearest to her approving of going to Los Angeles of which I know, and that was merely W.C.'s opinion.[17]

With the encouragement of the ladies, the motion was passed to erect what Ellen White might have described as "a large building in ~~Chicago~~ Los Angeles, which, in its erection and equipment, cost a large amount of money."

Same kind of building; same "requirement" for the building; same people promoting it, all lead us to ask whether or not the same inspired counsel would apply. If Los Angeles was the "lesson" of which Chicago was the "object," it seems the answer would be "yes."

If it can be said politely, the expensive building that was never built in Chicago... *was* built in Los Angeles.

---

16. Percy T. Magan Diary, November 17, 1895
17. Letter, Sanford P.S. Edwards to Dr. Claude E. Steen, June 15, 1962, quoted in David James Lee, *The Story of Loma Linda*, 1951–1952

Tell It Not In Gath[18]

One final episode in this regard remains to be acknowledged, distasteful though it is. The purpose of this account is, very frankly, to consider the possibility that two men—lifelong servants of the Lord and His church, men who stand head and shoulders above the accomplishments of their peers, men whose memory we justly honor, and whose loyalty deserves that honor—to consider the possibility that these two men may have had a blind spot, that in one particular area they may have unwittingly failed to grasp the Lord's ideal.

There seems to have been a tendency, on the part of Elder A.G. Daniels and Elder W.C. White, to have at times held the authority of the world in too high regard. We saw it in the "god of Ekron" mistake on the Avondale property. This volume is respectfully suggesting that something similar occurred in their favoring the association of the College of Medical Evangelists with the American Medical Association.

As early as 1907, Elder Daniells felt that the school must have that recognition or it wouldn't be "worth a nickel."[19] In 1908, Elder White preferred working toward AMA affiliation, over Elder Burden's suggestion that they avail themselves of the recently passed law.[20]

These were honest opinions, held in good faith by honest men. But was their judgment, in this case, in harmony with the ideal will of God? There is one more historical event which, sadly, suggests that these two men may have been human enough to have a blind spot, and it is simply this:

After the plans for the construction of a clinical hospital in Chicago had been disrupted by the counsel from Ellen White, during the time of confusion over the testimony she had written, the issue of the "need" for such a building was addressed at the 1901 General Conference session held in Battle Creek.

On April 15, Dr. Kellogg spent considerable time presenting his perspective on the need to purchase or construct a suitable building for the American Medical Missionary College. He asked the church to raise $100,000 for such a building. His description of what he wanted by way of a building, and even his inclusion of Dr. Holmes' volunteer work as a surgery professor, all mark this as another attempt to get the building he had wanted two years before.[21]

18. The allusion is to 2 Samuel 1:20
19. See page 180.
20. See page 179
21. *General Conference Bulletin*, April 17, 1901, 288–290

What happened during the next two days? We don't know. Who talked to whom? We don't know. Did someone lay out a plan? Or was it all spontaneous? We don't know.

What we do know is that two days later, with nothing in the minutes to indicate any sort of introduction or lead-in, the chair of the meeting, none other than John Harvey Kellogg, called on Elder W.C. White:

> *The Chair*—Brother White has a resolution, I believe.
>
> *W. C. White*—I am intensely interested in our schools, and in no school am I more interested than in this Medical Missionary College. Our schools should have their buildings without rent, and therefore I offer a resolution:
>
> Resolved, That we proceed to raise a fund for the purpose of providing necessary buildings for the American Medical Missionary College.
>
> I move the adoption of this resolution.

This is not the sort of motion that is going to be tossed out on the floor for random debate without having a few things in place beforehand. And the first issue is making sure someone will second your motion. Without a second, the motion dies... and you look foolish, so it's a good bet the second was already arranged.

But all we know for sure is what we can read in the minutes:

> *A.G. Daniells*—I second the motion.

Following the second, Elder White asked an appropriate question:

> *W.C. White*—This idea is not new to you. But brethren, the question with us is, Has the time come to make an earnest effort to lift in this matter, and put our medical missionary school where it will not have to pay rent?...

It's a fair question. Had the time come to build a large, expensive building in downtown Chicago? Two years before the answer was "No," but two years had passed. Is it possible that the answer had changed to "Yes"?

In actual fact, the response from the members was minimal. Following Elder White's comments, the minutes read:

> *The Chair*—Are you ready for this resolution, or are there further remarks? Perhaps as much was said the other day as need be said with reference to the Medical College, unless some one has a question he would like to ask....

O.A. Olsen spoke briefly, endorsing the motion, and then Dr. Kellogg told how much he wished he could tell everyone the private story of miracles which had blessed the school—but he was not at liberty to do so. And then—

The question was called and carried unanimously by acclamation. A rising vote was then taken, which was also unanimous.[22]

Unanimous, yes. But wise...?

This larger discussion has continued ever since.

For clarity, it should be pointed out that the differences of opinion which existed in 1915 were not over the question, "Should we train physicians?" nor even, "Should we train State licensed physicians?" All parties in the decision making process recognized the Spirit of Prophecy call for the training of at least "some" fully licensed physicians.

The differences centered on a single point: Should the College of Medical Evangelists affiliate with the American Medical Association and commit to achieving excellence as defined by their standards, or should the College decline that option to avoid "exalting men above God," and instead choose to "stand aloof, and labor with the advantages that you yourselves can offer." After all, those who questioned affiliation reasoned, we have been promised that God "will give us advantages that are far beyond all the advantages we might receive from worldlings."[23]

Again, it should be remembered that other legal options existed. AMA affiliation was not a State requirement.

The regret expressed by Elder Burden and others in later years was that the challenges of meeting and maintaining an acceptable rating from the AAMC so thoroughly overshadowed the school's efforts to establish the medical missionary evangelistic course that the main purpose of the institution never materialized in any viable form.

It was, after all, intended to be the College of Medical Evangelists, not the College of Evangelistic Physicians.

Was AMA affiliation a mistake? Predictably, there are honest opinions held on both sides of the question. For our purposes, there is no necessity that there be a single authoritative position. What seems undeniable, however, is that over time the emphasis on training "thousands" whose main purpose was to be the combining of the medical and the evangelistic work into a unified whole was largely lost sight of. Some see that mostly as a result of AMA affiliation, others do not. Whatever the cause, the outcome is to be regretted. But none of that meant that God had given up.

---

22. *General Conference Bulletin,* April 19, 1901, 341

23. The sentence fragments used here are from the September 20, 1909, interview of Ellen White that was discussed beginning on page 183.

Chapter Eighteen

To Take the Cities

WHEN Joshua was given the task of leading the children of Israel into the promised land, there was one major challenge: Cities. Jericho was only the first large center of heathen pride and arrogance that stood in defiance of God's plan. From the outset, the "Commander of the army of the LORD" wanted to make it clear that success was not based on human strength, but on human obedience. God's plans were not always such as would appeal to human logic; they were to be followed, nonetheless. Around and around for seven days, if called to do so.

Parallels between the conquest of Canaan and God's last-day conquest of the world are numerous and—sometimes—obvious. Just now we will consider only the two already mentioned. We today are faced with the challenge of the cities, and our greatest need is obedience to God's plan. But what *is* that plan?

Ellen White's interest in, and dealings with, cities were vastly increased when she went to Australia. More so than America at the time, Australia was a nation of cities with vast stretches of the famously unpopulated "Outback" in between. The people of the nation were urban, and that's where the battle for souls must be fought.

No wonder, then, that the medical missionary model of evangelism that developed in Australasia focused so much on the large cities, and the formation of small institutions like the Hydropathic Institute and the Helping Hand Laundry. Of course, Ellen White and her family of workers preferred to live in the country. That, too, was a part of the "new pattern" to be established in Australasia: Speaking of the Adventist population, rather than of evangelistic enterprises, she had this to say:

Let centers be no longer made in the cities. Let children no longer be exposed to the temptations of the cities that are ripe for destruction. The Lord has sent us warning and counsel to get out of the cities. Then let us make no more investments in the cities. Fathers and mothers, how do you regard the souls of your children? Are you preparing the members of your families for translation into heavenly courts? Are you preparing them to become members of the royal family, children of the heavenly King? What shall it profit a man if he gain the whole world, and lose his own soul? How will ease, comfort, convenience, compare with the value of the souls of your children?

There is not one family in a hundred who will be improved, physically, mentally, or spiritually, by residing in the city. Faith, hope, love, happiness, can far better be gained in retired places, where there are fields and hills and trees. Take your children away from the sights and sounds of the city, away from the rattle and din of streetcars and teams, and their minds will become more healthy. It will be found easier to bring home to their hearts the truth of the Word of God.

The Lord would have the believers in Melbourne consider the example set by Battle Creek, and not pattern after it. God has sent warning after warning that our schools and publishing houses and sanitariums are to be established out of the city, in places where the youth may be taught most effectively what is truth. Let no one attempt to use the Testimonies to vindicate the establishment of large business interests in the cities. Do not make of no effect the light that has been given upon this subject.

Men will arise speaking perverse things, to counterwork the very movements that the Lord is leading His servants to make. But it is time that men and women reasoned from cause to effect. It is too late, too late, to establish large business firms in the cities—too late to call young men and women from the country to the city.

Conditions are arising in the cities that will make it very hard for those of our faith to remain in them. It would therefore be a great mistake to invest money in the establishment of business interests in the cities....

The cities will become worse and worse. In them will be strife and bloodshed, and at last they will be visited by earthquakes. Buildings will be thrown down, and will be consumed by fire from heaven....

Will our brethren and sisters in Melbourne move without the counsel of God? Will they make large plants in Melbourne, when the world is growing worse and worse, when the cities are becoming as Sodom and Gomorrah? Will they put out the eyes of the people, that they shall not discern the signs of the times?

The cities must be worked. Those who are living in them must be warned of what is before us. Let time and means be wisely spent. See if you cannot do something in the highways and byways of the cities to proclaim the message of present truth. But do not locate your families in the city, and do not establish business interests there. If you do this, you will in the future be expected to conform to the observance of various holidays. Watchers will be set to seek occasion of complaint against the commandment-keeping people of God. ...

Though stormy times are before us, much missionary work still remains to be done in the cities. This work can be done better now than at any other time in the future. But this does not require the establishment of large business enterprises. Let us not move according to human ambition. We are living in too solemn a time to move impulsively. While missionary work is to be done in the cities and out of the cities, God does not desire His people to invest their means in large commercial interests in the cities. My brethren and sisters, if you have physical force, if you have money, invest them in the work of enlightening men and women, warning them to prepare for what is coming upon the earth.[1]

This is valuable counsel. Precious instruction from the Lord.... But how in the world are we supposed to make it actually happen? What were those "thousands" of medical missionaries that Loma Linda was going to train actually supposed to do?

Producing a Prototype

As it turns out, before a single MD ever graduated from the College of Medical Evangelists, the principles for which the school was founded had been turned loose on an unsuspecting world—to a small degree. The model developed in San Francisco had already come... and gone, unfortunately. And with those losses Ellen White became even more insistent on the virtues of *not* basing large enterprises in the cities.

What emerged as an adjunct to the multi-faceted approach to city ministry was an even lighter division of cavalry; a mobile, temporary (but not *too* short term), health-oriented approach to evangelism that was pioneered by a somewhat unlikely character. Here's the story:

John Tindall was raised a Methodist, but that all fell apart when his little brother, Willie, died. No matter how hard the adults in his life tried to explain, nothing they said about Willie made sense.

They said he was in heaven, but John had watched them put him in the ground. They said he could see what John was doing, but John had last seen him lying cold and lifeless with his eyes closed. Perplexed enough with all this, the arrival of an old-fashioned, hell-fire-and-brimstone preacher undid all the Christian belief anyone had managed to get into John Tindall's mind and heart.

---

1. *Manuscript Releases*, vol. 19, 335–337

Later exposure to skeptical sentiments, and the claim that "religion" had produced most of the world's war and oppression (an unfortunately easy position to support), led him to adopt a militant, evolutionistic, existentialist atheism. He had found his mission in life! It was to break the shackles of "God" from the minds and hands of mankind.

I Will Question You, And You Shall Answer Me[2]

Several years of high-flying, happy-go-lucky business ventures had gone well for him. He had enough money so he could do as he wished, and he didn't hesitate to do so. In this frame of mind, he bought a ticket for the maiden run of the Great Northern Transcontinental Flyer, an express train from Seattle, Washington, to Buffalo, New York. Here's how he told the story:

> A party of seven or eight gentlemen being gathered in the smoking room of the buffet car, after talking over everything from game shooting to politics, finally drifted into a discussion of religion. Always ready for an argument, and particularly so on this subject, as I was honestly at war with what I believed to be the greatest fraud ever perpetrated on mankind, I soon had things going my own way.
>
> After about half an hour or so, a tall, stately gentleman, with a very pleasant countenance, came in and took a seat almost directly in front of me and listened attentively to my arguments. After a little while he asked me a question which seemed at once to open the whole controversy anew. It took some time for me to give what I supposed to be an intelligent and logical answer to this question.
>
> When I finished, he asked me another, quietly and unobtrusively. His second question staggered me. I had hard work to handle it, but I did my best.
>
> After about ten minutes' reasoning, he asked a third question, which so completely upset my arguments that I was speechless. I verily felt dumbstruck. My mind failed me, and I was not able even to utter a word. After a few moments the gentleman arose and passed quietly out, and one by one the others followed until I found myself alone, humiliated, defeated. The more I thought it over, the more humiliated I became, until anger and grim determination to find this man took hold of me.
>
> As I tried to think of just what he had asked me I was unable to recall exactly the questions. That train did not stop within an hour or more, being a through train, making very few stops, and I hunted that train through and through, making inquiries of those who were in the smoking room, watching every door, leaving no corner unsearched, but the man could not be found.
>
> The train was running at least forty-five or fifty miles an hour—the man did not get off: who he was, where he came from, what became of him, is a mystery,

---

2. Job *38:3*

but I believe him to have been a messenger from God to me, and no ordinary be-ing. From that experience I passed into a state of agnosticism, for in my heart I felt I had been talking about a subject which I had better take the negative side of rather than the positive, and that I would never again say, "There is no God"; but I did not know there was a God.[3]

His reported activities during this time were varied. He was called a "Newspaper man," though that could mean a lot of things. He raised Thoroughbred horses for a time, and was, at one point, studying law. But evidently none of that was enough to rule out striking it rich when gold was reported down near the Mexican border. It was here that he actually found something worth keeping:

On a prospecting trip into the mountains of San Diego, I was told that we would stop at the humble home of a very peculiar man—a man of about 64 years, who would not wish me to smoke in his house, who ate no meat, and who was very peculiar in his religion and in many other ways, but who would make us in every way comfortable and at home. He received us cordially and gave us the best of everything in the house. When we went out prospecting he wished to go along, and in spite of his years and peculiar diet, we found he always led the party and came home in a far better condition than the rest of us. When we asked him where he got his strength without eating meat, he replied that real strength does not come from meat and that all the elements of value gotten from meat were taken secondhand and would better be taken direct from the vegeta-tion. I saw that he was keen mentally and strong physically and bethought to test his character and his peculiar religion, and so for many days I purposely did those things which I knew would displease him to see if I could make him show temper, and even made fun of his religion and his keeping part of Friday and part of Saturday for Sunday; but he was always of the same sweet temper. One day I told him I had been fooling with him, but now wished to ask him some se-rious questions. I said: "Why do you keep Saturday for Sunday?"

"Because I believe the Bible," he answered.

"Do you believe in the God set forth in the Bible, and do you get your pecu-liar religion out of that book?"

"Yes," he said.

Then I took him back to the hard questions my parents had faced in my childhood and asked him why a God of infinite love should torment a poor, help-less man in hell-fire always—asked him if man did not have an indestructible soul and that at death went either to heaven or burning hell forever. He replied:

3. *Gospel-medical Evangelistic Campaign*, conducted jointly by the Southeastern California Conference and the College of Medical Evangelists, under the direction of Evangelist John Tindall, Redlands, California, 1922, 161–162

"Let us not argue the matter, but let us see what the Bible really does say on that point."[4]

Naturally this led to Bible studies and a setting straight of all the concerns which had driven him from the Christianity of his youth. Time for all this study came to Tindall courtesy of a leg injury that laid him up for some while... out in the mountains at the older gentleman's cabin. It turned out that Tindall's host, "Daddy Bell" by name, was a pretty good nurse. He was also a pretty good evangelist who was not in the least afraid to tackle Tindall's objections and concerns, most notably the inspiration of the Bible, and—as an added bonus—the Spirit of Prophecy.

For one who had wandered through both atheism and agnosticism, the idea of a contemporary prophet had an obvious appeal. What an opportunity! A way to actually know what was what, from God's perspective. More than that, it was the *Desire of Ages* that reached his heart in a way commensurate with Daddy Bell's witnessing to his brain. This appreciation for the Spirit of Prophecy never left the man, and was successfully passed on to his converts in the coming years.

So... Now What?

All this left Tindall a new convert to Adventism. But when he was told that a school existed to train "medical evangelists," it was time to move to Loma Linda. The timing was providential, for he was to finish the course in the spring of 1910. Unbeknownst to him, that was perfect. Perfect, because of what transpired on the night of February 27, 1910.

Four hundred twenty-five miles north-northwest of him, the woman whose writings had been instrumental in his conversion was having a restless night. In a letter addressed "To Conference Presidents," she told about it:

> During the night of February 27, a representation was given me in which the unworked cities were represented before me as a living reality, and I was plainly instructed that there should be a decided change from past methods of working. For months the situation has been impressed on my mind, and I urge that companies be organized and diligently trained to labor in our important cities. These workers should labor two and two, and from time to time all should meet together to relate their experiences, to pray, and to plan how to reach the people quickly, and thus if possible, redeem the time.
>
> This is no time to colonize. From city to city the work is to be carried quickly....

4. *Gospel-medical Evangelistic Campaign*, 162–164

> Let companies now be quickly organized to go out two and two, and labor in the spirit of Christ, following His plans.[5]

And thus was born a concept eventually known as "company" evangelism. United with earlier instruction on reaching the cities, this word tended to be lost in the name "Gospel-Medical Missionary Evangelism," but the "company" concept was important in its own right.

When the responsibility to see this approach carried out was laid on the shoulders of the administration at CME, Elders Burden and Owen looked for a "point man" to pioneer the new technique. One student stood out. Slightly older than his classmates, solidly (though recently) converted, a gifted speaker, and one familiar with the higher walks of life, John Tindall was the obvious choice. After a period of prayer and deliberation, he accepted the call.

San Bernardino or Bust

With the task of incorporating the "health message" into an evangelistic outreach (hard enough), Tindall was told to do this in the nearby town of San Bernardino (even harder). Only a few miles from the College, San Bernardino had already been the focus of considerable evangelistic effort. The only problem was that the good people of the town had been remarkably resistant. San Bernardino was something of a proverb amongst those interested in soul-winning....

But, to everyone's surprise (O ye of little faith), the health approach appealed to the members of a high-society ladies' club, and they used their influence to gain free coverage of the meetings in the local newspaper.

One regular attendee was convinced, and seemed ready to commit.... but just never would. Direct inquiry found the problem; the man couldn't stop smoking. With a weak heart, he feared he'd die in the process, but—

> After being encouraged that God had given us knowledge along the line of diet and treatments which would aid him in giving up his tobacco, he finally consented to try, once more to give it up.
>
> Two things were now combined in the effort to save this precious soul from death. One was to bring him to the Savior with His power and willingness to help him. This kindly sympathy, linked with a demonstration of practical godliness, broke the old gentleman's heart and he wept like a child. God answered our prayer by the gift of the Holy Spirit, which strengthened his faith and he became a liberated man. And oh, such a grateful man as he was! This is but one case of many showing how the proper service of the "right arm" draws men and women

5. *Paulson Collection*, 69

to the "body"—the church. The combination of the evangelical and medical as demonstrated in the Savior's life, and carried on in this work, will ever be found efficient in saving souls.[6]

In the end, there were sixteen baptisms—one of which was Tindall's till-this-time hesitant wife. Sixteen baptisms! In San Bernardino!

That was enough to catch the attention of local conference officials, who requested that Tindall repeat the performance on a larger stage—Los Angeles—but with one minor alteration: leave the health stuff behind and do "real" evangelism.

Taking the Gospel to the Cities

It may have been a temptation. Los Angeles was a plum assignment for a rookie evangelist. But John Tindall had a calling to health evangelism, so he and his team took their experiment on the road, and accepted an invitation to Hartford City, Indiana. It's possible that the evangelist, by now commonly known as J.H.N. Tindall, had pulled some strings to get this location. It was home to his family. At the end of the series, his mother, a physician brother and his wife, and two sisters and their husbands—along with thirty-five others—were baptized.[7]

But there was more:

> Eventually even the editor of the local newspaper came to one of the health talks, and was so impressed with the work that he offered to open his paper to the campaign. C.E. Garnsey, nurse and medical evangelist, wrote some health articles for the papers and Elder Tindall was requested to write some columns concerning religion. So he wrote on our Adventist doctrines.
>
> About ten to twelve miles away there was a Church of God that didn't have a resident pastor. They took these articles of Elder Tindall appearing in the paper and read them for their Sunday services. They didn't realize what they were getting into and eventually half of that church accepted the truth and the Sabbath and were baptized.[8]

The team continued to move about the country, holding campaigns (usually about six months long) in Indianapolis, Indiana; Virginia; Farmersburg, Terre Haute, and Indianapolis, Indiana; Milwaukee, Wisconsin; Tulsa, and Oklahoma City, Oklahoma; and Dallas, Texas.

6. *Gospel-medical Evangelistic Campaign*, 6
7. Details of this and future evangelistic series are blended from *Gospel-medical Evangelistic Campaign*, 7–8; Calvin Thrash, *John H.N. Tindall: Fifty Years a Gospel-Medical Missionary Evangelist*; and *The Experiences of Elder J.H.N. Tindall, a Medical Evangelist for More than Fifty Years*, originally from Norman Gulley, *Gospel-Medical Evangelism*, Book 1
8. *Experiences of Elder J.H.N. Tindall*, 2–3

Following the team's work in Virginia, the right people had been impressed, and they arranged for Elder Tindall to meet in Washington, D.C., with all the evangelists, union conference presidents, and local conference presidents east of the Mississippi River. The potential of Gospel-Medical Missionary Company Evangelism impressed them enough that it was voted to create a joint training program operated by the sanitarium and the college in the D.C. area. Unfortunately, the lack of ministers comfortable working with a health emphasis doomed the program, and it soon folded with no apparent gain.

This experience highlighted a problem that many have recognized, but no one has yet solved.

Here Evil Lurks

Years before, Ellen White had written one of those mind-stretching superlative comments that she sometimes would make. It isn't pretty:

> I want to tell you that when the gospel ministers and the medical missionary workers are not united, there is placed on our churches the worst evil that can be placed there. Our medical missionaries ought to be interested in the work of our Conferences, and our Conference workers ought to be as much interested in the work of our medical missionaries.[9]

It's interesting to note where the damage is done when this disunity takes place. It's not the doctors... not a word about them. They seem to be doing just fine, thank you. But the churches? They get saddled with the "worst evil." This isn't just your run-of-the-mill evil; this is as bad as it gets. What would that be?

Perhaps it is simply the delusion of thinking we are doing something that will—one day—"finish the work," when the truth is that what we are doing is totally incapable of providing the demonstration that needs to be made.

Mid-Course Correction

Every campaign had its stories and memorable quotes. All are worth reading the full accounts, but space does not permit that here. The less interesting, but more convenient way to portray the success of the Gospel-Medical Missionary Evangelism approach is to simply cite statistics. This approach highlights something that might be overlooked, otherwise.

---

9. *Loma Linda Messages,* 59

When we crunch the numbers on Elder Tindall's first five campaigns, we find an average of thirty-six baptisms per campaign. That's not bad, actually. But there was something that continued to bother him. The testimony from Ellen White had called for "companies" of workers, and his little team of four to six didn't seem like a company. What was he to do, since there was no budget for more workers? In a sense, he did the same thing Jesus did; he recruited volunteers; *lots* of volunteers.

At the time, there were three paid positions: the evangelist, a medical "helper," and a Bible worker. To this core group, he added one businessman, one singer, six nurses, and ten general purpose volunteers. That's eighteen volunteers, a total of twenty-one... living on three salaries and the possibility of donations.

Interesting. But did it work?

The statistics are available for six campaigns after the switch to the "company" model. There was an average of one hundred twenty-one baptisms per series. Something was working right. The counsel of God through the little old lady from Elmshaven was good, again!

The Details, Please

In a document printed up in 1922, Elder Tindall gives a point by point run down on his approach to a six-month campaign. We can only give an overview here:[10]

- **Preliminaries**—Contact prominent community members to inform them of your work; secure a high quality hall, or possibly two, if separate facilities are required for health lectures; solicit donations from businesses for materials and supplies to be used in free classes; advertise both evangelistic and health lectures;
- **Public Meetings**—Evangelistic, once a week on Sunday nights; Health, twice a week with diet and healthful foods on Tuesday night, and disease and simple treatments on Thursday nights.
- **Ongoing Aspects**—Monday morning meeting with all team members for instruction, coordination, and prayer; Question Box service gives public opportunity to ask questions for either public or private answers; Classes offered on Bible topics, Cooking, Home nursing for public and often separately for church members; Free health consultations and treatments given by doctors and nurses; In-home physician or nurse visitation offered free; Baptismal classes and services.[11]

---

10. The documents concerning the work of J.H.N. Tindall are perfect examples of valuable materials that simply cannot all be included in a single book. Many of these documents are available for download at www.AdventistCityMissions.org

11. *Gospel-medical Evangelistic Campaign*, 8–11

Over all, the plan was working. Perhaps the best statistic was the long term retention rate which ranged from seventy-five, to as high as ninety percent of converts.[12]

In Oklahoma City, even the local newspaper chimed in with a comparison of Tindall's work and that of the far more famous evangelist, Billy Sunday, who just happened to show up in town at the same time. In an article titled "A New Evangelism," their comment was: "Sunday got the crowds, but Tindall got the converts."[13]

As the *Review and Herald* of January 6, 1921, put it: "Oklahoma City probably had the most successful single city effort ever held in the history of our work, which resulted in the addition of about 200 members to the church." Of course, that was written *before* the Dallas, Texas, campaign, which could hardly have been any less successful than something done in Oklahoma!

Truth be told, Dallas *was* a success:

> At that time there was only a small Adventist church in Dallas. Dr. Mary McReynolds from the Medical College assisted Elder Tindall during that campaign, and the Union asked that a training school be held in connection with the meetings for delegates from the churches of the Union. This lasted for three months. The Dallas meetings were quite successful, resulting not only in conversions but also in the acquiring of a beautiful new church which was valued at $23,000. Much of it was paid for by donations and conversions from among the higher strata of society in that city. Norman Gulley states: "That campaign finished with fifty-six people receiving certificates from the training school which were delegates from the churches in the Union, one hundred baptisms, $18,000 in cash and pledges for the new church and $10,500 in tithes.... Truly God had wonderfully blessed!"[14]

Things were going well; surely it must be time for the devil to crash the party.

12. *Gospel-medical Evangelistic Campaign*, 7

13. Calvin Thrash, *John H.N. Tindall: Fifty Years a Gospel-Medical Missionary Evangelist*; 5

14. Calvin Thrash, *John H.N. Tindall: Fifty Years a Gospel-Medical Missionary Evangelist*; 5

Chapter Nineteen

The Field School

T HEY say that it's in the water that you learn how to swim. That
seems to have been the basic philosophy of those who established
the Field School of Evangelism in San Francisco. Of course, perhaps they
didn't have a "philosophy." Maybe they just noticed that Jesus took His
disciples wherever He went and had them work along with Him.

The Dallas, Texas, evangelistic campaign had included a school
kind of like that, with students from all the Conferences of the Union.
Perhaps that got the idea rolling in minds out West. But it didn't happen overnight.

For one thing, the devil had finally found his agents following the out-
standing successes of the programs in Oklahoma City and Dallas. It
seems that a number of physicians who thought meat was an essential
part of the human diet began to make an issue about Tindall not being
"professionally trained." After all, he wasn't a doctor; he wasn't even a
nurse. This guy wasn't anything.

Actually, that was part of the beauty of it all. Tindall was a medical
missionary who happened to know more of value than some doctors, but
his two years at Loma Linda had mostly covered the sort of thing that a
diligent, self-motivated student could learn at home. (Certainly far more
easily today than back in the pre-Internet era. Hint: start by reading *Ministry of Healing*!)

What that meant, of course, was that there could easily be hundreds
of people, maybe even the "thousands" that Ellen White had foreseen,

out doing roughly the same thing Elder Tindall was doing. It really wasn't impossible.

Knowledge Is Power

Nonetheless, the high profile attacks of these physicians were starting to influence public opinion and make his work more complicated. Rather than fight these publicity seekers head-on, Elder Tindall decided to take some time off and learn more in the area of dietetics. If this was going to be an issue, he was going to be ready.

Besides, he knew that he could use the knowledge in his evangelistic work. Public interest in diet was high at the time, and Tindall knew that a familiarity with the science of nutrition would serve him well.

Not everyone saw it that way:

> While at Loma Linda taking my training in dietetics I had a very prominent man of our denomination say to me, "John, what are you doing here? What do you expect to do studying dietetics? Do you think it right to leave your great work as an evangelist, and come here and spend all this time studying dietetics?" In reply to my good friend, I said, "Time will show the wisdom of the plan, my brother. Did you ever read in [*Testimonies*] volume 9, page 112, 'There are some who think that the question of diet is not of sufficient importance to be included in their evangelistic work, but such make a great mistake'? It seems to me, my brother, that some people do not see the value of dietetics in evangelism; but I am certain there is wisdom in this statement and I am certain that evangelism needs dietetics; but a great mistake is made by leaving it out and I am here to get the training that someday will aid me greatly in carrying forward that evangelism which will demonstrate God's plan of soul-winning in the closing work."[1]

All Things, Working Together

His leave of absence from evangelism in 1923 was providential on another front as well. It seems that the Elder had some challenges with chemistry. Surely he's neither the first, nor the last, who has had a hard time working with whatever passed for state-of-the-art knowledge in the field of chemistry. Judging from the number of changes that have been made in our best understanding of what all those sub-atomic particles are actually doing down there, maybe it wasn't his fault. Maybe he was simply reacting negatively to the mistakes that no one else saw back then. Who knows? It could be....

In any case, he had the good fortune of making friends with Bill, a bright young scholar who seemed to take the chemistry classes in stride

---

1. *The Medical Evangelist*, March 15, 1928, 1

and gave him the help he needed. And "young" was something of an un-derstatement. Only seventeen, he had had a struggle to even gain accep-tance into the medical missionary course that fall. But he made it, and it's a good thing he did. The course which embodied the core purpose of the College of Medical Evangelists, the one for "thousands," was never off-fered again.

The established evangelist and the unknown youngster became friends there, both completing their studies in the spring of 1925. Then Tindall went back to evangelism; Bill—now all of nineteen—earned money printing evangelistic notices and flyers on a hand-powered letter-press and began to study nursing. Two years passed....

Out in California, the Conference president began thinking about what J.H.N. Tindall was doing, and wondering why no one else did the same. They *could* be doing it. Just about *anybody* could be doing the sim-pler things, at the very least. What would it take to get them going?

The answer, of course, was a school. Why not have an evangelism school? One that would teach people to do what Tindall was doing. Surely it wasn't impossible! He might even get Tindall to run it.

So Elder G.A. Roberts got hold of John Tindall and laid out his plan. Without a big budget available for the project, he could promise him only one additional salary. But, said Roberts, I'll get you the best man in the conference; just tell me whom you want.

Tindall asked for Bill. Roberts had never heard of him, and was not amused. Then he found out that "Bill" (technically it was "Wilmont") had not gone to Adventist schools (unless one counted his mother's parsonage-home classroom, something few were prepared to do in those days), was too young to vote, and had never held a Conference position. Roberts was even less amused than previously, and he hadn't been amused before.

Tindall insisted. "That's why I want him. He is fully dedicated to the Lord. He fully believes the Spirit of Prophecy, has grown up working in the family garden, has a printing press and publishing business, and is faithful in health reform. And because he has no professional experience, I can train him the way I want to. I won't have to re-educate him."[2]

Tindall won, and Bill (more commonly known as W.D. Frazee, in later years) became his partner in various capacities for the next decade.

2. Calvin Thrash, *John H.N. Tindall: Fifty Years a Gospel-Medical Missionary Evangelist*; 6–7; James and David Lee, *John H.N. Tindall and the Field Training School*, 4

What Sort of a School *Is* This?

Anyone who has ever started something new knows that it's a good way to generate misunderstandings. After all, if it's new, no one really knows what it is, and they're probably going to get the wrong idea long before they get the right one. So it was with the Field Training School for Gospel-Medical Evangelism launched by Elders Roberts and Tindall in San Francisco.

After three years, the team had made some progress, but there was clearly work to do. As W.C. White explained it, he had been hearing about the school:

> The course is too long. The course is too short.
>
> The course is unbalanced. The teachers are enthusiasts.
>
> Less time should be given to house-to-house work. More time should be given to house-to-house work.
>
> The students are bent toward too much effort for the very poor. The students are too anxious to work for the very rich.
>
> And so on without limit.[3]

"An Astonishing Degree of Emphasis..."

By this time, it seems that Elder White had developed quite an appreciation for this general kind of work. So much so that his letters on the subject present one of the most complete pictures of what the program was really like. It's interesting to see how he came to regard this work so fondly:

> I think that you are acquainted with my work, and know that, as Secretary of the Board of Trustees of the White Estate, with whom Sister Ellen G. White left the custody of her writings, it has been my privilege and duty to study very diligently the messages given through her to the remnant church. I refer to the messages found in her many published books and also especially to those that are found in the many hundreds of letters and manuscripts kept in her extensive manuscript file. These were kept in response to her direct instruction and were left by her for our benefit.
>
> As I and my associates have studied these writings, we have been surprised, encouraged, and amazed at the evidences therein presented that our heavenly Father has made wonderful provision for our enlightenment regarding success and victory in every phase of Christian Evangelism. We have been especially impressed by the clearness and forcefulness of the instruction regarding the importance and the urgency of the work of training a host of young people to be successful laborers in the spreading of the Gospel by every agency employed by the Master.

3. Letter, W.C. White to Elders Kneeland and Scoggins, May 30, 1931, 3

As we have read scores upon scores of pages regarding acceptable evangelistic work, we have found an astonishing degree of emphasis given to Medical Missionary work and Medical Evangelism. And we cannot evade the conviction that there is, pointed out to us very clearly, a line of work that is rarely followed in a truly serious way by other ministers or physicians, or by Bible workers or nurses.[4]

Now We See It; Now We Don't

To Elder White, of course, the work being promoted by Elder Roberts, et al., was not entirely new. He'd seen this sort of thing before, several times in fact... if only briefly:

I will now refer to one feature of the Field Training School which has given me great encouragement. That feature is its aim at permanency and the possibility of its continuance, You will appreciate my joy over the possibility of its continuance when you consider the numerous instances in which efforts for the training of workers for Medical Evangelism have been inaugurated and have grown and borne precious fruit for one or two years and then died. Here I will mention a few of the many instances of short-lived efficiency.

In Australia, Elders Starr, Haskell, and Baker, with their wives and other helpers did a wonderful work in health reform instruction in connection with evangelistic effort, and when they left the field there was no one to carry the work forward in the same lines with similar strength.

In New York City and in Boston and its suburbs, Elder Haskell, Starr, and Doctor Ingress did a work in Medical Evangelism that was far-reaching in its influence, but when they were called to other fields, there were no locally trained workers prepared to continue and maintain that line of effort.

In connection with the establishment of the Loma Linda Sanitarium, excellent work in Medical Evangelism was carried forward by Loma Linda students ably led in field work by Dr. Lillis Wood-Starr and others. It was a great success, and an eye-opener on house-to-house work and cottage lectures.

Sister White felt so keenly its value that she gave hundreds of dollars to keep it going. When three years of successful work had been accomplished, it was permitted to die of starvation.

Repeatedly Sister White pleaded with the teachers in Fernando School to take their students during vacation into the city of Los Angeles and give them a training in soul-winning work. One year they did so. It was a great success, and having made one great success, they never tried again.

None of the efforts were continuous. No leaders were trained from among the students. The question in my mind has been something like this: Shall we go on to the end of the controversy, seeing the world's need, and reading of Christ's

---

4. Letter, W.C. White to Elders Kneeland and Scoggins, May 30, 1931, 2

method of ministry, and reading the clear, pointed instruction regarding the need and value of Medical Evangelism, and let it pass as a pleasant song?

Or shall we ask our most experienced laborers to make a demonstration once in three years of what can be done, and in its connection give to a few co-laborers a brief, superficial training that falls short of efficiency.

Or shall we encourage the maintenance of the Field Training School in San Francisco, and hope and pray that we may soon see efforts of the same sort in other places?[5]

A Look at the Details

What kind of school was this? What were they teaching?

Elder Roberts outlined the course of study comprising forty-eight weeks, divided into three sixteen-week periods. The curriculum was outlined briefly as follows: Bible, one hundred ninety-two hours; campaign company meetings or round table discussions, one hundred ninety-two hours, with the Bible and Testimonies as the textbooks for both of these features; evangelistic services, sixty-four hours; field Bible work or evangelism was to comprise one hundred ninety-two hours; baptismal class organization and studies, sixteen hours; gospel salesmanship, thirty-two hours. This part constituted the strictly evangelical sections of the course.

As to the technical part, there would be anatomy and physiology, one hundred twenty-eight hours and taught by a doctor; hygiene, thirty-two hours; chemistry, eighty hours; foods, thirty-two hours; medical dietetics, sixty-four hours; cooking, forty-eight hours; disease and diagnosis, sixty-four hours, also taught by a doctor; home nursing, thirty-two hours; hydrotherapy, practical, sixty-four hours; and hydrotherapy lectures, thirty-two hours.[6]

The courses listed here don't include anything that should have struck any Adventist as inappropriate, at least not in the 1930s. Today some of us might scoff a bit at hydrotherapy, and others might warn about the legal implications of the "disease and diagnosis" course, but back then there was nothing to fault.

Well, maybe one thing. It wouldn't get anyone any sort of a degree. Nothing. Zero. In fact, the only chance to make a living with those skills was to work for the church, and Willie White had already pointed out the probable term for a job like that![7]

---

5. Letter, W.C. White to Elders Kneeland and Scoggins, May 30, 1931, 3

6. Calvin Thrash, *John H.N. Tindall: Fifty Years a Gospel-Medical Missionary Evangelist,* 7

7. To put the issue of professional recognition into context, remember that this was the year, 1931, that the Autumn Council felt forced to adopt an "emergency measure" to authorize the very careful selection of only experienced Seventh-day Adventist educators to be sent off for "advanced training" (often starting with undergraduate work) at non-Adventist colleges, so they could get an accredited

Doth this offend you?

And yet, even with that shortcoming, the Field Training School was such that Elder White seemed eager to recommend it. He made that clear in a remarkably frank address to the students on the opening day of the school's fourth year. Included here is a lengthy selection from that address, for the simple reason that his thoughts deserve to be heard again:

> My heart is filled with conflicting emotions as I meet with you this morning, I greatly rejoice to look you in the face and see so goodly a company that are taking part in the school for this, its fourth year. It has been my privilege to be present on the first day of the first terms of several of our largest denominational schools, and it is in none of them that I took more joy than in this school.
>
> Solomon says, "There is nothing new under the sun," and I want to call your attention very briefly to the burden that was laid on the heart of the pioneers of this denomination for the kind of work that you are training for....
>
> Joseph Bates was a leader in Temperance work. Goodloe Bell was chosen to demonstrate to our people simple methods of practical education and to show that simple, practical lines of education could develop strong characters, forcible men and women, much better than the ordinary lines of classical education. These leaders, whom God had chosen, were criticized. Elder Bates was laughed at. Goodloe Bell was derided because of his poverty, his simplicity, his thoroughness in discipline, and in his insistence in making a practical use of that which was studied in his classes.
>
> We may well understand and believe what the Scripture says, "They that will live godly, shall suffer persecution." From whom do we expect persecution? From the government, from the officers of the State, from the leaders of the popular churches? Yes, but that does not terrify us. The persecution that hurts is that which comes from our own brothers and sisters, leaders that we love. I pray God to give us courage.
>
> I pray God to give to every student here a clear understanding of the principles taught in this school and a heart knowledge of these principles through practice. Also that He may give a knowledge of the power of Medical Evangelism, through practical experience gained by students in the homes of the people....

---

degree to bring back to the Adventist college as an instructor, so that our colleges could become accredited by the non-Adventist agencies, so that they could provide accredited pre-medical studies, so that the AMA would stop threatening to revoke the "A" rating of the College of Medical Evangelists, thus disqualifying all CME graduates from taking State Boards.

The "safety measures" that were discussed with such care were totally ineffective, of course, and a large number of Adventist young people immediately opted to head off to the secular universities themselves. If an accredited degree was the thing to get, they were going to get it.

As the president of CME, Percy Tilden Magan, would write to his counterpart at Emmanuel Missionary College: "Our necks are in the noose of advancing knowledge, and a kind heavenly Father only knows what the end is going to be." (Letter, P.T. Magan to H.J. Klooster, July 1, 1937, quoted in James M. Lee and David J. Lee, *A Compendium on Outpost-City Ministry*, fourth edition, 590).

When, in the providence of God, the Loma Linda Sanitarium was being established, a great burden was laid upon Sister White to make it known to our people that God's purpose in giving us that magnificent institution was that it might be a center of influence from which an educational work would be carried on in surrounding cities. Redlands, Riverside, San Bernardino, and Los Angeles were repeatedly named as places where the principles of healthful living as given to us for the world, should be taught and demonstrated.

But what could they do? The Sanitariums at Glendale and Paradise Valley were just getting on their feet and the burden of this larger institution at Loma Linda looked formidable, and for such an institution, struggling to round out this work by securing a strong faculty and a wise management, to undertake immediately a field work, seemed more than they could do. How could they at such a time take up this work for the surrounding country! But the message kept coming, urging that it be done, and Elder Burden who had carried much responsibility regarding the purchase of the place, prayed and planned and Sister White prayed and planned, and after a time Dr. Lillis Wood-Starr was encouraged to take the leadership of this outside work....

Meetings were held in our churches and classes organized to be held in the homes of our people where the principles of better living could be taught. Very soon our sisters were deeply interested, and they were encouraged to bring in their neighbors. Soon the rooms used for these classes were over-crowded, and when the leader was asked what could be done, some well-to-do matron (not an S.D.A.) would say, "I have a room larger than this. You may have the meetings in my house if you choose."

This is exactly what the leader desired, and when the meetings were transferred to the big dining room of some influential lady, the way was thus opened for her and her associates to bring in other women who were non-Adventists. Thus practical lessons were given on diet, food, clothing, rest and exercise, and simple nursing to a large number of influential women. This educational work in the homes of the people was carried on, as I remember it, for about three years. This is quite a contrast to the many good efforts put forth elsewhere which continued for only a few months and then ceased.

Try, Try Again...

In many places many wonderful efforts have been made in these and similar lines which have proved a great success, but quietly they have died and gone into history. I was about to say that they are nothing, only in memory, but this is not true because their influence on the people has been lasting and powerful in the matter of teaching better ways of living and of developing a friendly interest toward the people to whom God has committed the knowledge of history and prophecy for these last days.

When the managers of Loma Linda Sanitarium said, "We cannot support this field work. It is largely evangelical and should be supported by the Conference"—then the Conference manager said, "We cannot support this health work; it is largely in the interest of the Sanitarium."

Then Sister White said, "It is in the interest of both. God has revealed to me that such work should be done in many places. Now if the Conference will pay one-third of the expense of this campaign, and the Sanitarium will pay one-third, I will pay one-third." And it is this encouragement that helped in the matter of the work being continued in a vigorous way for about three years....

When the Fernando Academy was at the height of its career, Sister White urged the teachers to take their older students into Los Angeles and teach them to do city missionary work during the vacation. One year they took this seriously and Prof. Lucas as head of the school with Elder Warren as Bible teacher, and Dr. Lillis Wood-Starr as matron and leader in medical work, with Brother Horsman as leader in the Canvassing work, united their efforts to carry out the counsel of Sister White.

Nearly twenty students were led by them in a summer campaign in Los Angeles. The results were a joyful surprise to many. Some sold [*Christ's*] *Object Lessons* and *Ministry of Healing*. Some held Bible readings, and others did nursing. Every day they met and reported their experiences and all the workers were greatly benefited by the experience, and a far-reaching work was done in behalf of the people.

We who were watching this remarkable undertaking, felt greatly rejoiced. We thought that this would lead many other schools to do a similar work. In this we were disappointed. With this one magnificent effort, wonderfully blessed of God, the work ceased.

Many other efforts to do in our cities the work outlined in the Testimonies have been undertaken, and have proved a great success, but after one successful experience, the work has died. A few years ago there was developed a method of sending out specially trained canvassers with the medical book and health journals, with which was connected the privilege of membership in a health school. This work proved successful. The people appreciated what they learned, and in one place a small church was raised up as a result; but because strong churches were not raised up in every place, and because those bearing the chief burden of this work became weary, these efforts were discontinued.

A beautiful combination work was done for two or three years in these lines in Utah, Salt Lake City, and Ogden, but where is it today! These one-year efforts, these two-year efforts, and three-year efforts, have all died for lack of nourishment. That we may be nerved to action we must remember that "we wrestle not against flesh and blood, but against principalities, against powers, against the rulers of the darkness of this world, against spiritual wickedness in high places."

I know of nothing that seems to be hated more by Lucifer and all his hosts than our efforts to encourage the education and training of men and women to do a work similar to that of the Master.

Our friends say, "That is all good, but conditions have changed. You can not now work the way the Master did. Conditions have changed—present conditions make it necessary to do something entirely different."

It is very true that conditions have changed and will change to the end of time, and in minor plans and details our work must change and be adapted to present conditions. We must meet the people where they are, but we must also remember that God has not changed—that the power of the Holy Spirit has not been withdrawn from the world, and that God will open the way for us to follow the instruction of the Master....

Our most important study is to learn how to get access to the homes and to the hearts of the people.

There is another work which I believe that the students of this school can do just now to great advantage. It is the matter of placing before their friends and brethren, and before church officers and conference officers with whom they may be acquainted, the wonderful advantages of this school.

Very largely the criticism of any new line of work for the Master comes from those who do not understand it. I think your teachers will be ready to admit that I have been continually a thorn in their side, urging that more be done to make known what is being done in this school. One Monday morning in October, it was my privilege to be present at the round-table held in this room, and I made request that students and teachers should tell us what they felt they were getting here, in this school. Their remarks were so interesting, that we urged them to write out their statements. Some of these statements have been passed to the printer, and soon we shall have them in leaflet form, and I suggest that you use them quite freely. Send them to your friends and church officers and in a simple, modest way, make known your confidence in the way that God is blessing this work....

Now if you want to double the membership of your school, write to your friends, giving personal experiences in which you have had contact with the people in soul-winning work, and in sowing seeds of present truth.

I pray God that He may, through our self-denial, through our consecration, through our heart-to-heart converse with one another, with our teachers, with our ministers, and with our young people and leaders of our Sabbath school work, win their confidence.

I pray that by our earnest consecration to the work in general, by our effort to improve every opportunity to help where help is needed, that we may establish confidence in this work of medical evangelism, and carry to the hearts of the people a belief that it is of primary importance.[8]

Opinions Vary

It's safe to say, after all that, that Elder W.C. White was hopeful the Field Training School would be a blessing. But one of the key lessons to learn in life is that not everyone thinks alike. Willie knew it; he gave a bit of a warning to the students that day: "The persecution that hurts is that which comes from our own brothers and sisters, leaders that we love. I pray God to give us courage."

Viewed from our perspective, that comment may not sound like much, but in the 1930s such a thing would have seemed rather pointed. And then, of course, if that wasn't enough, he filled in whatever may have been missing with this: "I know of nothing that seems to be hated more by Lucifer and all his hosts than our efforts to encourage the education and training of men and women to do a work similar to that of the Master."

He doesn't seem to be holding out any rosy pipe dreams for these students! He may have known quite well of which he spoke.

Information is sparse (probably just as well), but there are indications of challenges in the working relationship with other Church entities and officers, and perhaps even a trace of human imperfection on Tindall's part. None of this is cause for shock. "We have this treasure in earthen vessels...."

While working on his research paper that has been quoted here, Dr. Calvin Thrash had the opportunity to personally interview both Tindall and Roberts, and he provides a convenient summary of these issues. For economy of space, we will look only at selections:

> There is evidence that, from the beginning, many of the church leaders did not understand the objectives nor see the necessity for the establishment of the Field Training School....
>
> A main point of friction was, apparently, with some of our established schools who seemed to feel that the Field Training School was competing with them for students during those difficult days early in the depression....
>
> Another letter from a highly placed church official complained that the catalog of the school, in its section entitled, "The Call for Such a School," was misusing certain Spirit of Prophecy quotations which this leader felt were directed to Loma Linda alone. This section was later removed from the Catalog....
>
> There were also some criticisms of Elder Tindall's leadership; one suggestion being that he was too egotistical. Others criticized Elder Roberts for starting the

8. Elder W.C. White's Address to the Field School in its fourth year, January 19, 1931, quoted in Norman R. Gulley, *Gospel-Medical Evangelism*, Book 1, 107–115

school without sufficient counsel. That this was not so is attested by his numerous letters of counsel and encouragement from a wide range of Union and General Conference leaders and medical leaders....

Despite some degree of opposition in high places, Elder Roberts felt that the Field Training School was generally well accepted by the public in San Francisco, and he says that benefits were attested to during its period of operation by a considerable increase in tithe, increased mission offerings, and increase in missionary work among the members, to say nothing of the souls that were converted as a result of the evangelistic meetings held by members and faculty. Also, treatment rooms were established, a new church was built, and much good will was built up among city leaders as the result of lectures to various clubs, civic groups, police, and fire departments, etc.

Elder Roberts tells of a rather amusing case, demonstrating Elder Tindall's value and versatility to the conference. A boy had been adopted into an Adventist family in San Francisco, and his previous family had attempted to sue the Conference because the boy was being deprived of meat to eat. With his legal and nutritional training, Elder Tindall defended the Adventist family in court, presenting scientific evidence on the values of vegetarian diets and the hazards of eating meat. He also presented Bill Frazee as a young man who had never tasted meat. The judge and jury were favorably impressed, apparently, as the case was dismissed and the family bringing suit was ordered to pay all court costs.[9]

Every challenge should end so well!

Our other major source for this chapter, the father-son team of James and David Lee, also interviewed Tindall. Their summation statement is shorter, less detailed, but perhaps just as accurate:

In 1932, Elder Roberts was moved to another position. The new conference president, under the pressures of the depression, had less interest in the program, and it died an untimely death.[10]

Forgetting Those Things Which Are Behind

Our final document, a letter from Elder Roberts to Elder Tindall about the time the Field Training School was closed down, suggests the sort of comment that one Purple Heart recipient might make to another:

Dear Elder Tindall...

I am just as sure as you are that God called you to San Francisco that you and I might work together and demonstrate to the denomination what could be done in combining the two lines of work. And even though much opposition arose and Satan did everything in his power to discourage, dishearten us, and

---

9. Calvin Thrash, *John H.N. Tindall: Fifty Years a Gospel-Medical Missionary Evangelist*; 8–9
10. James and David Lee, *John H.N. Tindall and the Field Training School*, 4

wreck us, still I am glad we held on and carried the program through to a very practical demonstration. Out of that demonstration, Brother Tindall, Brother Troy[11] established a work in Chicago that has been the admiration of the whole denomination, and will never lose his vision, I am sure, and that example in Chicago has been and is being repeated in other places. Then, of course, what Elder Scoggins and Elder Frazee and Elder Neil and others have done and are doing, is perpetuating the example, and some day, I believe, out of the example of that San Francisco Field Training School will be crystallized a denominational program that will be world-wide. So our sufferings there will not have been in vain.[12]

Praise the Lord for all who carried the banners of the Lord before us! And may the "denominational program that will be world-wide" soon fulfill the dreams of those who died, "having obtained a good testimony through faith, [but who] did not receive the promise."[13]

Of course, there is no call to idolize either this particular program or these particular people. They provided a helpful illustration of an encouragingly successful approach to the Lord's work, but it's unlikely that either the program or the people represent the final word on perfection. Still, we can afford to learn from every helpful illustration we can find.

11. The author could find no leads on "Brother Troy." Any information on this individual would be much appreciated.
12. Letter, G.A. Roberts to J.H.N. Tindall, April 6, 1937, quoted in Norman R. Gulley, *Gospel-Medical Evangelism*, Book 1, 133
13. Hebrew 11:39

Chapter Twenty

Voices in the Wilderness

SOME things are just too good to pass over, and this chapter is de-voted to noticing a couple of them. These are the words of just two who caught the vision of God's last-day church making a world-wide demonstration of Christ-like service, using the same general methods that He used, and embracing *both* body and soul.

Elder W.C. White's address to the Field Training School would be here, but his thoughts were noted in the last chapter so we'll move on to hear from Elder W.D. Frazee, who played Elisha to Elder Tindall's Elijah. Thousands have been blessed by his recorded sermons and books, but we'll consider selections from a very practical article of his, published in *Ministry* magazine in 1942:[1]

> We are happy to give a brief report of some of the methods followed in our medi-cal evangelistic campaigns, and the results obtained under the blessing of God.
>
> The value of medical missionary work in connection with evangelism is ap-parent when we consider the fact that it accomplishes, as nothing else can, two great purposes. The first of these is the revelation of God's love in practical min-istry to the needs of humanity. The second is the preparation of the mind for the understanding and appreciation of gospel truth by bringing the physical habits into harmony with the laws of life.
>
> 1. Preliminary Work—As soon as we enter a city, contacts are made with vari-ous clubs, schools, lodges, and other organizations, and appointments are ar-ranged for health lectures. Through these health lectures many friends are made and a following of honest seekers after truth is gathered. We have been able to trace in the experience of some converts a direct connection between these

---

1. For space and readability, the selections in this chapter (and *only* this chapter) have been "con-densed" rather than "excerpted." In other words, deletions are not shown by ellipses (...).

health lectures and their attendance at the evangelistic meetings, resulting in the acceptance of the full message.

One young man contacted at an anti-tobacco lecture in a large city high school was baptized a few months later, together with four other members of his family. After a period of preparation in our schools, he was called to the mission field, and is now occupying a position of responsibility. In another city, five adults from one family were baptized as the result of a medical evangelistic campaign. Their first contact was the temperance lecture in the local high school which the son attended. The father of this family later became the elder of the church in that place.

While these health lectures are being given throughout the city, we seek to carry on a training program for the church members in medical missionary service. Rather than emphasize a negative attitude in health reform, it is our plan to stress the positive, practical side.

Nurse-Bible workers, connected with our company, work with the church members in visiting their friends and neighbors, especially those who have asked for physical help. Thus the church and the medical evangelistic company are fused together, and made ready for a united effort in soul winning.

2. The Public Effort—We present throughout the series of meetings a broad, well-balanced program of health, based on a knowledge of the human body. Physiology is made the basis of every lecture, and the audience is taught that the laws of the body are as truly divine as are the precepts of the Decalogue. The thought that the Creator has made us for health and happiness, not for disease and misery, is kept before the people. (This lays a strong foundation for an appreciation of the moral law.)

As those attending the meetings change their habits of life, they begin to experience an improvement in health which makes them very thankful for the instruction received. In many cases liquor, tobacco, tea, coffee, and other poisons are abandoned before we reach the testing truth of the Sabbath. The minds of the people are in much better condition to weigh and appreciate the special message for this time. Having experienced the blessed results of obedience to natural law, they are prepared to see the importance of obedience to every command of the moral law.

3. Work in the Homes—Many desire further instruction, and thus the way is opened for personal interviews in the homes of the people. Classes in cooking and in other phases of health are also held, using *Ministry of Healing* and the little twenty-five-cent books as texts. We like the plan of holding some of these classes in the homes. This gives our workers close contact with the people, and affords precious opportunities to help them personally.

It is rare today to find a home without sickness. Many cases of acute or chronic illness furnish opportunities for simple treatments which are given by our nurses or other trained workers. Many times we have seen one treatment in the home do more to break down prejudice than any number of public lectures or sermons could do. As ministers and Bible workers, we are usually thankful if we can get into one room of the house and sit down with the people to study. As medical missionaries, it is our privilege to enter every room as we give treatments and demonstrate healthful cookery, and thus enter into the very lives of the people.

4. Christian Help Work—The Saviour spent much of His time among the poor, ministering to their physical and spiritual necessities. It our large cities today, there are thousands of poor people. They greatly need health instruction, but they need more than this. In many cases, food and clothing must be provided. To do this is an essential part of medical missionary work—a phase that every church member can share in.

The great medical missionary chapter, Isaiah 58, is very practical in its instruction. "Deal thy bread to the hungry," clothe the naked, "bring the poor that are cast out to thy house"—these are the commands of our heavenly Father.

5. Reaching the Higher Classes—In the cities are many who can never be reached by meetings. Occupied as they are with business and social life, they must be reached by special efforts. We have found that health lectures given before their business or social groups are a means of contact with some. Most important of all for this class is personal ministry in the home.

We think of one case in which a few treatments that were given by one of our nurses resulted in the conversion of several members of a prominent family, with a resulting inflow of means which amounted to more than the cost of the entire campaign. Efforts to help these neglected classes build good will for Seventh-day Adventists, even among many who do not accept the full message. It is worth a great deal for us to be known as a medical missionary people by judges, legislators, physicians, and ministers of other denominations.

6. The Medical Evangelistic Company—To carry on the medical evangelistic program outlined in the Spirit of prophecy writings, we have found it necessary to have a company made up of workers with varied talents and training. The instruction upon this matter is clear: "There should be companies organized and educated most thoroughly to work as nurses, as evangelists, as ministers, as canvassers, as gospel students, to perfect a character after the divine similitude." *Counsels on Health*, 541.

Few conference budgets can provide for all the necessary workers in a city evangelistic effort, but we have found that in answer to prayer, God will send efficient helpers who are willing to work on a sacrificial, self-supporting basis. For a number of years we have had graduate nurses and other trained workers associated with us in every effort we have held. These workers always testify to the great blessing they receive.

It is essential that we do more than put together the minister and the physician, the nurse and the Bible worker, and call the group a medical missionary company. In the ideal program, every evangelistic worker is to be a medical missionary and every health worker must be a soul winner.

Have we not reached the hour when hundreds of our medical missionary workers should be linked with the ministry in aggressive, soul-winning effort? We have been told that "it is as these lines of work are united that we may expect to gather the most precious fruit for the Lord." *Medical Ministry*, 27.[2]

Our second essayist is one who may seem an unlikely candidate for this category. Widely seen as the most driving force in both the establishment of the White Memorial Hospital in Los Angeles, and in the push for academic accreditation in 1931, the "Invincible Irishman," P.T. Magan, held his views tenaciously and worked doggedly to see them accomplished, but few saw his underlying goals clearly. Many have been perplexed at the seeming incongruity of his "reformer" image from the Madison days, and his later, more "accommodative" positions. Before writing him down as a "liberal apostate," consider this "Memorial to the Officers of the General Conference," which he penned in 1932:

Our physicians are quite fond of citing us to certain expressions alleged to be found in the Spirit of Prophecy to the effect that the last work ever to be done on earth by Seventh-day Adventists will be our medical work. However, the intrinsic idea which Ellen G. White expressed seems to have been almost altogether lost sight of. The words were spoken at the 1901 General Conference. The exact language is as follows:

"I wish to tell you that soon there will be no work done in ministerial lines but medical missionary work." *General Conference Bulletin*, 1901, 204. It must be very clear from this that the medical work to which we are called is in its nature ministerial, spiritual, and soul saving. Otherwise, it would not be stated that soon there will be no ministerial work amongst us except medical missionary work. Therefore, it is most essential that the training in the medical school be of a ministerial and missionary nature. It must be spiritual as well as scientific. This thread must be woven into the warp and woof of its fabric. Anything short of this is fraught with disaster.

The ultimate aim of our effort must be to equip and send forth into the harvest field an army of *medical ministers* of the Word of God.

Very many of our graduates are engaged in private work and only comparatively a few are in the great lands beyond the homeland. Unless a different state of affairs can be brought about in this regard, our school will be failing in a lamentable manner to fulfill the great mission to which it has been called.

In the Gospel of Luke, at the time when the Great Physician was commissioning his twelve disciples it is written: "And He sent them to preach the king-

---

2. W. D. Frazee, "Medical Evangelism in Action," *Ministry*, October 1942

dom of God and to heal the sick." And in Matthew it is written concerning the same event, "And as ye go, preach, saying, the kingdom of heaven is at hand. Heal the sick, cleanse the lepers, raise the dead, cast out devils; freely ye have received, freely give."

Later, at the time of the appointment of the seventy, the Master admonished them saying, "Heal the sick.... and say unto them, the kingdom of God is come nigh unto you." There can be no gainsaying that these comments form a pattern for our medical work in the last hours of time. Clearly do they make manifest that the medical minister is not only to have a care for the body but also for the soul. He is charged to preach that the kingdom of God is at hand as well as to heal the sick.

And now, should it be written down that it is at this point that our training in the College of Medical Evangelists is faulty? Our men go forth as good scientific doctors. A very large number of them go forth as Seventh-day Adventist Christian men and women. But they are not trained to go forth blending the two ministries into one, the ministry of the preaching of the kingdom and the ministry of the healing of the body. Nevertheless, the molding of these two into one unified ministry is the producing once more in the earth of the divine plan upon which our Lord and Saviour Jesus Christ formed his whole effort during his sojourn on earth. And how clearly did he teach the twelve disciples, as well as the seventy, that this unified gospel of cleansing soul and body must be the foundation stone of all their effort. If the College of Medical Evangelists is to fulfill its divine mission amongst the remnant people and for earth's sinsick and diseased souls it will be fundamentally necessary to train the students in gospel medical missionary work.

From all of the above, we conclude that the medical College owned and operated by the Remnant Church—if it is going to be true to its trust—must educate its students that their work is to be that of teaching the gospel equally with healing the sick.

Through the long, sad role of the years since sin first soiled the souls of man's first parents there have ever been from age to age godly groups of men who have preached the Word of Salvation in living power to the lost of earth. Each band in its turn has been commissioned of God to admonish, cheer, and bless the sons and daughters of this old world.

Abraham and the "souls he had gotten" shed radiance upon longing hearts with the gospel which he had learned. The great company of prophets, ordained as mouthpieces for God to the nations, have borne a testimony which time and again has saved men and nations who would otherwise have been doomed to destruction.

Those disciples who spread abroad the glad tidings will have their names inscribed upon the twelve foundations of the wall of the holy city as a tribute of their loving labor in bringing to its birth the Church of Christ.

Between eleven and thirteen hundred long, dark years go by and another sacred battalion sweeps forward to its task of keeping alive the holy spark.... I speak of the Albigenses and Waldenses. What a wondrous verse will be theirs to sing as their part of the song of the Lamb.

There was Wicklif—the "Morning Star"; the fearless Militz of Prague; that godly Augustinian monk—Conrad of Waldhausen; the learned Matthias of Lanow; John Huss—burned at the stake for the testimony which he bore.

It is now the dawn of the sixteenth century, and Martin Luther was not to call the church to repentance. Never in the forceful manner of his predecessors did he do this. On the contrary, his message was "forsake her!" He electrified men with the cardinal doctrine of righteousness by faith in Jesus Christ.

The picture fades once more. And then two hundred years ago we hear sweet voices preaching in the fields to thousands upon thousands of sin-torn souls. They are the voices of John and Charles Wesley, George Whitefield and their brethren speaking wondrous flowing words of *grace* and of a new birth.

Finally, in the last hours of time there come upon the spiritual stage a group of most devoted, sacrificial-hearted men. That they have toiled and wept and prayed brooks no denial. With great yearning of soul they have called to earth's teeming millions: "Prepare to meet thy God."

And yet, as the Divine Master gazes upon the different throngs who in the ages that have come and gone have borne the message of the hour, each in his appointed time and generation, methinks, I hear him say—"'One thing thou lackest'—of ministerial bands there have been many who have nobly trod the hard and narrow way. But mine eye beholdeth not anywhere in time's long day as much as one company, save that one which I did train for a pattern, who have made it their role on earth to blend two ministries in one, even as I their Master did, and concerning which I commanded, 'And as ye go preach, saying, The Kingdom of Heaven is at hand. Heal the sick, cleanse the lepers, raise the dead, cast out devils: freely ye have received, freely give.'"

There has never yet gone forth on earth a godly group of medical ministers to do a set and certain work, combining the cleansing of the soul and healing of the body.

The great privilege of doing this still stands untouched in this late hour. To the Remnant People, God offers the holy joy of doing that which otherwise will be lacking as a trophy of His grace when the story of His work on earth is reviewed amid all the glories of heaven. True, in this matter, we have been the foremost of sinners, nevertheless we may yet obtain mercy "for the purpose of furnishing Christ Jesus with the chief illustration of His utter patience."—I Timothy 1:15-16, Moffatts Translation[3]

---

3. Memorial to the Officers of the General Conference from Officers of the College of Medical Evangelists, Part II, Percy T. Magan

How many more voices have been raised to proclaim the need for doing Christ's service in the manner He did it? Impossible to say. It's tempting to begin listing off those who justly deserve credit, but the list would never be complete, and those most worthy of commendation would be most embarrassed.

Many thousands more may never have understood the theory of what they were doing, and may never have spoken a word in defense of their course. They have simply responded to the Spirit's call and done whatever they could, be it as simple as a cup of cold water or as complex as the proverbial brain surgery. Every such act, done from a selfless desire to serve, we are assured, is recorded in heaven:

> And whoever gives one of these little ones only a cup of cold water in the name of a disciple, assuredly, I say to you, he shall by no means lose his reward.[4]

And every such act bears witness to the truth that it is more blessed to give than to receive, for God will surely repay.

---

4. Matthew 10:42

Chapter Twenty-one

The Works of Atonement

AS Seventh-day Adventists, we tend to have more interest in the idea of atonement than most other Christians. We often think of it in connection with the day of atonement, and by extension, the 2,300 day prophecy of Daniel, chapter eight. Those are good and valid associations, to be sure.

It was William Tyndale, back in the 1530s, who went looking for an English noun to translate the Hebrew *yom ha-kippurim*. Not satisfied with the idea of "expiate" as used in the Latin Vulgate, he turned to the phrase "at one." Tyndale took the adjective phrase and turned it into a noun by tacking on the suffix "ment," which means "a state of." And that's where the word at-one-ment came from.

Our interest in the word, though, is more basic, along the lines of the root meaning of "united," or "in harmony." As it turns out, the idea of "oneness" is pretty important in the Bible's scheme of things. One of the more famous examples is:

> Hear, O Israel: The LORD our God, the LORD is one![1]

Deuteronomy 6:4 is pretty much the foundation of the whole idea of monotheism. Judaism just wouldn't be the same without it. You may remember that Jesus quoted this passage once, and it seems He saw more than ordinary importance in it. It was His response to a scribe's inquiry:

---

1. Deuteronomy 6:4

Jesus answered him, "The first of all the commandments is: 'Hear, O Israel, the LORD our God, the LORD is one. And you shall love the LORD your God with all your heart, with all your soul, with all your mind, and with all your strength.' This is the first commandment."[2]

But Jesus had a lot more to say about "oneness."

I and My Father are one.[3]

When Jesus made this comment, He wasn't speaking in some offhand manner. The circumstances were tense enough that He was very much aware of what He was saying. The account continues:

Then the Jews took up stones again to stone Him.

Jesus answered them, "Many good works I have shown you from My Father. For which of those works do you stone Me?" The Jews answered Him, saying, "For a good work we do not stone You, but for blasphemy, and because You, being a man, make Yourself God." Jesus answered them,... "If I do not do the works of My Father, do not believe Me."[4]

Notice this: Jesus was defending His claim to oneness with the Father, and what did He say? "Look at My works! If they don't match the Father's works, then don't believe Me!" And this isn't the only time He made that point:

The works which the Father has given Me to finish—the very works that I do —bear witness of Me, that the Father has sent Me.[5]

Notice what is cited as the evidence for Christ's Messiahship—"the very works that I do." Don't miss the concept: the similarity of a person's works to the works of his or her "Father" is evidence of that relationship. And that seems to be true in both a positive and a negative way,

It Works Both Ways

Jesus answered them... "I speak what I have seen with My Father, and you do what you have seen with your father."

They answered and said to Him, "Abraham is our father." Jesus said to them, "If you were Abraham's children, you would do the works of Abraham."[6]

In this situation, what the scribes and Pharisees were doing was just as much evidence of their "father," as Jesus' own works were evidence of His Father. To dispel any remaining doubt, in verse forty-four, Jesus told

---

2. Mark 12:29–30
3. John 10:30
4. John 10:31–37
5. John 5:36
6. John 8:38–39

them point blank, "You are of your father the devil, and the desires of your father you want to do." But the link between "oneness" and "works" is most emphatically expressed in chapter fourteen:

> Do you not believe that I am in the Father, and the Father in Me? The words that I speak to you I do not speak on My own authority; but the Father who dwells in Me does the works. Believe Me that I am in the Father and the Father in Me, or else believe Me for the sake of the works themselves.[7]

There may have been many reasons to believe that Jesus was "in the Father," and that "the Father" was "in" Jesus. But the last, best argument, the most convincing evidence, is always the "works" that come from that relationship. Just hold that thought for a moment, because we need to look at another idea.

The Work of the Priest

When we read about "atonement," perhaps the single most consistent detail is this:

> ...the priest shall make atonement...

In fact, a simple search of the New King James Version finds twenty occurrences of this exact phrase.[8] The most obvious implication of this is that we should expect Jesus' role as our Priest to be connected with the idea of being one with God. So it's no surprise to find these ideas showing up prominently in John, chapter seventeen, Jesus' "High Priestly Prayer."

> I do not pray for these alone, but also for those who will believe in Me through their word; that they all may be one, as You, Father, are in Me, and I in You; that they also may be one in Us, that the world may believe that You sent Me. And the glory which You gave Me I have given them, that they may be one just as We are one: I in them, and You in Me; that they may be made perfect in one, and that the world may know that You have sent Me, and have loved them as You have loved Me.[9]

This is one of those Bible passages which is obviously a step or two beyond normal human thinking. It's hard to imagine how "Item A" can be "*in*" "Item B" at the same time as "Item B" is "*in*" "Item A." So for the sake of time and sanity, let's just get over it. God is smarter than we are. That's good; now let's move on.

7. John 14:10–11
8. Leviticus 4:20, 26, 31, 35; Leviticus 5:6, 10, 13, 16, 18; Leviticus 6:7; Leviticus 12:8; Leviticus 14:18, 20, 31; Leviticus 15:15, 30; Leviticus 16:30; Leviticus 19:22; Numbers 15:25, 28
9. John 17:20–23

Notice that "oneness" is again cited as the evidence to the world of Jesus' Messiahship. But this time it's not just His "at-one-ment" with the Father, it's *our* "at-one-ment" with both of them that is the evidence He was sent to earth by God. This is not something to be taken lightly!

And another detail: notice the provision Jesus says He made to accomplish all this:

> ...the glory which You gave Me I have given them...

What is the "glory" of the Lord? When Moses prayed "show me Your glory," the revelation of God that was given was His character:

> ...merciful and gracious, longsuffering, and abounding in goodness and truth, keeping mercy for thousands, forgiving iniquity and transgression and sin...[10]

That would mean that it is Jesus' gift to us of the attributes of mercy, grace, longsuffering, goodness, and truth, and our resultant one-ness with the Godhead, that provides the evidence of Jesus' Messiahship. That's a big issue, and no small thing "done in a corner"! Let's go back to a verse we looked at a while ago:

> Do you not believe that I am in the Father, and the Father in Me? The words that I speak to you I do not speak on My own authority; but the Father who dwells in Me does the works. Believe Me that I am in the Father and the Father in Me, or else believe Me for the sake of the works themselves.[11]

We've seen this already, but it sets the context for the verse which follows:

> Most assuredly, I say to you, he who believes in Me, the works that I do he will do also; and greater works than these he will do, because I go to My Father.[12]

Jesus says that those who believe in Him will do even greater works than He did. How is that supposed to happen?

A partial answer, at the very least, is that oneness with Christ enables believers to carry on far more extensive "works" than Jesus did while He was here—at least geographically. That may sound like a cop-out of sorts, but we're talking about world-wide, 100% population exposure, and that's no small task.

Once again, we will lay that thought to one side for a moment—along with the last one—while we look at something else.

---

10. Exodus 34:6
11. John 14:10–11
12. John 14:12

What Kind of Works?

It seems fair—if works are a sign of both Jesus' role as God's Messiah and our oneness with God—to ask what kind of works we are talking about. It may be tempting to think of the dramatic, obviously supernatural miracles: Walking on water, multiplying bread, raising the dead... that sort of thing.

But is there anywhere in the Bible that Jesus actually specifies what kind of "works" it is that provides this evidence? Well, "Yes," and "No."

This time the story is in Luke:

> And John, calling two of his disciples to him, sent them to Jesus, saying, "Are You the Coming One, or do we look for another?"
>
> When the men had come to Him, they said, "John the Baptist has sent us to You, saying, 'Are You the Coming One, or do we look for another?'" And that very hour He cured many of infirmities, afflictions, and evil spirits; and to many blind He gave sight.
>
> Jesus answered and said to them, "Go and tell John the things you have seen and heard: that the blind see, the lame walk, the lepers are cleansed, the deaf hear, the dead are raised, the poor have the gospel preached to them. And blessed is he who is not offended because of Me."[13]

Jesus doesn't explicitly say, "OK everyone! Please notice that these six categories of good works are the specific evidence of My Messiahship." But providing the evidence of His Messiahship was exactly what He was doing for John. And when the report of Jesus' works came back to him, John the Baptist caught sight of a truth he had never quite understood before:

> The evidence of [Christ's] divinity was seen in its adaptation to the needs of suffering humanity. His glory was shown in His condescension to our low estate....
>
> The principle of the Baptist's own life of self-abnegation was the principle of the Messiah's kingdom.[14]

So here we have the "greatest of all the prophets" who had been quite seriously confused about the work of God. He had not understood the work of the very Messiah he had heralded! And yet God accepted his work and honored him with success in reaching the multitudes of Judea!

That's amazing, really. What a comfort for all of us who struggle trying to understand what God would have us to do. Perhaps there's hope yet!

But notice: John's mistake was in thinking that the Messiah would take a *less* self-sacrificing role than he himself had been called to. Unfor-

---

13. Luke 7:19–23
14. *Desire of Ages*, 217

tunately, we tend to be at fault in exactly the opposite way. We've grown up with the idea of Jesus' basic goodness, so it seems normal for Him to be merciful, gracious, and all the rest. "What would you expect? He's the Son of God!"

The inevitable side effect is thinking that it's normal that our circumstances should be better than His, that we should be *less* merciful, gracious, and all the rest. "What would you expect? We're only human!"

A Point of Reference

What Jesus said to the messengers—"the blind see, the lame walk, the lepers are cleansed, the deaf hear"—reminded the Baptist of Isaiah 61:1. Significantly, this is the same passage Jesus chose when He "stood up to read" in the synagogue at Nazareth.

The issue in both cases was the same: Is Jesus the Messiah?

And Jesus' answer was the same: "Look at the works I'm doing." But unlike John the Baptist, the people of Nazareth weren't impressed with that sort of thing—and especially not when Jesus brought up the widow of Zaraphath, and Naaman the Syrian. The idea that God had been generous to Gentiles was so offensive to them, that—

> All those in the synagogue, when they heard these things, were filled with wrath, and rose up and thrust Him out of the city; and they led Him to the brow of the hill on which their city was built, that they might throw Him down over the cliff.[15]

So Jesus' fulfillment of Isaiah chapter sixty-one was the evidence that He was the Messiah. John recognized it when Jesus pointed it out; the people of Nazareth did not. As a result, John was strengthened prior to his martyrdom and the people of Nazareth tried to kill Jesus.

Once you have the idea in your head, it's pretty obvious, really. But let's look at the passage to see if it makes sense:

> The Spirit of the Lord GOD is upon Me, because the LORD has anointed Me to preach good tidings to the poor; He has sent Me to heal the brokenhearted, to proclaim liberty to the captives, and the opening of the prison to those who are bound; to proclaim the acceptable year of the LORD.[16]

Is there anything here that would label this as a passage about the Messiah? If you don't see it, you can probably blame it on not knowing Hebrew. Here's a clue: What does "Messiah" mean?[17]

---

15. Luke 4:28–29
16. Isaiah 61:1–2
17. For those who have really never heard, it means "the anointed one."

Jesus wasn't making some strained application of an obscure Bible passage. He read a verse about the Messiah, and then told them, "Today this Scripture is fulfilled in your hearing." They knew what He meant, so they wanted to kill Him. But that's not the point right now.

Our interest is to understand what kind of works Jesus was citing as the evidence of His Messiahship. Why? Because they are important to us, too, in determining what sort of "works" deserve our time and effort.

What About Us?

With all the emphasis on the oneness of the believers with Christ, it should be no surprise that there would be a similarity between His "works" and our "works." But where do we find that Biblically? If you want the satisfaction of solving the puzzle for yourself, read through the sixty-first chapter of Isaiah, think of its general tone, ponder the specifics, and ask yourself where you might find something similar that would apply to God's people in the end of time.

Or take a hint from Dr. Kellogg, and turn back three chapters to find the works that God has "chosen."

> Is this not the fast that I have chosen...?[18]

The fifty-eighth chapter of Isaiah has "Seventh-day Adventist" written all over it. This chapter is for us just as much as Isaiah sixty-one was for Jesus. Notice the closing verses:

> If you turn away your foot from the Sabbath, from doing your pleasure on My holy day, and call the Sabbath a delight, the holy day of the LORD honorable, and shall honor Him, not doing your own ways, nor finding your own pleasure, nor speaking your own words, then you shall delight yourself in the LORD; And I will cause you to ride on the high hills of the earth, and feed you with the heritage of Jacob your father. The mouth of the LORD has spoken.[19]

There is an interesting comparison to be made between the two chapters. Here's the first verse of Isaiah sixty-one:

> The Spirit of the Lord GOD is upon Me, because the LORD has anointed Me to preach good tidings to the poor; He has sent Me to heal the brokenhearted, to proclaim liberty to the captives, and the opening of the prison to those who are bound.

Notice the imperatives, and the direct object pronouns: "The Spirit... is upon *Me*," "the Lord has anointed *Me*," "He has sent *Me*."

---

18. Isaiah 58:6
19. Isaiah 58:12–14

By comparison, in the fifty-eighth chapter, the words "you," "your," and "yourself" are used fifty times! The contrast in that regard is clear, chapter sixty-one is for Jesus; chapter fifty-eight is for us.

Another point—consider the focus of the first three verses of the sixty-first chapter:

> The Spirit of the Lord GOD is upon Me, because the LORD has anointed Me to preach good tidings to the poor; He has sent Me to heal the brokenhearted, to proclaim liberty to the captives, and the opening of the prison to those who are bound; to proclaim the acceptable year of the LORD, and the day of vengeance of our God; to comfort all who mourn, to console those who mourn in Zion, to give them beauty for ashes, the oil of joy for mourning, the garment of praise for the spirit of heaviness; that they may be called trees of righteousness, the planting of the LORD, that He may be glorified.

There is a progression and a purpose in this passage worth noting:

1. Christ is anointed
2. to do what we might call medical missionary work
3. so that "they" (His church) will be recognized as connected to the Lord,
4. so that God "may be glorified."

Verse four continues, specifying the manner in which the church is to bring glory to God:

> And they shall rebuild the old ruins, they shall raise up the former desolations, and they shall repair the ruined cities, the desolations of many generations.[20]

And that, of course, is exactly what Isaiah fifty-eight calls us to do:

> Those from among you shall build the old waste places; you shall raise up the foundations of many generations; and you shall be called the Repairer of the Breach, the Restorer of Streets to Dwell In.[21]

The connection is irrefutable, and the application of Isaiah fifty-eight to the last day church is clear. Even more direct is this comment—and many others—from the Spirit of Prophecy:

> I cannot too strongly urge all our church members, all who are true missionaries, all who believe the third angel's message, all who turn away their feet from the Sabbath, to consider the message of the fifty-eighth chapter of Isaiah. The work of beneficence enjoined in this chapter is the work that God requires His people to do at this time. It is a work of His own appointment.

---

20. Isaiah 61:4
21. Isaiah 58:12

We are not left in doubt as to where the message applies, and the time of its marked fulfillment, for we read: "They that shall be of thee shall build the old waste places: thou shalt raise up the foundations of many generations; and thou shalt be called, the repairer of the breach, the restorer of paths to dwell in." God's memorial, the seventh-day Sabbath, the sign of His work in creating the world, has been displaced by the man of sin. God's people have a special work to do in repairing the breach that has been made in His law; and the nearer we approach the end, the more urgent this work becomes.

All who love God will show that they bear His sign by keeping His commandments. They are the restorers of paths to dwell in. The Lord says: "If thou turn away thy foot from the Sabbath, from doing thy pleasure on My holy day; and call the Sabbath a delight... then shalt thou delight thyself in the Lord; and I will cause thee to ride upon the high places of the earth."

This is familiar stuff. We know about keeping the commandments and honoring the Sabbath. But notice what all this means! This quotation continues on, and Ellen White's next word is "thus."

What does "thus" mean? It means "as a result or consequence of."

So... what is the natural result or consequence of all this?

Thus genuine medical missionary work is bound up inseparably with the keeping of God's commandments, of which the Sabbath is especially mentioned, since it is the great memorial of God's creative work. Its observance is bound up with the work of restoring the moral image of God in man. This is the ministry which God's people are to carry forward at this time. This ministry, rightly performed, will bring rich blessings to the church.[22]

And this is not an isolated statement, a one-off sort of thing that she happened to write when she got distracted one day. There are many more:

The fifty-eighth chapter of Isaiah contains present truth for the people of God. Here we see how medical missionary work and the gospel ministry are to be bound together as the message is given to the world. Upon those who keep the Sabbath of the Lord is laid the responsibility of doing a work of mercy and benevolence. Medical missionary work is to be bound up with the message, and sealed with the seal of God.[23]

Did you notice the word "responsibility." What does that mean?

A responsibility is a contractual obligation, in this case, one for which God's church will be required to give account of their actions, and accept the results. Responsibilities can be serious issues, and this one looks to fit

22. *Testimonies*, vol. 6, 265–256
23. *Evangelism*, 516–517

into that category, since it involves the divinely ordained evidence of Christ's whole mission to earth.

That's important. No matter what we think, say, do, prefer, or promote, it's important and God treats it that way.

The counsel continues:

> I have been instructed to refer our people to the fifty-eighth chapter of Isaiah. Read this chapter carefully and understand the kind of ministry that will bring life into the churches. The work of the gospel is to be carried by means of our liberality as well as by our labors. When you meet suffering souls who need help, give it them. When you find those who are hungry, feed them. In doing this you will be working in lines of Christ's ministry. The Master's holy work was a benevolent work. Let our people everywhere be encouraged to have a part in it.[24]

> [Isaiah 58] is the work God requires His people to do.... With the work of advocating the commandments of God and repairing the breach that has been made in the law of God, we are to mingle compassion for suffering humanity. We are to show supreme love to God; we are to exalt His memorial, which has been trodden down by unholy feet; and with this we are to manifest mercy, benevolence, and the tenderest pity for the fallen race. "Thou shalt love thy neighbor as thyself." As a people we must take hold of this work. Love revealed for suffering humanity gives significance and power to the truth.[25]

Think about that last sentence. Have you ever done something "evangelistic" and wondered how it was that so many people, even really "good" people, could just ignore you?

"I mean, come on, people! I mailed you a flier with the coolest looking multi-headed red dragon that has ever been painted! What more does it take to get you out to a meeting!"

Would a little "significance and power" injected into the situation help? Maybe this "love revealed for suffering humanity" thing might be something worth trying.

And there will be a temptation to respond, "Seriously? That's a lot of work... and what these people really need is to understand the Sabbath!"

And it's true, they do need to understand the Sabbath, but maybe we need to understand it better, too:

> "We cannot keep [the Sabbath] holy unless we serve the Lord in the manner brought to view in the Scripture...

---

24. *Medical Ministry*, 263
25. *Welfare Ministry*, 32

As you can see from the ellipsis, this statement continues, and it does so by quoting a Bible passage. Would you care to guess which passage?

Before we do away with the suspense, stop and consider the significance of this assertion. "We cannot keep the Sabbath holy unless...."

"Cannot" is a very strong term. In our individualistically oriented, Western society, with its worship of unlimited "personal empowerment," it has as much appeal as a jail cell. We idolize those who thrive on the challenge of proving wrong the assertion that something can't be done. But when God says "cannot," we would do well to give careful thought before we commit our energies to trying to prove Him wrong.

And, as you have no doubt guessed, the full statement reads:

> We cannot keep [the Sabbath] holy unless we serve the Lord in the manner brought to view in the scripture: 'Is not this the fast that I have chosen, to loose the bands of wickedness, to undo the heavy burdens, and to let the oppressed go free, and that ye break every yoke? Is it not to deal thy bread to the hungry, and that thou bring the poor that are cast out to thy house? when thou seest the naked, that thou cover him; and that thou hide not thyself from thine own flesh?' This is the work that rests upon every soul who accepts the service of Christ.[26]

> Let the instruction given in the fifty-eighth chapter of Isaiah be studied.... Wonderful would be the results if ministers and church members would be converted, and adopt Christ's manner of witnessing to the power of the Lord.[27]

"Adopt Christ's manner...." Really? Do we have to? Only if we want to succeed. We know that, of course. We've all heard the statement:

> Christ's method alone will give true success in reaching the people. The Saviour mingled with men as one who desired their good. He showed His sympathy for them, ministered to their needs, and won their confidence. Then He bade them, "Follow Me."[28]

Perhaps we still have some lessons to learn.

---

26. *Manuscript Releases*, vol. 5, 33
27. *Paulson Collection*, 297
28. *Ministry of Healing*, 143

Chapter Twenty-two

d'Sozo!

YOU have certainly read the back cover of this book by now, and seen the "definition" given there. You may have even been a "good" boy or girl and read straight through from chapter one. But you are probably still a bit fuzzy on what the title of the book is all about. That's OK. This is the chapter you've been looking for.

In one sense, this is a continuation of the last chapter. Both address the question of whether or not medical missionary work could really play as important a role as Dr. Kellogg implied in 1893, but this chapter takes in a bigger picture, a wider swathe of the end of time. This chapter gives a more complete idea of what d'Sozo embraces. Simply put, it's "a work identical with the work that Christ did,"[1] and "the true interpretation of the gospel."[2] Is there anything else we need?[3]

Failure Is Not an Option

Let's start with an encouraging thought:

> When our churches will fulfill the duty resting upon them, they will be living, working agencies for the Master. The manifestation of Christian love will fill the soul with a deeper, more earnest fervor to work for Him who gave His life to save the world....

---

1. *Medical Ministry*, 24
2. *Review and Herald*, March 4, 1902
3. Of course, this volume makes no pretense of fully explaining d'Sozo, nor does the author pretend to fully understand d'Sozo. But what a joy to know that such a thing exists! Let's just be happy for what we've been given, and pray and study to master what yet remains beyond our grasp.

> We shall see the medical missionary work broadening and deepening at every point of its progress, because of the inflowing of hundreds and thousands of streams, until the whole earth is covered as the waters cover the sea.[4]

We looked briefly at the last sentence a few chapters back, but we didn't take time to specifically notice the Biblical allusion. Ellen White seems to have been thinking of one or the other—maybe both—of these verses:

> They shall not hurt nor destroy in all My holy mountain, for the earth shall be full of the knowledge of the LORD as the waters cover the sea.[5]

> For the earth will be filled with the knowledge of the glory of the LORD, as the waters cover the sea.[6]

The parallelism makes it clear that the knowledge of the Lord that covers the earth is not just doctrinal information, but the glory, or character, of the Lord. That is never simply doctrine; it *is* always simply demonstrated. Which is why medical missionary work is the perfect medium for the final promulgation of "this gospel."

But there is a troublesome question which intrudes into our thinking, perhaps only subconsciously, at times. It is this: What if it just never happens? What if God's people never get their act together? There is no disrespect of divine foreknowledge intended here; this is serious stuff. After all, how many Old Testament verses are there that promise the triumph of Jerusalem and the conversion of the Gentiles? We just looked at two of them, didn't we?

We pass over all that pretty easily now, and say that those prophecies will be fulfilled by Spiritual Israel (meaning "us"). But remember—the Jews' failure led to their rejection, and there isn't any reason to assume there is a new third option that allows us to fail and still succeed. So let's at least be honest and admit the magnitude of what we're talking about.

Looking Over the Cliff

Now, look back at the quotation we started this chapter with and notice the first word, "When."

Logically speaking, a "When" statement, implies two possible outcomes. Either "our churches fulfill the duty resting upon them" and all the rest happens, or our churches *never* fulfill the duty resting upon them, and... and then what?

---

4. *Notebook Leaflets*, book one, 18
5. Isaiah 11:9
6. Habakkuk 2:14

Do we actually think the Lord is going to say, "Oh well, that's fine, we didn't really *need* a demonstration to convince the world that Jesus was sent from heaven," and then just go ahead with the second coming anyway?

That's hard to imagine, but the only alternative in case of perpetual and irreversible human failure is not inviting at all. Consider:

> Should all the inhabitants of this little world refuse obedience to God, He would not be left without glory. He could sweep every mortal from the face of the earth in a moment, and create a new race to people it and glorify His name. God is not dependent on man for honor.[7]

> It was in order that the heavenly universe might see the conditions of the covenant of redemption that Christ bore the penalty in behalf of the human race. The throne of Justice must be eternally and forever made secure, even though the race be wiped out, and another creation populate the earth. By the sacrifice Christ was about to make, all doubts would be forever settled, and the human race would be saved if they would return to their allegiance.[8]

> Before Christ's first advent.... With intense interest God's movements were watched by the heavenly angels. Would He come forth from His place to punish the inhabitants of the world for their iniquity? Would He send fire or flood to destroy them? All heaven waited the bidding of their Commander to pour out the vials of wrath upon a rebellious world. One word from Him, one sign, and the world would have been destroyed. The worlds unfallen would have said, "Amen. Thou art righteous, O God, because Thou hast exterminated rebellion."[9]

> He has worlds upon worlds that give Him divine honor, and heaven and all the universe would have been just as happy if He had left this world to perish.[10]

Now, we ought to be careful how we interpret these statements. Given the holy character of unfallen beings, Ellen White certainly isn't implying a callous, who-cares-about-them attitude. But sin is bad enough that, once the evil of it is understood, the rest of the universe just doesn't have a problem getting rid of it. So... could that really happen? Or were those statements written "just for effect"?

At this point, human wisdom should fall silent, and focus on how to ensure that "the earth will be filled with the knowledge of the glory of the Lord, as the waters cover the sea." That's pretty much what Ellen White did:

---

7. *Review and Herald*, March 1, 1881

8. *Signs of the Times*, July 12, 1899

9. *Signs of the Times*, August 27, 1902. This article together with the article published the following week, September 3, 1902, are an excellent portrayal of the issues upon which the Great Controversy is being fought out. Highly recommended reading!

10. *Review and Herald*, March 9, 1886; see also *Signs of the Times*, August 27, 1902

Three times Christ prayed, "Father, if it be possible, let this cup pass from me."... What if His request had been granted, and the cup had passed from Him? The scene that was presented before me as the result of such a decision made me for a time lose all consciousness. When I aroused the scene was presented to me again and again until it had passed before me three times.

As I have thought of that cup trembling in the hands of Christ; as I have realized that He might have refused to drink it and left the world to perish in its sin, I pledged that every energy of my life should be devoted to Christ, that I may win souls to Him.[11]

Her response was logical, wouldn't you say? Doesn't that logic hold just as true today as it did back then?

But let's move on:

We are to work the works of Christ.... Isaiah says, "Thy righteousness shall go before thee; the glory of the Lord shall be thy rearward."... This is the work that must be done before Christ shall come in power and great glory.... Man is the agent through whom God works for man, and yet how few have given themselves unreservedly to work the works of God. Man can accomplish nothing without Jesus, and yet it is so arranged in the plan of salvation, that its great object cannot be consummated without human co-operation.[12]

Why does God require human co-operation? It seems like it would be so much simpler if He just did it Himself. But it is the propriety of taking us to heaven that is at stake here, and if you strip out all the fascinating details, the issue boils down to one simple fact—some things require action and demonstration, not just words and theory.

So here are some ideas on how we might move forward with all this:

There are some who withhold themselves from their fellow men, and shut themselves within themselves, and the gospel of Jesus Christ is made void by their practice. Their words go as far as expressions of warmth, but the poor are not clothed, nor fed, nor warmed, nor taught, nor given personal labor.

These indolent, slothful servants are abundant; but they say, and do not. They themselves are destitute of hope, faith, and love, and they are not helped by the gospel, because they are not doers of the word.

Some moral expressions are made, and some frozen exhibitions are shown, but the bright beams of the Sun of Righteousness do not penetrate the heart, brighten the life, and give vitality to their religious experience. They do not know what service, unselfish service, to God means. Many consider that it will sometime be their duty; but it cannot be now. They contemplate it afar off, as some-

11. *General Conference Bulletin*, June 6, 1909
12. *Review and Herald*, November 1, 1892

thing we are not ready for, when it should have been brought into their life at the very beginning of their religious experience....

Just a note—isn't the "very beginning of their religious experience" pretty much at baptism... or before? Something to ponder, but let's go on:

> The moral apathy that is prevailing in the churches today, would be largely corrected, if they would consider that they are under service to God to do the very work Christ did when he was upon the earth and "went about doing good."...
> This work is the work the churches have left undone, and they cannot prosper until they have taken hold of this work in the cities, in highways, and in hedges.

Another interjection—some people thrive on a sense of challenge. They don't want a routine job, they want something that puts all their talents to the stretch. There's something admirable about that... up to a point. But if all you want is a challenge, consider taking up a project that God says cannot be done. Try to make a church prosper without the members "going about doing good," and see how it works out. If all you want is a challenge... or did you want at least some chance of success?

But enough of that. The statement continues:

> Then angels of God will co-operate with human instrumentalities, and a religious system will be inaugurated to relieve the necessities of suffering human beings who are in physical, mental, and moral need.[13]

Checking Connections

You may recall that back in chapter nine the question was raised as to whether or not Isaiah fifty-eight and the medical missionary work could really be tied so closely to the loud cry as Dr. Kellogg had suggested. One idea was to see if other related theological concepts were linked to Isaiah fifty-eight. That's the question we take up now.

For starters, let's consider the opening verse of the chapter:

> Cry aloud, spare not; Lift up your voice like a trumpet; Tell My people their transgression, and the house of Jacob their sins.[14]

Is there anything here that might remind us of the loud cry? Like the first two words, perhaps? Or consider the imagery of the trumpet and its use to announce the day of atonement:

13. *Home Missionary*, November 1, 1897
14. Isaiah 58:1

> Then you shall cause the trumpet of the Jubilee to sound on the tenth day of the seventh month; on the Day of Atonement you shall make the trumpet to sound throughout all your land.[15]

Admittedly, these examples are not profound theology, but we should not dismiss them out of hand on that account, because the Bible and the Spirit of Prophecy both tie Christlike works of sacrificial kindness to just about every aspect of last day events.

For instance, there's this familiar statement about the beginning of the loud cry:

> The time of test is just upon us, for the loud cry of the third angel has already begun in the revelation of the righteousness of Christ, the sin-pardoning Redeemer. This is the beginning of the light of the angel whose glory shall fill the whole earth.[16]

We commonly associate this with 1888, Jones, Waggoner, Minneapolis, and "righteousness by faith." And that's fine... as long as we include this statement in the mix:

> Faith in Jesus Christ as our personal Saviour, the One who pardons our sins and transgressions, the One who is able to keep us from sin and lead us in His footsteps, is set forth in the fifty-eighth chapter of Isaiah. Here are presented the fruits of a faith that works by love and purifies the soul from selfishness. Faith and works are here combined....
>
> "Thy righteousness shall go before thee." What does this mean? Christ is our righteousness.[17]

So let's take another look at Isaiah fifty-eight:

> "Why have we fasted," they say, "and You have not seen? Why have we afflicted our souls, and You take no notice?" In fact, in the day of your fast you find pleasure, and exploit all your laborers. Indeed you fast for strife and debate, and to strike with the fist of wickedness. You will not fast as you do this day, to make your voice heard on high. Is it a fast that I have chosen, a day for a man to afflict his soul? Is it to bow down his head like a bulrush, and to spread out sackcloth and ashes? Would you call this a fast, and an acceptable day to the LORD?[18]

Look at the flow of ideas, and notice that there is no railing accusation here, no thundering threat of retribution. God simply tells His children—the people who are seeking Him every day, the ones who delight to know His ways—He tells them, "This approach isn't working. It never will work."

15. Leviticus 25:9
16. *Review and Herald*, November 22, 1892
17. *Review and Herald*, March 17, 1910
18. Isaiah 58:2–5

Why won't it work? Because it is completely foreign to the methods and the character of Jesus. It's separate from Him. It is utterly opposed to the work of at-one-ment.

Then there comes a divine prescription: "Here," Jesus says, "try this approach. Try loving the people, not in word, not in theory, but in actual helpful service." And He offers a few specific examples for our consideration:

> loose the bonds of wickedness... undo the heavy burdens... let the oppressed go free...break every yoke... share your bread with the hungry... shelter the poor who are cast out... clothe the naked... extend your soul to the hungry... satisfy the afflicted soul.[19]

So... does this sequence sound at all familiar?

A church that doesn't know it has a problem... a stunningly negative divine diagnosis... a prescription for treatment of the condition... and finally a conditional promise of success, honor, and glory.

Ever hear anything like that?

Perhaps it's going out on a theological limb to say this, but isn't there an exact parallel between Isaiah fifty-eight and the message to the church of Laodicea? Consider the sequence from Revelation three. Here's the church:

> And to the angel of the church of the Laodiceans write,

Here's the diagnosis:

> These things says the Amen, the Faithful and True Witness, the Beginning of the creation of God: I know your works, that you are neither cold nor hot. I could wish you were cold or hot. So then, because you are lukewarm, and neither cold nor hot, I will vomit you out of My mouth. Because you say, 'I am rich, have become wealthy, and have need of nothing'—and do not know that you are wretched, miserable, poor, blind, and naked—

And in passing, notice the basis for this diagnosis. Jesus doesn't say, "I know your theology." Nor does He say, "I know your diet, musical tastes, dress, or Internet viewing habits." Those things are not what Jesus is talking about. He says, "I know your works." What kind of works might those be? The works that would indicate a oneness with Christ, perhaps?

Now, before we move on, it should be said that diet, music, and all the rest are not irrelevant. They all affect our spiritual lives—and that means they all affect the "works" that Jesus says mark us as lukewarm. Far from

19. Isaiah 58:6–10

irrelevant, faithfulness in these "little" issues is what prepares us to be "faithful also in much."

And anything that we might call "faithfulness" in the little things, that leaves us unfaithful in that which is much, is flawed at its core.

But let's go on to the prescription:

> I counsel you to buy from Me gold refined in the fire, that you may be rich; and white garments, that you may be clothed, that the shame of your nakedness may not be revealed; and anoint your eyes with eye salve, that you may see. As many as I love, I rebuke and chasten. Therefore be zealous and repent.

And, finally, the promises:

> Behold, I stand at the door and knock. If anyone hears My voice and opens the door, I will come in to him and dine with him, and he with Me. To him who overcomes I will grant to sit with Me on My throne, as I also overcame and sat down with My Father on His throne.[20]

So... isn't that moderately interesting? We can find a direct literary parallel between Isaiah fifty-eight and the last half of Revelation three.

At the risk of sounding disrespectful of scholasticism, we might notice that that is the sort of thing someone could turn into a pretty good MDiv thesis paper. And then we could all read it, weigh the many arguments and counter arguments, consider the historical exegesis of the passages, even conclude that we essentially agree with the author's main points... and stay just as lukewarm and nauseating to Jesus as we had been all along.

We could do that, but let's not.

Shaking Laodicea... Or Not...

If there is a link between Isaiah fifty-eight and righteousness by faith, and a link between Isaiah fifty-eight and the Laodicean message, then that means we should probably be able to find a link between righteousness by faith and the Laodicean message. Something a lot like this, perhaps?

> Since the time of the Minneapolis meeting, I have seen the state of the Laodicean Church as never before.[21]

But no matter how you describe our situation, it always seems there is something missing. If you're talking 1888, Jones, Waggoner, etc., you're left wondering what happened to the loud cry. It had started by late 1892; so where is it now? Or what happened to it?

---

20. Revelation 3:14–21
21. *Review and Herald*, August 26, 1890

The missing piece in the history of the Laodicean message isn't quite so glaring, perhaps, but it is just as real. What's missing is impact.

Some of our more conservative brethren bemoan the disappearance of the "Message to Laodicea" from the Adventist preaching schedule. And they have a point. Seriously, when was the last time you heard a sermon on Revelation three? But worse than not preaching it, is the impotence of the subject when it is presented! The last time you did hear a sermon on the message to Laodicea, did it do this?

> I asked the meaning of the shaking I had seen and was shown that it would be caused by the straight testimony called forth by the counsel of the True Witness to the Laodiceans. This will have its effect upon the heart of the receiver, and will lead him to exalt the standard and pour forth the straight truth. Some will not bear this straight testimony. They will rise up against it, and this is what will cause a shaking among God's people.[22]

Can you blame preachers for not wanting to touch the subject? It's like saying that you're going to pull a rabbit out of your hat, and then coming up empty handed—not something that helps anyone, especially when it's done on a public stage.

So why is this message so powerless? Have we misplaced the "straight testimony"?

Over the years, there have been quite a few self-proclaimed "straight testimony" ministries. They have tended to emphasize different issues that they felt were being neglected by the Church as a whole. It's fair to say that some of them have done some good; others... well, maybe not so much. But none of them have brought on the loud cry, latter rain, sealing, etc.

We know that much, because *we're still here.* It's undeniable. Some of these well-meaning presenters have managed to become rude enough that they have produced a "shaking" of sorts, but if that's where it all stops it hardly bears the divine credentials. Something is missing, but what is it?

> Says the true Witness, "Behold, I stand at the door and knock."...
> The heavenly Guest is standing at your door, while you are piling up obstructions to bar His entrance. Jesus is knocking through the prosperity He gives you. He loads you with blessings to test your fidelity, that they may flow out from you to others. Will you permit your selfishness to triumph? Will you squander God's talents, and lose your soul through idolatrous love of the blessings He has given?[23]

---

22. *Early Writings*, 270
23. *Review and Herald*, November 2, 1886

Notice the references to the "True Witness" and the "heavenly Guest... standing at your door." That's right out of the message to Laodicea. This is "straight testimony" stuff,... but not, perhaps, as straight as this next one:

> All His gifts are to be used in blessing humanity, in relieving the suffering and the needy. We are to feed the hungry, to clothe the naked, to care for the widow and the fatherless, to minister to the distressed and downtrodden. God never meant that the widespread misery in the world should exist. He never meant that one man should have an abundance of the luxuries of life, while the children of others should cry for bread. The means over and above the actual necessities of life are entrusted to man to do good, to bless humanity.
>
> The Lord says, "Sell that ye have, and give alms." Be "ready to distribute, willing to communicate." "When thou makest a feast, call the poor, the maimed, the lame, the blind." "Loose the bands of wickedness," "undo the heavy burdens," "let the oppressed go free," "break every yoke." "Deal thy bread to the hungry," "bring the poor that are cast out to thy house." "When thou seest the naked,... cover him." "Satisfy the afflicted soul." "Go ye into all the world, and preach the gospel to every creature." These are the Lord's commands.[24]

For Laodiceans—said to feel themselves "rich and increased with goods"—and especially, perhaps, for those of us living in the richer nations of the earth, the question of "actual necessities" may need some serious thought. What are we going to do about "the Lord's commands"?

At some level (and, please, let's be mature enough to grant that there *will be* different levels, and that what the Lord calls one to do is not necessarily the same as He calls another to do), this issue loops back around to the question of "the Lie." Can God be trusted to provide for us... or not?

It's not a new idea. Back at the General Conference of 1891, when John Kellogg was making his first plea for an orphanage, he touched on this:

> I have given quite a good deal of thought and study to this subject. My wife and I have given considerable attention to this work for a number of years. We have been planning to raise forty or fifty children ourselves. Just as fast as we get any money, we will invest it in children. I have done that for several years. Every single dollar that can be saved from other necessary expenses goes into the education of children. I do not believe we have any right to accumulate money. I think as long as we are well, and have God's blessing upon our work, it is our duty to spend what we earn in God's work. I do not believe that in this age any man has a right to accumulate money.[25]

---

24. *Christ's Object Lessons*, 370
25. *General Conference Daily Bulletin*, March 20, 1891, 178

It's hard to say how long or how firmly Dr. Kellogg held to this position. He and his wife did raise forty-two children, so it's hard to dismiss his comments as just hot air.

And that makes a point that may be the answer to our dilemma about the missing influence of the Laodicean message. Perhaps what has been lacking is "the power of demonstration." As Kellogg mentioned repeatedly in his 1893 sermons, "talk is cheap." Perhaps every presentation on the Laodicean message, including this one, is doomed to irrelevance until it can be seen carried out in an obvious and inspiring manner. Then, perhaps, it will shake someone else into doing the same, and that influence may spread to still more, until—finally—the knowledge of the Lord covers the earth as the waters cover the sea.

Keeping It All In Balance

Here's another "straight testimony" type of statement, again based on Isaiah fifty-eight:

> The work of the people of God is to enlighten the world, in accordance with the directions given in the fifty-eighth chapter of Isaiah. Here is presented the plan of work which is to be carried on in every place where the truth takes hold of minds and hearts. In connection with the proclamation of the message is to be done the work of relieving families who are in distress. Those who take their position on the Lord's side are to see in Seventh-day Adventists a warm-hearted, self-denying, self-sacrificing people, who cheerfully and gladly minister to the needy.[26]

This isn't some disconnected, pointless, warm-fuzzy social gospel approach. This isn't something we should let the Salvation Army take care of for us. This isn't a replacement for Bible truth. This is what needs to be done "in every place where the truth takes hold of minds and hearts."

This kind of work is to be done "in connection with the proclamation of the message." And there are intelligent limits placed on this work—it's not supposed to absorb all our time and money. That's what happened in the late 1890s, when Dr. Kellogg distorted the medical missionary work.

Notice Ellen White's next sentence:

> But the work of providing for all the depraved, all the drunkards, and all the prostitutes, has not and never will be given by the Lord to Seventh-day Adventists.[27]

The key word here is "all." Of course there will be *some* depraved, *some* drunkards, *some* prostitutes who accept the truth. And, yes, there will even be *some* time and *some* money spent on some people who never respond.

---

26. *Manuscript Releases*, vol. 1, 224
27. *Manuscript Releases*, vol. 1, 224

After all, how many lepers came back to thank Jesus?

The point is, there needs to be a balance. Kellogg went overboard in one direction and then flipped the traces theologically. So we disfellowshiped him (sad, but necessary) and proceeded to throw the baby out with the bath water (sad, and completely unnecessary).

Fire Retardant

You may recall that there were two disastrous fires in Battle Creek in 1902. The Sanitarium burned down in February, and the Review and Herald burned down in December.

Ellen White explicitly said that, "The Lord signified His displeasure by permitting the principal buildings of these institutions to be destroyed by fire." She spoke of a number of specific issues and problems which brought these "judgments" upon Battle Creek. Each concern she mentioned was no doubt valid, but there is an interesting statement in which she speaks more generally of the cause:

> Notwithstanding the plain evidence of the Lord's providence in these destructive fires, some among us have not hesitated to make light of the statement that these buildings were burned because men had been swaying things in directions which the Lord could not approve.
>
> Men have been departing from right principles, for the promulgation of which these institutions were established. They have failed of doing the very work that God ordained should be done to prepare a people to "build the old waste places" and to stand in the breach, as represented in the fifty-eighth chapter of Isaiah. In this scripture the work we are to do is clearly defined as being medical missionary work.
>
> This work is to be done in all places. God has a vineyard; and He desires that this vineyard shall be worked unselfishly. No parts are to be neglected. The most neglected portion needs the most wide-awake missionaries to do the work which, through Isaiah, the Holy Spirit has portrayed: "Is not this the fast that I have chosen?..."[28]

As mentioned, this seems to be a more general concern, rather than the specific sort of things like printing infidel books and grasping for high wages.

But because it's a more general concern... does that make it less important, or more important? No matter how we might approach that question, there's one statement that puts a pretty strong exclamation point on the seriousness of the issue:

---

28. *Testimonies*, vol. 8, 218

The word was spoken, "God will cleanse and purify His temple in His displeasure."

In the visions of the night, I saw a sword of fire hung out over Battle Creek.

Brethren, God is in earnest with us. I want to tell you that if after the warnings given in these burnings, the leaders of our people go right on, just as they have done in the past, exalting themselves, God will take the bodies next. Just as surely as He lives, He will speak to them in language that they cannot fail to understand.[29]

Praise God for conditional prophecies! May we never meet the conditions and understand what this one means!

The Last Call to the Supper

Another end-time motif that comes into this whole discussion is the parable of the last call to the supper. Used almost synonymously with the loud cry to represent the final warning to the world, this parable provides a slightly different angle from which to view the closing work of the church:

The medical missionary workers are doing the long-neglected work which God gave to the church in Battle Creek—they are giving the last call to the supper which He has prepared.

In order to be carried forward aright, the medical missionary work needs talent. It requires strong, willing hands, and wise, discriminating management. But can this be while those in responsible places—presidents of conferences and ministers—bar the way?

The Lord says to the presidents of conferences and to other influential brethren:"Remove the stumbling blocks that have been placed before the people."...

Time is short, and there is a great work to be done. If you feel no interest in the work that is going forward, if you will not encourage medical missionary work in the churches, it will be done without your consent; for it is the work of God, and it must be done. My brethren and sisters, take your position on the Lord's side and be earnest, active, courageous co-workers with Christ, laboring with Him to seek and save the lost.[30]

Above and beyond the imagery of the call to the supper, part of what makes this striking is the idea that in this particular arena it might be proper to resort to a kind of "sanctified insubordination" and move forward without the consent of conference officials. And notice the phrase, "take your position on the Lord's side." Do you recognize it? It's a subtle indication of the magnitude of the issue.

29. *Manuscript Releases*, vol. 4, 367
30. *Testimonies*, vol. 8, 71, 75

The wording is from Exodus 32:26. It's what Moses said when he came into the camp and interrupted the celebration around the Golden Calf. It was the tribe of Levi which responded to his call, and—at Moses' direction—they then proceeded to kill about three thousand of the idolaters. Ellen White was not promoting homicide, but she clearly placed medical missionary work as a high priority.

This material was written originally as a private letter to the president of the Michigan Conference. In that form the dividing line was made very clear:

> Doctor Kellogg is doing the very work which God has given to the church in Battle Creek—the last call to the supper He has prepared....
>
> Time is short, and there is a great work to be done. If you feel no interest in the work that is going forward, if you will not encourage medical missionaries to work in the churches, they will do it without your consent, for this work must and will be done. Brother _____, Brother _____, Brother _____, Brother _____, in the name of the Lord, I call upon you to take your position on the Lord's side. Do not be found fighting against God.[31]

To restrict and retard the medical missionary work was effectively equated with "fighting against God," obviously a serious issue. But this wasn't the first time the question was raised by Ellen White; some years earlier, speaking of medical missionary work carried on in the setting of city missions, she had written:

> There is enough wealth in your conference to carry forward this work successfully; and shall the prince of darkness be left in undisputed possession of our great cities because it costs something to sustain missions? Let those who would follow Christ fully come up to the work, even if it be over the heads of ministers and president.[32]

Again, there is this intimation of a "sanctified insubordination." To the anti-establishment mindset of the modern world, this doesn't sound like much, but for Ellen White, this was seriously out of her comfort zone. To appreciate the magnitude of this, you have to remember all the effort she and her husband had put into getting God's people into some sort of working order.

From the "passing of the time" in 1844, to the organizing of the Seventh-day Adventist church in 1863, was nineteen years! And Ellen White had lived through every disorganized episode of that whole period.

Looking back to those early days, she summed it up like this:

31. *Manuscript Releases*, vol. 11, 218
32. *Testimonies*, vol. 5, 369

As our numbers increased, it was evident that without some form of organization, there would be great confusion, and the work would not be carried forward successfully. To provide for the support of the ministry, for carrying the work in new fields, for protecting both the churches and the ministry from unworthy members, for holding church property, for the publication of the truth through the press, and for many other objects, organization was indispensable....
We had a hard struggle in establishing organization.[33]

Why is this of interest? Because there was only one other issue which raised this same level of concern and commitment. It happened in the city of Minneapolis, in the fall of 1888:

Now, this is the last ministers' meeting we will have unless you wish to meet together yourselves. If the ministers will not receive the light, I want to give the people a chance; perhaps they may receive it."[34]

Again we see a message, more significant even than the existing structures of the church, which led Ellen White to adopt a less organized but more populist approach to spreading it. Some months later, Ellen White penned an even more ominous recollection of the event:

I was confirmed in all I had stated in Minneapolis, that a reformation must go through the churches. Reforms must be made, for spiritual weakness and blindness were upon the people who had been blessed with great light and precious opportunities and privileges. As reformers they had come out of the denominational churches, but they now act a part similar to that which the churches acted. We hoped that there would not be the necessity for another coming out.[35]

When this passage was quoted by the compilers of the book *Last Day Events*, they underscored the uniqueness of this private letter like this:

This is the only known statement from the pen of Ellen White indicating that she might have lost confidence in the Seventh-day Adventist church organization. The doubt which she expressed here was never repeated during the remaining twenty-six years of her life.[36]

While this is certainly true, it is significant that only these two issues—righteousness by faith and medical missionary work—rose to this level of commitment by the prophet. They appear to have been very closely related in her mind. Nearly identical....

33. *General Conference Daily Bulletin*, January 29, 1893
34. *Ellen G White 1888 Materials*, 152
35. *Ellen G. White 1888 Materials*, 356–357
36. *Last Day Events*, 48

Revealing God's Character

Another attribute of practical medical missionary work that ties it to final events is its unique ability to reveal the character of God. A well known statement from the book *Christ's Object Lessons* serves as a useful springboard for this point:

> Christ is waiting with longing desire for the manifestation of Himself in His church. When the character of Christ shall be perfectly reproduced in His people, then He will come to claim them as His own.[37]

This truth has, at times, been misrepresented and applied in any number of questionable ways. Perhaps the best perspective is shown in another quotation from the same volume:

> The completeness of Christian character is attained when the impulse to help and bless others springs constantly from within.[38]

There is an interesting tension between the commonly recognized Christian grace of humility, and a willingness to actually attract attention, which is then to be directed away from ourselves:

> As Christians we are to have a righteousness that shall be developed and seen—a righteousness that represents the character of Jesus Christ when He was in our world.[39]

> Those who wait for the Bridegroom's coming are to say to the people, "Behold your God." The last rays of merciful light, the last message of mercy to be given to the world, is a revelation of His character of love. The children of God are to manifest His glory. In their own life and character they are to reveal what the grace of God has done for them.[40]

These quotations present a fascinating responsibility that is laid on God's church. We are to live in such a way that we can point the people of the world to our own lives and conduct as a revelation of God's grace, glory, and character. And notice, it is said to be a "*revelation* of His character," not a "proclamation." That difference is significant.

How are we ever going to accomplish this? There are times when the task simply seems too great, and humanity too degraded. Something about silk purses and sows' ears comes to mind.[41]

---

37. *Christ's Object Lessons*, 69
38. *Christ's Object Lessons*, 384
39. *Seventh-day Adventist Bible Commentary*, vol. 4, 1151
40. *Christ's Object Lessons*, 415
41. For those who are too young to understand this comment, try Google.

What we need is something powerful. Really powerful. Perhaps even the "most powerful":

> Search heaven and earth, and there is no truth revealed more powerful than that which is made manifest in works of mercy to those who need our sympathy and aid. This is the truth as it is in Jesus. When those who profess the name of Christ shall practice the principles of the golden rule, the same power will attend the gospel as in apostolic times.[42]

And the challenging fact of the matter is that there is no gray area between doing it right and doing it wrong:

> The standard of the golden rule is the true standard of Christianity. Anything short of it is a deception.[43]

Really living by the Golden Rule brings apostolic power; anything short of that is deception. Where have we been on this scale? Where do we want to be?[44]

Here's another well-known statement to consider. Have you ever wondered what stimulus is supposed to set this into motion?

> Before the final visitation of God's judgments upon the earth there will be among the people of the Lord such a revival of primitive godliness as has not been witnessed since apostolic times.[45]

Turns out there isn't any particular mystery about reviving primitive godliness. It hinges on the principle of benevolence:

> God's work is ever to be a sign of His benevolence, and just as that sign is manifest in the working of our institutions, it will win the confidence of the people, and bring in resources for the advancement of His kingdom. The Lord will withdraw His blessing where selfish interests are indulged in any phase of the work; but He will put His people in possession of good throughout the whole world, if they will use it for the uplifting of humanity. The experience of apostolic days will come to us when we whole-heartedly accept God's principle of benevolence.[46]

Need Some Help?

If you're feeling a little weak in the knees, ready to give up on yourself and the rest of the human race (something that long ago occurred to everyone else in the universe, as you recall), you may feel like you could

---

42. *Mount of Blessing*, 137
43. *General Conference Bulletin*, July 1, 1900
44. For a rather graphic depiction of how sharp this divide is, read Isaiah fifty-nine and consider this inspired snippet, "[Isaiah] chapter fifty-nine describes the character of the priests and rabbis." *Desire of Ages*, 458
45. *Great Controversy*, 464
46. *Special Testimonies*, Series B, No. 4, 10

use some help. As seems to be common when dealing with this topic, Ellen White holds out hope for, not just help, but top-flight, industrial-strength help:

> Nothing will help us more at this stage of our work than to understand and to fulfill the mission of the greatest Medical Missionary that ever trod the earth; nothing will help us more than to realize how sacred is this kind of work and how perfectly it corresponds with the lifework of the Great Missionary. The object of our mission is the same as the object of Christ's mission. Why did God send His Son to the fallen world? To make known and to demonstrate to mankind His love for them....
>
> God's purpose in committing to men and women the mission that He committed to Christ is to disentangle His followers from all worldly policy and to give them a work identical with the work that Christ did.[47]

So *that's* what medical missionary work is supposed to do... get us disentangled from all worldly policy. That in itself says something about what might qualify as medical missionary work, doesn't it? And, sadly, what might not qualify:

> All heaven is looking on with intense interest to see what character medical missionary work will assume under supervision of human beings. Will men make merchandise of God's ordained plan for reaching the dark parts of the earth with a manifestation of His benevolence? Will they cover mercy with selfishness, and then call it medical missionary work?[48]

What can we say? The first nineteen verses of Daniel chapter nine come to mind. But perhaps this one verse sums it up well:

> I said, "LORD, be merciful to me; Heal my soul, for I have sinned against You."[49]

If understanding the work of the greatest Medical Missionary that ever trod the earth is what would help us most, is it any surprise that we have this prescription for the best way to further God's work?

> In no way could the Lord be better glorified and the truth more highly honored than for unbelievers to see that the truth has wrought a great and good work upon the lives of naturally covetous and penurious men. If it could be seen that the faith of such had an influence to mold their characters, to change them from close, selfish, overreaching, money-loving men to men who love to do good, who seek opportunities to use their means to bless those who need to be blessed, who visit the

---

47. *Medical Ministry*, 24
48. *Special Testimonies*, Series B, No. 1, 19
49. Psalms 41:4

widow and fatherless in their affliction, and who keep themselves unspotted from the world, it would be an evidence that their religion was genuine.[50]

Again we see the one weapon in the Lord's arsenal that He tells us will get something done: The influence of intelligent and *joyful* self-sacrifice. What else but the vision of people with more joy than money, constantly doing humanly impossible acts of blessing to others, will bring the riches of the Gentiles in to finish the work?[51]

"Humanly impossible" doesn't necessarily mean "miraculous," in the sense of defying the laws of physics. Sometimes the greater miracles are the ones that defy the laws of psychology. The change from self-seeking to self-sacrificing is a huge miracle, and it carries a lot of influence. It's this sort of thing that holds out hope for finishing the task that the Lord has assigned His people.

The Catalyst

Speaking of "finishing the work," have you given any thought to the close of probation? Sure, we know that "this gospel" has to go to all the world before that happens, but have you wondered what actually marks the final tipping point where probation's door closes with a thud, never to open again?

Here's something to ponder. In the fifteenth chapter of John, Jesus was talking with the disciples on the night of His arrest. In verse fourteen He calls them "friends," and says the difference is that a servant doesn't know what the master is doing, but He is calling them friends because He has told them everything the Father had told Him.

In verse eighteen, He begins a series of comparisons between Himself and His work, and them and their work:

> If the world hates you, you know that it hated Me before it hated you. If you were of the world, the world would love its own. Yet because you are not of the world, but I chose you out of the world, therefore the world hates you. Remember the word that I said to you, "A servant is not greater than his master." If they persecuted Me, they will also persecute you. If they kept My word, they will keep yours also. But all these things they will do to you for My name's sake, because they do not know Him who sent Me.

---

50. *Testimonies*, vol. 2, 239
51. A word to the wise: Though "intelligent and joyful self-sacrifice" may seem innocent enough, bear in mind that it runs directly counter to the way the world gets things done. The movers and shakers of the world will gladly embrace those who are willing to sacrifice, if they can find a way for themselves to profit in the process. But when our sacrifice is intelligent enough that the glory goes to God, and any profit goes into His work, the embrace of the world either drops away in disgust or becomes chains to be broken.

In all these details, Jesus established a parallel between the world's re-lationship to Him, and the world's relationship to them. Then He adds two more slightly puzzling comments about His relationship to the world, but He doesn't spell out any parallel in His followers' experience. But, if there *is* a parallel, what would it be?

> If I had not come and spoken to them, they would have no sin, but now they have no excuse for their sin. He who hates Me hates My Father also. If I had not done among them the works which no one else did, they would have no sin; but now they have seen and also hated both Me and My Father.

The Basis of the Judgment

This next line of evidence is almost a re-run, because Dr. Kellogg talked about the parable of the sheep and the goats back in 1893. But he didn't have *these* quotes; Ellen White hadn't written them yet:

> "When the Son of man shall come in His glory, and all the holy angels with Him, then shall He sit upon the throne of His glory: and before Him shall be gathered all nations: and He shall separate them one from another." Thus Christ on the Mount of Olives pictured to His disciples the scene of the great judgment day. And He represented its decision as turning upon one point. When the na-tions are gathered before Him, there will be but two classes, and their eternal destiny will be determined by what they have done or have neglected to do for Him in the person of the poor and the suffering.[52]

> There is a work to be done by our churches that few have any idea of. "I was an hungered," Christ says, "and ye gave me meat; I was thirsty, and ye gave me drink; I was a stranger, and ye took me in; naked, and ye clothed me; I was sick, and ye visited me; I was in prison, and ye came unto me."... there is a work, as yet untouched, that must be done. The mission of Christ was to heal the sick, en-courage the hopeless, bind up the brokenhearted. This work of restoration is to be carried on among the needy, suffering ones of humanity.

> God calls not only for your benevolence, but your cheerful countenance, your hopeful words, the grasp of your hand. Relieve some of God's afflicted ones. Some are sick, and hope has departed. Bring back the sunlight to them. There are souls who have lost their courage; speak to them, pray for them. There are those who need the bread of life. Read to them from the Word of God. There is a soul sickness no balm can reach, no medicine heal. Pray for these, and bring them to Jesus Christ. And in all your work, Christ will be present to make impressions upon human hearts.

---

52. *Desire of Ages,* 637

This is the kind of medical missionary work to be done. Bring the sunshine of the Sun of Righteousness into the room of the sick and suffering. Teach the inmates of the poor homes how to cook.[53]

How to *cook*? She's kidding, right? What happened to Daniel Two, the Second Coming, State of the Dead, and the Sabbath?!

Don't worry, they're all still here. It's just that this practical ministry needs to be "in connection with the proclamation of the message."

We might think it's an exaggeration to say that the judgment "turns upon [this] one point" of how we treat the "poor and suffering," but the Spirit of Prophecy doesn't back down on that. After telling the story of the Good Samaritan (another parable Kellogg referred to in 1893), Ellen White has this to say:

> Here the conditions of inheriting eternal life are plainly stated by our Saviour in the most simple manner. The man who was wounded and robbed represents those who are subjects of our interest, sympathy, and charity. If we neglect the cases of the needy and the unfortunate that are brought under our notice, no matter who they may be, we have no assurance of eternal life; for we do not answer the claims that God has upon us.[54]

And in that classic volume of encouragement and love, the *Desire of Ages*, there is still room for this challenging statement:

> The sufferings of every man are the sufferings of God's child, and those who reach out no helping hand to their perishing fellow beings provoke His righteous anger. This is the "wrath of the Lamb."[55]

We have a tendency, when faced with this sort of divine requirement, to throw up our hands and say, "Well, that's ridiculous. I can't help all those people." God isn't demanding that we help "all those people"; He'd probably be pleased to see us help the nearest one. As our skills and faith grow over time, He may ask us to take on greater responsibilities, but it's bogus to use a fear of that as a reason to not help the nearest one.

Here's a more accurate picture of the kind of thing that holds most of us back from helping the needy:

> You may say you have been taken in and have bestowed your means upon those unworthy of your charity, and therefore have become discouraged in trying to help the needy. I present Jesus before you. He came to save fallen man, to bring salvation to His own nation; but they would not accept Him.... Though

---

53. *Call to Medical Evangelism*, 23
54. *Testimonies*, vol. 3, 524
55. *Desire of Ages*, 825

your efforts for good have been unsuccessful ninety-nine times, and you received only insult, reproach, and hate, yet if the one-hundredth time proves a success, and one soul is saved, oh, what a victory is achieved![56]

As a steward, it's commendable to seek a good return on investment of the Master's funds... but not if it leads us to disobey orders! If the Master is happy with a one-out-of-a-hundred success rate, but we aren't, it's a good sign that we've forgotten our stewardship, and we're trying to manage what we think is our own portfolio of assets. This, by the way, is a blatant violation of the Law of Life, another example of "the Lie."

Our place in God's scheme, like everyone and everything else in the universe, is to "take to give." When we lose faith in His willingness and ability to supply what He wants us to "take," we very quickly lose our willingness to "give."[57] And yet, His instruction is still, "Freely you have received, freely give."[58]

56. *Testimonies*, vol. 2, 31
57. *Desire of Ages*, 21; *Education*, 103; *Signs of the Times*, January 22, 1902
58. Matthew 10:8

Chapter Twenty-three

Personal Observations

Just so there is no confusion about the chapter title, this is where I largely put aside the mechanisms of objective documentation and say what I think on a few topics. You're certainly entitled to your opinions, and I hope it's OK if I have one or two of my own, so take the next few pages in that light. You may agree, you may disagree. No hard feelings. But please don't throw out anything that's actually inspired counsel because I might say something here that strikes you as stupid or heretical. Fair?

WHERE do we go from here? What does all this mean for God's people, God's remnant church, today? The central need is simple:

The world needs today what it needed nineteen hundred years ago—a revelation of Christ. A great work of reform is demanded, and it is only through the grace of Christ that the work of restoration, physical, mental, and spiritual, can be accomplished.

Christ's method alone will give true success in reaching the people. The Saviour mingled with men as one who desired their good. He showed His sympathy for them, ministered to their needs, and won their confidence. Then He bade them, "Follow Me."

There is need of coming close to the people by personal effort. If less time were given to sermonizing, and more time were spent in personal ministry, greater results would be seen. The poor are to be relieved, the sick cared for, the sorrowing and the bereaved comforted, the ignorant instructed, the inexperienced counseled. We are to weep with those that weep, and rejoice with those that rejoice. Accompanied by the power of persuasion, the power of prayer, the power of the love of God, this work will not, cannot, be without fruit.[1]

---

1. *Ministry of Healing,* 143

Simply put, this *revelation* of Christ is what must accompany our *proclamation* of His truth. This revelation of Christ is an essential element of "this gospel," without which the work will never be complete.

And in making that revelation, we will find that this "right-doing" can only be done through faith in Christ's promise to supply our need. As we grow in faith, making increasingly large demands on God's pledged word (which will eventually grow to proportions that would currently leave us feeling hopelessly overextended beyond our own abilities and resources), we will see His faithfulness exemplified time and again. With every such experience our own faith will grow, and our witness to others will more clearly show that we are simply channels. We take from Christ and give to those in need. In doing this, our own needs are supplied, and we find joy in helping others.[2] Plus, we gain the opportunity to say, "You can live this way, too! 'Imitate me, just as I also imitate Christ.'"[3]

Remember the green cord of faith that provides "hold from above"?[4]

Only as we exemplify this faith can we inspire others with the same faith. Only as this faith is grown to maturity can the demonstration of the time of Jacob's trouble be made. And, apparently, the only way to accomplish all this is through the combined teaching/preaching, physical/spiritual, medical/ministerial approach that Jesus demonstrated for us. He did say, after all, "And as you go, preach, saying, 'The kingdom of heaven is at hand.' Heal the sick, cleanse the lepers, raise the dead, cast out demons. Freely you have received, freely give."[5]

How to Relate?

Perhaps a passing comment on the practice of medicine today would be in order. I'm no expert, but in the areas that are most likely to affect me, modern medicine is amazing. Having enjoyed the documented benefits of the "Adventist lifestyle" for many years (except for "adequate sleep," which I still find an incredibly boring challenge), I suspect my most likely reason to visit a hospital as a patient any time in the next decade or two would be a car accident or something similar. In that kind of trauma care, I give modern medicine extremely high marks. The ability to keep badly damaged bodies alive and to eventually restore them is incredibly impressive.

---

2. There is all sorts of research that shows this. Go to TED.com and search "happiness." Since most of the presenters are atheistic psychologist types, I make no defense of whatever else they may say, the vocabulary they may use in saying it, or the goals they promote as a result of it. Take it for what it's worth if "more blessed to give" isn't enough.

3. 1 Corinthians 11:1

4. See the chapter "An Impressive Dream," in *Testimonies*, vol. 2, 594.

5. Matthew 10:7–8

Fortunately, it's unlikely that I'll be needing much input from the medical establishment on basic lifestyle-related conditions. And that's good... I'll be working to keep it that way.

And so I'd like to reassure my health-professional friends that I respect the high-tech wonders of modern medicine. And while I don't believe those techniques are ideally adapted to the kind of large scale medical evangelism we as a church have been called to do, neither do I believe the AMA is the beast of Revelation thirteen. I was doubly convinced of that when I went to a lot of trouble recently learning how to setup a spreadsheet function that enabled me to type in "American Medical Association" and easily add up the number of its name. I think anyone trying to make that case will have a hard time coming up with a way to get 2,854 back down to 666.

But did the dragon of Revelation twelve use the AMA to distort our perception of God's call for blended Gospel-Medical Missionary Evangelism? It does seem that way to me. One thing should be obvious: Our evangelistic work has never been the AMA's primary concern. They are focused on a different set of goals, and to the degree that their goals sometimes overshadowed ours, I believe we lost opportunities and hindered our primary work for the Lord.

But, still, I'm thankful for the improvements the AMA has brought to the general field of health care, and wish them well. If they're ever interested in what they could learn from the "rest of the story" on Loma Linda, I'd love to meet with them!

Speaking of Loma Linda.... More than a century later and the place is still in business. As Percy Magan said back in 1932, it's no doubt still a challenge to maintain and promote the spiritual when students are wrestling with such a massive load of the scientific. We can well pray that the Lord will give wisdom to all concerned with the University's management, that they will know how best to make the institution's considerable influence count, not in gaining the esteem of the world, but in winning souls to Christ. Not in merely training professionals to the world's standard, but in seeking to inspire and equip every student to serve as a true medical missionary as envisioned by Christ. May the best days of Loma Linda be yet to come!

All that having been sincerely said, it should be noted that wiser heads than mine foresee rocky days coming for the medical field. It takes little imagination to see the possibility of serious challenges coming from political, legal, and financial issues that no one can accurately predict. On what to do about all those challenges, in my ignorance I will keep silent, except to pray for those who are called to face them.

Get Out Ahead of the Game

But since the same uncertainties that will affect healthcare will also affect society as a whole, I'll make a couple of comments intended primarily for church members who are not healthcare professionals.

It seems to me that there is a common line of thought in the Spirit of Prophecy that encourages us all to become familiar with a low-tech approach to medical care—what Ellen White calls "simple treatments"—especially adapted to treat "common ailments."[6] I suspect that the inspired encouragement for us to learn these simple treatments is because the final events of planet earth will stress our current medical, financial, and social structures, first to confusion, and eventually to collapse.[7]

I make no predictions as to a time for this to happen, or for the immediate cause of such a thing. Any pessimist worth his salt can point us to a dozen potentially civilization-destroying crises on any given day of the month. And with the precarious state of things, it might only take one.

But I suspect that through war, famine, and disease, the Lord will provide His people with an unprecedented opportunity to serve others when no one else is ready or willing. I also suspect that doing so will extract a heavy price of self-sacrifice. In a time of great distress, such a display of old-fashioned Christian Help work in the middle of despair will be a powerful tool to touch hearts... but a tool which only those who've learned to love self-sacrifice and depend on God will be prepared to use.

That's all in the future, of course, and until then, you might not feel called to, or interested in, medical missionary work. But you *are* called,[8] so you might as well go ahead and get interested. You may want to look over that sequence of quotations on page 114 again. Go ahead! Bite the bullet! *Do what you know you need to do,* and God will give you the love for it.

By the way, did you notice that "simple treatments" were for "common ailments"? You don't have to worry about curing CJD, or HIV, or even XDR-TB. Why not? Because God is calling you to help—and influence—as many people as possible. Stick with common ailments; you'll have more chances to help more people.

---

6. See *Testimonies*, vol. 6, 113

7. See *Counsels on Health*, 506, quoted in the Foreword on page twelve of this volume.

8. "We have come to a time when every member of the church should take hold of medical missionary work." —*Testimonies*, vol. 7, 62

And you did see the quote on page 279, didn't you? Come on now! Get out there and help some of these people people learn how to cook food that's worth eating. God is serious about this. Check out all the YouTube videos on things like nutrition and hydrotherapy. You may never be a doctor or a nurse, and that's fine. But the day will come when you'll be glad for what you learned. If nothing else, practice on a pet. (Hydrotherapy works fine on dogs, not so well on cats.)

With the Lord's blessing and some common sense health reform, you and everyone you know may just stay fit and happy, and you'll never get a chance or have a need to play nurse or doctor. That's great. Praise the Lord for good health. Just be ready with your knowledge of simple treatments when it's needed.

Something for Everyone

One of the beauties of medical missionary work is that anyone and everyone can find a part to play, from the simplicity of raking leaves for an elderly neighbor on up as far as the case may call for. In the hands of an informed and committed Christian, any act of selfless service is powerful.

But there is nonetheless a special power exerted by those two lines of gospel work that most closely approach Jesus' ministry. Our ministers and our doctors hold a unique level of influence, which can either combine for the greatest good, or separate and produce the worst evil. To each of these two groups, the question is inevitably, which will it be? Good or evil?

So, if you *do* have a medical license, you have a special opportunity and responsibility to represent the Great Medical Missionary. Use the privileges you have earned and that God has blessed you with; make them count for eternity... because that's *all* that really counts. (Eternity is also one of the few things certain to last longer than Med School.)

Or are you a pastor? Why not team up with some health workers and aim for a more complete, a more "true interpretation of the gospel"? You might want to get in touch with AMEN; *the health folks are looking for people like you!*

And for all God's church: give some thought to the needs of the people and the world around us. Jesus said "It is more blessed to give than to receive," and even the psychologists agree with Him now. So when He asks you to do something for Him, it's OK. You can trust Him.

Make it a point to look for opportunities to help others. *Choose* to learn to trust God and serve others. Spend some time, spend some money on those who need help. Give God a chance to pay you back like He said He would. Just be careful that you don't start setting conditions and telling the Lord that you'll do His work as long as such and such happens, or you get such and such, or....

Think of it this way: If Jesus sees that you need $500 a week to live on, but you make up your mind that you need $510 a week, you're going to have trouble. If every time your income drops below that $510 level, you decide that God isn't taking care of you and you stop doing what you were doing for Him so you can take care of yourself instead, you're never going to learn to trust Him, and you'll lose your soul over $10 a week! That's "the Lie," the devil's favorite pick-up line, right there in full view.

On the other hand, the idea that "my God shall supply all your need,"[9] doesn't mean everyone ought to quit their job and go on some sort of heavenly welfare. Just start doing what God puts in front of you to help others. If He sees it's time to kick things up a notch, He'll let you know.

Honor the Dead and Love the Living[10]

And a final request concerning the people this book has mentioned: No matter how well they may or may not have conformed to your ideal in terms of theology, policy, or human decency, deal gently with them. Every one of them has sacrificed more and accomplished more than I have, and maybe more than you, too. It won't hurt us a bit to stay down off our high-horse.

I'm sure their love for the Lord would prompt them to encourage us all to learn from their experience, so let's do that. Let's work together, Ministers, Doctors, and Laymen. Let's re-unite the medical and the ministerial; let's find ways to use medical missionary work to reach the cities and especially the neglected classes at the top and bottom of the social ladder. Let's learn that God wants us to take all we need from Him, and then just as freely to share what they need with others. In short, let's master d'Sozo, and reverse the worst evil.

It's time for a demonstration of what Christ's method alone can do.

---

9. Philippians 4:9

10. *S.P.S. Edwards—Memoirs of SDA Pioneers*, 14. This was the petition of Dr. Edwards in his memoirs written out for Emmett K. Vande Vere. It is good counsel for us as well.

Medical missionary work must have its representatives in our cities. Centers must be made and missions established on right lines. Ministers of the gospel are to unite with the medical missionary work, which has ever been presented to me as the work which is to break down the prejudice which exists in our world against the truth.

The medical missionary work is growing in importance, and claims the attention of the churches. It is a part of the gospel message, and must receive recognition. It is the heaven-ordained means of finding entrance to the hearts of people. It is the duty of our church members in every place to follow the instruction of the Great Teacher. The gospel message is to be preached in every city; for this is in accordance with the example of Christ and His disciples. Medical missionaries are to seek patiently and earnestly to reach the higher classes. If this work is faithfully done, professional men will become trained evangelists.

—Ellen G. White
Medical Ministry, 241

NEWSTART GL●BAL
HEALTH
Health Evangelism And Leadership Training for Him

HEALTH & GOSPEL
REUNITED

The comprehensive training needed to reunite the health message with the gospel is now available! **HEALTH** (Health Evangelism And Leadership Training for Him) is the program specifically designed to produce effective outreach leaders who utilize NEWSTART® *health principles* to spread the *gospel* around the globe.

The HEALTH program is a key a component of Weimar Institute's NEWSTART Global initiative to reunite the proclamation of the gospel with the ministry of health.

Ministers and physicians are now joining forces! They are coming together through the aid of HEALTH graduates trained to implement a unique multiphase plan that closely tracks Ellen White's counsel to use medical missionary work as the "entering wedge" to accelerate the proclamation of the gospel.

HEALTH is the program that equips today's health outreach professional with the materials, systems, and training necessary to lead churches and health organizations of all sizes on the path to becoming true *centers of influence*.

Program Features
- *A comprehensive four-month health evangelism leadership curriculum infused with practical experience and real world application.*

- *An integrated leadership module where participants work together in health evangelism teams.*

- *A program track tailored for licensed medical professionals desiring to incorporate health evangelism in their day-to-day practices and become health evangelism leaders in their churches and communities.*

Apply Online at newstartglobal.com (click on "I want to be Trained")
Additional Questions? Call 530-422-7911 or email globalhealth@weimar.org